THE SINGLE INDIVIDUAL AND THE SEARCHER OF HEARTS

T&T Clark Enquiries in Theological Ethics

Series editors
Brian Brock
Susan F. Parsons

THE SINGLE INDIVIDUAL AND THE SEARCHER OF HEARTS

A Retrieval of Conscience in the Work of Immanuel Kant and Søren Kierkegaard

Jeff Morgan

LONDON • NEW YORK • OXFORD • NEW DELHI • SYDNEY

T&T CLARK
Bloomsbury Publishing Plc
50 Bedford Square, London, WC1B 3DP, UK
1385 Broadway, New York, NY 10018, USA
29 Earlsfort Terrace, Dublin 2, Ireland

BLOOMSBURY, T&T CLARK and the T&T Clark logo are trademarks of
Bloomsbury Publishing Plc

First published in Great Britain 2020
This paperback edition published in 2022

Copyright © Jeff Morgan, 2020

Jeff Morgan has asserted his right under the Copyright, Designs and Patents Act, 1988, to
be identified as Author of this work.

For legal purposes the Acknowledgments on p. vii–viii constitute an extension
of this copyright page.

All rights reserved. No part of this publication may be reproduced or transmitted
in any form or by any means, electronic or mechanical, including photocopying,
recording, or any information storage or retrieval system, without prior permission
in writing from the publishers.

Bloomsbury Publishing Plc does not have any control over, or responsibility for, any
third-party websites referred to or in this book. All internet addresses given in this
book were correct at the time of going to press. The author and publisher regret any
inconvenience caused if addresses have changed or sites have ceased to exist, but can
accept no responsibility for any such changes.

A catalogue record for this book is available from the British Library.

A catalog record for this book is available from the Library of Congress.

ISBN: HB: 978-0-5676-9463-8
PB: 978-0-5676-9772-1
ePDF: 978-0-5676-9464-5
eBook: 978-0-5676-9466-9

Series: T&T Clark Enquiries in Theological Ethics

Typeset by Newgen KnowledgeWorks Pvt. Ltd., Chennai, India

To find out more about our authors and books visit www.bloomsbury.com
and sign up for our newsletters.

CONTENTS

Acknowledgments	vii
List of Abbreviations	ix

INTRODUCTION	1
The Thesis: Knowing Myself as God Knows Me	1
The (Non)place of Conscience in Contemporary Christian Ethics	3
What Kant and Kierkegaard Have to Offer	5
What's Ahead	7

Chapter 1
THE DISMISSAL OF CONSCIENCE IN TWENTIETH-CENTURY
CHRISTIAN ETHICS

	11
Introduction	11
MacIntyre and Hauerwas on the Rise of Modernity	15
Lehmann and O'Donovan on Modern Morality and the Decline of Conscience	17
Revising Conscience Out of Existence: From Niebuhr to Hauerwas	25
Between Niebuhr and Hauerwas: MacIntyre's Narrative Self	31
The Disappearance of Conscience: Hauerwas on Corporate Self-Awareness	33
Summary and Conclusion	37

Chapter 2
SELF-KNOWLEDGE AND THE APPROXIMATION OF DIVINE
JUDGMENT: CONSCIENCE IN THE PRACTICAL PHILOSOPHY AND
MORAL THEOLOGY OF IMMANUEL KANT

	41
Introduction	41
Conscience as Tribunal	41
Conscience and Autonomy	44
Conscience and the Approximation of Divine Judgment	50
Conscience as Means to Knowledge of the Heart	54
Conscience as Antidote to Self-Deception	59
Conscience and "Moral Repentance"	65
Conscience and Perseverance	69
Conscience and Community	72
Summary and Conclusion	74

Chapter 3
SELF-KNOWLEDGE AND THE ENORMOUS WEIGHT OF GOD: CONSCIENCE IN THE SØREN KIERKEGAARD'S SECOND AUTHORSHIP — 75

- Introduction: Conscience in Kierkegaard's Second Authorship — 75
- Defining Conscience — 76
- Understanding Conscience from Its Absence: The Crowd — 80
- Defining the "Single Individual" — 83
- Isolating the Relationship of Conscience — 88
- Singularity and Authenticity as the Disclosure of Conscience — 94
- The Indicative-Imperative Disclosure of Conscience — 95
- Colliding with the World, Drawing Closer to God in Conscience — 99
- Conscience and the Consciousness of Guilt (or Conscience in Judgment) — 100
- Conscience and the Self before Christ — 103
- The Help of Christ: The Mirror of God's Word — 107
- To See Oneself before Christ in the Mirror of God's Word — 110
- Summary and Conclusion — 115

Chapter 4
CONSCIENCE AS SINGULAR MORAL SELF-AWARENESS: AN OUTLINE — 117

- Introduction: Conscience as Singular Moral Self-Awareness before God — 117
- The Unwelcome Individual in Contemporary Theology and Ethics — 119
- The Consequent Communitarian Turn and the Implications for Moral Self-Awareness — 123
- Beyond the Dichotomy: An Individual Not Sovereign but before God — 125
- Conscience as Tribunal and Self-Testimony — 133
- The Passive Experience of Conscience and the Activity of Conscientiousness — 137
- Conscience against Self-Deception — 144
- Repentance, Conversion, and the Universality of Conscience — 149
- Singularity, Sociality, and Authority — 154
- Summary and Conclusion — 163

Bibliography — 167
Index — 175

ACKNOWLEDGMENTS

A central theme of this book is that other people do not give us our conscience but other people can help us hear it, act conscientiously, and stand responsibly on our own two feet. I hope this book can be a tribute to the people who have helped me in this regard in so many ways. Many of the ideas found in this book began during my time as a doctoral student at the University of Notre Dame (Indiana), a place I cherish as a vibrant, rigorous, and authentic community. I am deeply grateful to the many friends and teachers who made my time there so rich, but a special thanks must go to my advisor, mentor, and friend Gerald McKenny, who is, for me, in his work and life a true exemplar. I would also like to thank David Clairmont, Cyril O'Regan, Jean Porter, and Randall Zachman, who have each played a vital role in my development as a scholar and in the writing of this book. Randall Zachman deserves additional mention for the many ways he has helped me refine the argument of this book—especially in the parts devoted to Kierkegaard—well after my time at Notre Dame.

My reading of Kant has benefited immensely from conversations with John Hare, Eric Bugyis, and Karl Ameriks. I am very grateful to Karl Ameriks for carefully reading and commenting on early drafts of the chapter on Kant as well as for allowing me to audit his class on Kant's practical philosophy. Conversations with Jennifer Herdt and Lisa Cahill (who I am grateful to have had as my first teacher of Christian ethics) have enriched my understanding of Christian ethics greatly over the years and have helped me sharpen the stakes for this book. Conversations with friends and colleagues during my time as a Catherine of Siena Fellow in the Ethics Program at Villanova University also greatly enriched how I thought about the central claims of the book. I'd especially like to thank Mark Doorley, Brett Wilmott, Mark Wilson, Vincent Lloyd, Jesse Couenhoven, Sally Scholz, Ian Clausen, Matt Puffer, Albert Chinn, Willa Swensen-Lengyl, Audra Goodnight, and Allison Covey. Vincent Lloyd deserves special mention here for reading and commenting on the entire manuscript (and the title, which thanks to Vincent is now more fitting than it once was).

I would like to thank the editorial team at T&T Clark. Anna Turton and Veerle Van Steenhuyse have offered so much help in bringing this book together. And I am deeply grateful to Brian Brock and Susan F. Parsons for their enthusiasm for the book and for their fruitful editorial suggestions.

I am grateful to our families for their love and support over the years that this book has taken shape. Above all I am grateful to Rebecca, John, Julia, and Hannah, my four children who constantly remind me of the things that matter most, and my wife Courtney. Courtney has been a calm, wise, patient, and loving companion and support to me throughout the highs and lows and the routine periods of self-doubt that come with a project like this (and with the pursuit of an academic career). She has listened and advised on big and small aspects of this book. It would not exist without her.

Portions of this book have appeared previously and are reproduced here with the kind permission of the publishers:

> Portions of Chapter 1 previously appeared in Jeffrey Morgan, "A Loss of Judgment: The Dismissal of the Judicial Conscience in Recent Christian Ethics," in *Journal of Religious Ethics*, vol. 45, no. 3 (August 2017): 539–61.
>
> Portions of Chapter 2 previously appeared in Jeffrey Morgan, "Self-Knowledge and the Approximation of Divine Judgment: Conscience in the Practical Philosophy and Moral Theology of Immanuel Kant," *Journal of the Society of Christian Ethics*, vol. 36, no. 1 (Spring/Summer 2016): 107–22.
>
> Portions of Chapter 4 appeared previously in Jeffrey Morgan, "Guilt, Self-Awareness, and the Good Will in Kierkegaard's Confessional Discourses," *Studies in Christian Ethics*, published online (January 2019).

Unless otherwise noted, Scripture quotations in this book are from the Holy Bible, New International Version® of the Bible. Copyright© 1973, 1978, 1984, 2011, Biblica. All rights reserved throughout the world. Used by permission of Biblica.

ABBREVIATIONS

Immanuel Kant's Writings

"Enlightenment"	"What Is Enlightenment"
Groundwork	Groundwork of the Metaphysics of Morals
Lectures	Lectures on Ethics
Metaphysics of Morals	The Metaphysics of Morals
Practical Reason	Critique of Practical Reason
Religion	Religion within the Bounds of Reasons Alone

Søren Kierkegaard's Writings

CD	Christian Discourses
CUP	Concluding Unscientific Postscript
DCF	Discourses at the Communion on Friday
FSE	For Self-Examination
JFY	Judge for Yourself!
JP	Journals and Papers
LR	A Literary Review
PC	Practice in Christianity
SUD	The Sickness unto Death
TA	Two Ages
UDVS	Upbuilding Discourses in Various Spirits
WL	Works of Love

INTRODUCTION

The Thesis: Knowing Myself as God Knows Me

The aim of this book is simple: I examine and retrieve a theory of conscience as a person's moral self-awareness before God. In other words, I examine and retrieve the idea that God makes a claim upon us and God knows us as God sees our hearts and judges us, and to have a conscience is to share with God in this knowledge. As a historical retrieval, this thesis seems uncontroversial to me. There are implicit warrants for it from the Hebrew Bible all the way to Ignatius of Loyola and there are explicit precedents for it from the New Testament to patristic theologians, from Bernard of Clairvaux to John Calvin to John Henry Newman.[1]

---

1. From the Hebrew Bible I have in mind passages like Isaiah 6 or Psalm 139 wherein the presence of God to the individual is singularly self-disclosing. But I also have in mind a common pattern in which God singles out an individual, calls an individual out from a group (the patriarchs and prophets are all good examples), and the individual has a clear sense of self in light of this summons. I will develop these thoughts at greater length in the concluding chapter. The Daily Examen of Ignatian spirituality, in which an individual quietly, prayerfully reflects on God's intimate presence to her throughout her day has close connections with the theory of conscience I lift up here (see http://www.ignatianspirituality.com/ignatian-prayer/the-examen/how-can-i-pray); conscience as singular moral self-awareness appears throughout the Pauline corpus, but I have in mind, in particular passages like Rom. 2:15-16 and 1 Cor. 12:11; we can hear Chrysostom working in this Pauline vein when he asks how it is that God has set within us a conscience to act as a watchful judge, holding us accountable before God (John Chrysostom, *On Wealth and Poverty* (Yonkers, NY: St. Vladimir's Seminary Press, 1999), 88); and on the similarity between figures as diverse as Calvin and Newman, consider the following claims: Conscience, Calvin writes, is a voice or witness within a person that brings a person before God; it "stands ... between God and man, not suffering man to suppress what he knows in himself"(*Institutes of the Christian Religion*, ed. John T. McNeil, trans. Ford Lewis Battles (Louisville, KY: Westminster John Knox, 1960), III.19.15). Newman, in a similar spirit, writes, "If, as is the case, we feel responsibility, are ashamed, are frightened, at transgressing the voice of conscience, this implies that there is One to whom we are responsible, before whom we are ashamed, whose claims upon us we fear. ... Thus conscience is a connecting principle between the creature and his Creator." In conscience, Newman concludes, striking a chord with Calvin, that

Such a thesis is controversial nonetheless, because it states that the knowledge we share with God in our conscience ultimately is distinct from the knowledge we have of ourselves before others. I retrieve the idea that our moral self-awareness before God is our *singular* moral self-awareness before God—it is a knowledge derived from a singular relation to God that cannot ultimately be reduced to our relationship with any particular community. This is not to say a community cannot be of help to an individual as she strives to hear her conscience. And it is not to say that our distinct, singular accountability before God precludes God claiming us through our neighbors (cf. Mt. 25). Nor is it to say that the conscientious individual cares little for the flourishing of community. As a conscientious individual, in fact, she cares a great deal. The knowledge we have of ourselves before God that is distinct from the knowledge we have of ourselves before others does profoundly concern our relationships with these others. Moreover, I do not mean to deny wholesale the ecclesial mediation of God's presence to us here and now. There is nothing inconsistent with the affirmation, for example, that Jesus Christ is known to us "in Scripture and the breaking of bread,"[2] and the affirmation that there is something deeply personal, private, and singular in our relation to God, that God knows us, claims us, and holds us each accountable for the life we live before God. But if we lose sight of this latter affirmation—and I think in contemporary Christian ethics we have lost sight of it—then we have lost something central about the Christian faith.

But none of these concessions will seem sufficient in our communitarian era of Christian ethics. Stanley Hauerwas's particular brand of ecclesial communitarianism has come under much scrutiny and criticism in recent years, but no one challenges the basic communitarian commitment. We can summarize this commitment as the belief that our moral identity comes into being as we are embedded in a public world, as we are given a role in the life of a particular, historical moral culture that lives according to particular sociolinguistic conventions. The task for the moral agent is one of acclimating to these conventions, finding her given role within them, and learning to live into that role. Theological renderings of this commitment find God working in and through the historical community. And so as the people of this time and place equip me to live into the identity they have given to me, I can believe God is at work in and through these people.

But in this case, it would probably be best not to make much of the individual's singular moral self-awareness in relation to God. If a community mediates to an individual her relationship to God, then it would be better to emphasize an individual's self-awareness in relation to the norms and prohibitions, habits,

---

God's creatures "are brought into His presence as that of a Living Person, and are able to hold converse with Him, and that with a directness and simplicity, with a confidence and intimacy" ("God in Conscience," in *The Heart of Newman*, ed. Erich Przywara, S. J. (San Francisco: Ignatius Press, 1997), 26, 30).

2. This is from the "Collect for the Presence of Christ" in *Book of Common Prayer* (New York: Church Hymnal Corporation, 1979), 70.

practices, and conventions of the community. And it might be better not to work this out in terms of conscience because conscience carries with it too many strong individualistic connotations.³ Conscience might suggest a buffer space between the individual and the community and this buffer is untenable, so it goes, in our era of Christian ethics. It would be better to work out a theory of corporate casuistry, such as Hauerwas does, which sublimates the individual into the tradition-bearing community as the *community* examines the congruity between its actions and its principles.⁴

The (Non)place of Conscience in Contemporary Christian Ethics

I offer this brief account of the fate of conscience in contemporary Christian ethics as a plausible suggestion about why conscience as moral self-awareness has such a marginal place in it. I should note that in Catholic moral theology a trajectory of thinking about conscience is alive and well. Conscience in this trajectory plays a significant role in the practical application of prudence; it is, in this regard, a kind of God-given internal moral director.⁵ This trajectory and the one I retrieve in this book are not mutually exclusive, and I am not raising objections here. But they are different trajectories with different emphases. I also do not mean to say that one trajectory is Catholic and the other Protestant. Conscience as an individual's singular moral self-awareness, as I have already suggested above, has strong precedents throughout the broader Christian tradition.⁶

Nonetheless, this tradition of thinking about conscience is marginal at best and dangerous at worst in contemporary Christian ethics. A significant reason for this is the association of conscience with the work of Immanuel Kant. Douglas Langston's book *Conscience and Other Virtues* is representative in this regard. Langston finds Kant at the climax of a trajectory he thinks Luther inaugurates that takes conscience to be a faculty or "independent entity" that mediates God's judgment. Langston thinks this development is a "most unfortunate turn in the history of the concept of conscience," since Kant's theory of conscience, after

---

3. Cf. Oliver O'Donovan, *Resurrection and Moral Order: An Outline for Evangelical Ethics*, second edition (Grand Rapids, MI: Eerdmans, 1994), 168.

4. Stanley Hauerwas, *The Peaceable Kingdom: A Primer in Christian Ethics* (Notre Dame, IN: University of Notre Dame Press, 1983), 120.

5. For an excellent recent discussion, see William C. Mattison III, *Introducing Moral Theology: True Happiness and the Virtues* (Grand Rapids, MI: Brazos Press, 2008), 95–112.

6. There are hints and echoes of the theory of conscience I advance in this dissertation in *Gaudium et Spes* as well as in the work of John Paul II and Benedict XVI. See, for example, *Pastoral Constitution on the Church in the Modern World—Gaudium et Spes*, in *The Documents of Vatican II*, ed. Walter Abbott S. J. (London: Chapman Press, 1966), 16–17; John Paul II, *Veritatis Splendor* (Boston, MA: Pauline Books, 1983), 57–8, 61; Benedict XVI, *On Conscience* (San Francisco, CA: Ignatius Press, 2007).

Kant, becomes the "standard view."[7] This is "most unfortunate" because it is just a short step from this view to the view that each individual is his or her own moral authority by virtue of conscience. In other words, it is just a short step from Kant's theory of conscience to the view that, so long as I'm OK and you're OK, I know myself as responsible to act in such and such a way, and who are you to tell me otherwise?

The appeal of Langston's argument against the theory of conscience he associates with Kant depends upon an overwrought assumption in contemporary Christian ethics, namely, that Kant is one of the principal architects (if not *the* architect) of the modern, self-asserting, atomistic, autonomous moral subject. The assumption is that Kant bequeaths to modernity the philosophical framework in which an individual is justified to create the personal morality he or she sees fit to create. As such, each individual is accountable to a self-given (i.e., self-created) law. Conscience, in this scheme, helps the individual monitor the consistency between his or her self-posited morality and actual behavior. It is a person's means to be consistent with his or her self-created principles.[8] This is not an attractive picture for the majority of Christian ethicists today, nor should it be. It is also not lacking in merit as a description of the present state of our contemporary cultural mores. And if this is what conscience has become in modern life, thanks to Kant, then it would be best to keep a healthy distance both from conscience and from Kant.

Over the past few decades, however, many scholars of Kant's practical philosophy and philosophy of religion argue that Kant is not the ogre of modern autonomy many take him to be. In this picture Kant is a philosopher of divine command, in a certain sense, who is deeply committed to the absolute, transcendent, object lawfulness of law and, in turn, to the establishment of truly cosmopolitan goods.[9] The verdict is still out in contemporary Christian ethics on the status of this relatively new picture of Kant. The communitarian turn in Christian ethics still has momentum and this turn has gained a great deal of traction by pushing against Kant as the villainous foil.

Kant is not an unproblematic figure, but he is also not unambiguous. There might actually be something in his thought worth our attention. Indeed, central

---

7. Douglas Langston, *Conscience and Other Virtues: From Bonaventure to MacIntyre* (State College: Penn State University Press, 2007), 77.

8. This account of Kant, modern moral autonomy, and conscience will be a central concern of Chapter 1.

9. See, for example, John Hare, *The Moral Gap: Kantian Ethics, Human Limits, and God's Assistance* (New York: Oxford University Press, 1996); Karl Ameriks, *Kant and the Fate of Autonomy: Problems in the Appropriation of the Critical Philosophy* (Cambridge: Cambridge University Press, 2000), and "Vindicating Autonomy: Kant, Sartre, and O'Neill," in *Kant on Moral Autonomy*, ed. Oliver Sensen (Cambridge: Cambridge University Press, 2012); Andrew Chignell, "Rational Hope, Moral Order, and the Revolution of the Will," in *Divine Order, Human Order, and the Order of Nature*, ed. Eric Watkins (New York: Oxford University Press, 2013).

elements of basic Christian ethics persist in his thought and we do well to consider what he makes of them. Conscience is one such element. His theory of conscience is not a buoy for the modern, autonomous, self-asserting individual; rather, it is corroborative of an important biblical and theological witness about the good for the moral life of self-examination and self-knowledge before the claim God makes upon us. We find this witness in Psalm 139, for example, a text I come back to at various points in this book. The central theme of the Psalm is that God sees each of our hearts and knows the quality of our hearts as we live before God. And if we would live well before God we have to have at least a glimpse of what God sees, we have to have some kind of share in the knowledge God has of us. It is this dynamic of being singularly known by the one who sees our hearts and of acquiring a share of this knowledge that New Testament writers and later theologians annex to conscience. My claim, so far, is that Kant's theory of conscience belongs in this trajectory; Kant, in his own way, directs us to this way of thinking about conscience.

What Kant and Kierkegaard Have to Offer

I have given this attention to Kant so far because I propose to defend a theory of conscience that has been dismissed in Christian ethics in large part because of its association with Kant and the alleged ramifications of Kant's practical philosophy. And so finding some leverage to put this claim for conscience back on the table requires these prefatory remarks about Kant and the theological witness his theory of conscience calls to mind. But Kant is not alone as he directs us in his own way to this witness. Søren Kierkegaard also offers his own distinct version of a theory of conscience as an individual's singular moral self-awareness in relation to God.

I am struck by how much Kierkegaard's theory of conscience sounds like Kant's theory of conscience. And this is reason enough to turn to Kierkegaard. They clearly seem to be operating within a common conceptual scheme about the nature and function of conscience. If there were but world enough and time we could consider more figures. But there are also strategic reasons to turn to Kierkegaard. Kierkegaard fares better than Kant in contemporary Christian ethics, but he too has come under criticism for fostering the detached interiority of the modern moral subject. Just as with our treatment of Kant, then, our treatment of Kierkegaard provides an opportunity, from a different rendering of this theory of conscience, to correct misinterpretations and challenge overreactions.

In short, Kierkegaard, as I will present him, shares in the tradition of thinking about conscience we find in Kant. But he does offer a distinct rendering of this understanding of conscience. Significantly, he differs from Kant on the final end conscience serves. While Kant thinks our moral self-awareness in relation to God helps us as we strive to conform our lives increasingly to the moral law that we should believe God gives to us, Kierkegaard believes this moral self-awareness ultimately serves us as we draw deeper into our relationship to God. And so I present Kant and Kierkegaard as each offering a distinct rendering of conscience as our singular moral self-awareness before God. Kant conceives of conscience as a kind of knowledge we have in relation to God who, as Supreme Lawgiver, holds us accountable to the law we discern through our practical reason. Kierkegaard conceives of conscience as our singular moral self-awareness in relation to God who, as our loving creator, holds us accountable to live as one whom God has created for a distinct relationship to God.

But these distinctions are intramural. My claim is that Kant and Kierkegaard each in their own way extend a tradition of inquiry about conscience as an individual's singular moral self-awareness before God. They each argue that this moral self-awareness is ultimately distinct from our moral self-awareness before our communities, including our ecclesial communities. Given the poor status of this tradition in contemporary Christian ethics, I do not want to distract from my broader goal of recommending it, and I am afraid that staging an adjudication between Kant and Kierkegaard that aims to find a hero for the book will be such a distraction. We will adjudicate between these figures from time to time in order to clarify what is going on in each figure's thought. But I do not mean to present Kant and Kierkegaard in a trajectory fashion, from good to better. Different readers will respond in different ways to these distinct renderings of conscience. But I leave such judgments to the reader. My aim is to present these theories of conscience thoroughly, clearly, and fairly. I hope this will provide at least a modest contribution to contemporary Christian ethics as well as to scholarship on Kant and Kierkegaard, since the secondary literature on conscience in their work is almost nonexistent.[10]

---

10. J. B. Schneewind's magisterial *The Invention of Autonomy* (New York: Cambridge University Press, 1997), to take a prominent example, offers an account of Kant's moral theory grounded in an extensive account of its background, but conscience is no more than an incidental matter. Michael Despland (nearly fifty years ago) pays some attention to conscience but in the service of a larger effort to defend Kant's understanding of hypocrisy and sincerity (see Despland, "Can Conscience Be Hypocritical? The Contrasting Analyses of Kant and Hegel," *Harvard Theological Review*, vol. 68, no. 3–4 (July–October 1975), 357–70); Thomas Hill situates some explication of conscience within an account of Kant's theory of punishment (see Hill, "Punishment, Conscience, and Moral Worth," in *Kant's Metaphysics of Morals: Interpretive Essays* (New York: Oxford University Press, 2002), 233–54). In short, what is lacking in scholarship on Kant and Kant's moral theory is a thorough treatment of Kant's theory of conscience as it appears across Kant's moral theory. A similar lacunae also characterizes scholarship on Kierkegaard, though there are several articles and book chapters that offer a glimpse into Kierkegaard's theory of conscience, either by exploring it in comparison to other figures or by locating the role of conscience in a particular work. See Philip Ziegler, "A Christian Context for Conscience? Reading Kierkegaard's *Works of Love* Beyond Hegel's Critique of Conscience," *European Journal of Theology*, vol. 15, no. 2 (2006); Randall Zachman has written two short, excellent treatments of Kierkegaard's understanding of conscience, one in relation to Luther's theory of conscience, and the other in relation to Calvin's (Zachman, "Conscience in the Theology of Martin Luther and Soren Kierkegaard," *Journal of Lutheran Ethics*, vol. 10, no. 12 (December 2010); *Reconsidering*

But, as I have said, I also intend to recommend the broader tradition of thinking about conscience they each distinctly uphold. That is my normative, constructive aim in these presentations of conscience. The Christian tradition certainly bears witness to a God who makes a covenant with a people, orders their life, and is present to them through their life together. Again, I do not mean to present this theory of conscience as a necessary denial of that affirmation. But the Christian tradition also clearly bears witness to a God who claims us and knows us as individuals, and who wants us as individuals to examine ourselves and live well singularly before God. And this means there is something about our relation to God, including our moral self-awareness before God, that is not mediated through or reducible to our relationships with others. To take the particular trek we are going to take through the work of Kant and Kierkegaard is to be reminded of this latter witness that has been dismissed in Christian ethics today.

What's Ahead

But first we have to understand how this witness has been forgotten. In Chapter 1 we will consider the contemporary dismissal of conscience. This dismissal comes in two stages. The first stage is constituted by a worry about the relationship between conscience and modern moral autonomy. MacIntyre and Hauerwas both argue that Kant bears significant responsibility for the presence in our midst of the self-asserting, atomistic autonomous individual. Paul Lehmann and Oliver O'Donovan, meanwhile, both find Kant's theory of conscience playing a central role in the rise of this modern moral subject. These diagnoses help to explain why there was a sense around the middle of the twentieth century that conscience was in need of a serious revision. But I conclude that this effort to revise conscience constitutes a Pyrrhic victory. I begin with H. Richard Niebuhr and turn, once again, to Stanley Hauerwas and find a trajectory of thinking about self-knowledge, moral identity, and moral accountability that begins as an effort to wrest conscience from its alleged Kantian captivity and ends with conscience quietly vanishing as the work of conscience dissipates in an emphasis on the priority of corporate life and corporate self-understanding.

In Chapter 2 I begin my challenge to this trajectory by offering a different interpretation of Kant's theory of conscience. I argue that for Kant conscience is the knowledge we have of ourselves in our relation to God as God judges us and holds us accountable to the moral law. To be more precise, I argue that for Kant conscience is an approximate knowledge in which we strive to recognize and endorse the knowledge God has of us in our actions. Kant claims that conscience is the "subjective principle" of our accountability to God, and I argue that he really

---

John Calvin (New York: Cambridge University Press, 2013)). Jamie Ferreira has a short chapter on the role of conscience in *Works of Love* in *Love's Grateful Striving: A Commentary on Kierkegaard's Works of Love* (New York: Oxford University Press, 2001)).

means this, even as there is also an "as if" element to his theory of conscience (we should think of our conscience as holding us accountable to the moral law, and we do this well when we think of conscience "as if" it holds us accountable to God). Conscience, furthermore, becomes the means, Kant thinks, with which we strive to know the quality of our hearts before God. In this regard, conscience plays an essential role, according to Kant, in our duty to know ourselves. I conclude that the dismissal of conscience from Christian ethics rests, at least in part, on a severe misinterpretation of Kant's theory of conscience. And in this overreaction to a misinterpretation of Kant's theory of conscience, there has been, again, a consequent omission in Christian ethics of an important biblical and theological witness that Kant's theory of conscience captures well: that God knows each individual and that each individual is singularly accountable before God.

I argue, in short, that for Kant an adequate, full understanding of conscience requires the belief that there is a God who sees our hearts and judges us. In Chapter 3 I turn to Kierkegaard who, like Kant, presents conscience as our singular moral self-awareness before God. But unlike Kant, Kierkegaard is not squeamish about the very personal and distinct relationship we each have with God and in which we are each personally disclosed. God creates each of us for a very distinct relationship to God. Kierkegaard insists that this distinct relationship to God is at the heart of the Christian faith. And he claims that we discover our distinct relationship to God as God encounters us in our conscience. As we break away from the many people who want to silence our conscience, we begin to hear conscience tell us who we are in relation to God and summon us to live into that relation. As we hear this summons and draw near to God, we find ourselves, Kierkegaard argues, before God's self-revelation in Jesus Christ. And here we discover that we are sinners who reject God and the summons God lays on us in our conscience; but here we also discover the help we need if we are to strive to be who God has created us to be.

In each of the chapters on Kant and Kierkegaard I bring their view of conscience into conversation with the communitarian trajectory we encounter in Chapter 1. I briefly suggest in these moments why the view of conscience Kant and Kierkegaard offer is preferable to the view of this trajectory. Kant and Kierkegaard each present a theory of conscience that effectively calls into question both the sublimation of self-knowledge to corporate self-understanding and the correlative conflation of our accountability before God and our accountability before others. Without something like conscience as Kant and Kierkegaard understand it, it is very difficult to understand on what grounds an individual formed by one community can come to identify with the cause of another community, or how an individual formed in one community can end up calling that community's life into question. Kant and Kierkegaard have an answer here that resists the inadequate dichotomy the alternative, prevailing trajectory poses. This inadequate dichotomy contrasts the atomistic autonomous individual with the communitarian, socially constructed self. Kant and Kierkegaard resist this dichotomy because, each in his own way, they ground the individual's moral identity and correlative moral self-awareness in the individual's relation to God as God claims the individual with a claim that transcends the life of any particular community. In the final chapter, I present an outline and defense of this way of thinking about conscience that draws on central themes from the chapters on Kant and Kierkegaard and situates those themes within a broader biblical and theological witness that deeply resonates with them. The aim is neither simply to "proof text" Kant's and Kierkegaard's theory of conscience nor to present a theory of conscience that is unqualifiedly Kantian or Kierkegaardian. The aim is to make the case that to pass through Kant's and Kierkegaard's theory of conscience as we do in this book is to be reminded of a deeply rooted Christian commitment to nature of an individual's singular accountability and corresponding self-awareness before God. Neither Kant nor Kierkegaard would necessarily endorse the outline I present in the final chapter, but the point is that they can help us think more sharply about this Christian commitment and make good theological sense about what it means to have a conscience.

Chapter 1

THE DISMISSAL OF CONSCIENCE IN TWENTIETH-CENTURY CHRISTIAN ETHICS

Introduction

What is it that enables a person to make a decisive change in the direction of his or her life? How does a person undergo a conversion from one way of life to another? Take a person who has not thought very much about where his food comes from, the omnivorous person who enjoys his weekly steak and routine trips to the fast-food chain. One day as he lifts his fast-food pork sandwich for another bite, he sees a report on the news about the abuse of pigs in factory farms. He puts his sandwich down and starts to pay closer attention to the story, with disgust slowly rising about the inhumane treatment of these animals who, even he as an omnivore believes, make some moral claim, and deserve at the very least not to be tortured; but his disgust also rises—perhaps more quickly—at the sandwich in his hand; and his disgust rises yet again, but this time at himself for his complicity in the abuse. He realizes that, even though he was not fully aware of the many horrors that transpired from "farm" to this particular pork sandwich or his other routine meals, he also knew, deep down, that food so cheap probably comes with some collateral damage. And he, like so many, has those annoying relatives that don't eat meat at the occasional family get together and, like so many, simply chose—as he subtly felt the moral challenge communicated by their behavior—to shrug his shoulders and quietly dismiss them as hippies or idealistic dreamers. But now he has begun to see himself as a participant in something that is not just gastronomically but morally gross and he feels pangs of guilt. What is significant here is not necessarily the facts that have come to bear on this person that illustrate the moral compromise embodied by industrial food. What is significant is that having lived in a culture that is indifferent to this compromise and having (at least semiconsciously) made food choices his entire life that echo such indifference, having been inculcated or habituated in this system, he is able to become aware of himself and his relation to it in a new way and to resolve on a new course of conduct. What is significant here (for our purposes) is not so much the knowledge of right and wrong that has come to clearer light for this person, but the moral self-awareness that accompanies it and that fuels his moral repentance. It is in this moral self-awareness and its life-changing power, as I am going to argue in this book, that conscience does its work. In other words, if human beings are, to some extent, products of their environments, socially conditioned creatures, what is it that enables a person no longer to identify in significant ways with his or her formative culture? How can a person become morally self-aware in a way that might cut against the grain of all the forces that have shaped him or her? A theory of conscience as moral self-awareness can answer these questions.

But conscience can be a slippery moral category. "I've been writing about Christian ethics my entire life," a leading Christian ethicist once told me when I mentioned I was writing about conscience, "and I am still not sure what exactly conscience is." Is it a person's innate sense of right and wrong? Is it the feeling of guilt that accompanies bad behavior? Is it a person's inviolable sense of the core principles that makes him or her who she is? Is it a cricket? I think it is fine for conscience to mean any of these things (except the cricket)—given the philosophical or theological system in which conscience lives—but it cannot mean all of them at once. If it does then it becomes a nebulous thing, stretched so thin it can be wrapped around whatever purpose a person might have for it. This, as we will see, is part of the frustration many ethicists have with conscience; the slipperiness of its meaning allows it fairly easily to become a safeguard for whatever self-assertion a person might want to make: I don't feel guilty buying a fancy car or house just outside of my means (while others who could use my help live in abject poverty), and I enjoy spending valuable time watching reality TV and doing other frivolous things; these all makes me happy, so keep your judgment to yourself. I am just being who I am, following my conscience. (Such a person might not necessarily invoke conscience, but its moral relativism and justifying power lurk in the background.) An important point, then, is that we need to be very clear and precise when we talk about conscience. Conscience, in a broad and general sense, does not need a rehabilitation or retrieval (as this book's subtitle promises to be). *Specific* theories of conscience need retrieval. A theory of conscience, that is, needs to state clearly what conscience is, identify where this particular theory of conscience can "go off the rails," and examine how it might make a distinct contribution to our understanding of the moral life—the Christian moral life in the case of this book.

Theories of conscience typically pertain to one of two kinds of moral knowledge. Theories of conscience can be theories about how we know what we should or should not do. These theories of conscience depict conscience as a moral guide or director that tells a person prospectively what should be done or retrospectively what should have been done. As a moral guide or director, conscience might be a person's moral knowledge, or it might be distinct from a person's moral knowledge but indissolubly related to it, as in Thomas Aquinas's theory of conscience as the practical application of the first principles of practical reason.[1] But in general, whether or not conscience is the locus of a person's moral knowledge, theories of conscience that concern how we know what we should or should not do depict conscience as a moral guide or director.

---

1. Thomas Aquinas, *Summa Theologica* (Notre Dame, IN: Christian Classics, English Dominican Province Translation, 1981), I. 79.

Distinct from theories of conscience about how we know what we should or should not do are theories of conscience about how we know ourselves as moral agents. It is this theory of conscience as a person's moral self-awareness that I examine in this book as I retrieve it from the work of Immanuel Kant and Søren Kierkegaard. I argue that for Kant and Kierkegaard alike conscience pertains to the knowledge we have of ourselves in our relation to God. I argue, specifically, that for Kant and Kierkegaard conscience is a person's singular moral self-awareness in relation to God as God holds each person accountable for the quality of his or her life before God. For Kant conscience is not itself the knowledge of the claim on us; he thinks we have knowledge of this claim by means other than conscience. Conscience, then, is for Kant, the knowledge we have of ourselves in light of this claim as God holds us accountable to it. Conscience is for Kierkegaard also primarily a person's moral self-awareness in relation to God. Kierkegaard, however, does not distinguish, as Kant does, between conscience as a person's moral self-awareness before God and the claim God makes on us. For Kierkegaard the knowledge of the claim God makes upon us and the knowledge of ourselves before this claim are forms of knowledge that both belong to conscience. That is a broad claim we will qualify as we treat Kierkegaard's theory of conscience in detail. But what is salient for the moment is that Kant and Kierkegaard each develop a distinct version of a theory of conscience that concerns the knowledge we have of ourselves. And they each develop a theory of conscience that concerns the knowledge we have of ourselves in relation to God.

It might be that this theory of conscience sounds especially Protestant. And there are indeed strong echoes of this kind of language that reverberated throughout the Reformation and were developed by later Protestant theologians. Calvin, to take a prominent example, writes, "when [persons] have a sense of the divine justice added as a witness which allows them not to conceal their sin, but drags them forward as culprits to the bar of God, that sense is called conscience. For it stands as it were between God and man, not suffering man to suppress what he knows in himself."[2] A few decades after Calvin, English Puritan William Perkins writes, in language close to Calvin's, that "conscience is appointed of God to declare and put in execution his just judgments against sinners ... conscience is of a divine nature, and is a thing placed of God in the midst between him and man, as an arbitrator to give sentence and to pronounce either with man or against man unto God."[3] Similar to Perkins's definition of conscience is the definition of his student William Ames who writes that the "conscience of man ... is a man's judgment of himself, according to the judgment of God of him."[4] We can see how this way of thinking about conscience within Protestant thought continues into the nineteenth century in Abraham Kuyper's claim that the Christian should submit to his or her

---

2. Calvin, *Institutes*, III.19.15.
3. Perkins, *Conscience* (Nieuwkoop B. De Graf, 1966), 3, 7.
4. Ames, *Conscience* (Leyden: Imprinted W. Christiaens, E. Griffin, J. Dawson, 1639), 1.

conscience "as to a direct *sensus divinitatis* through which God Himself stirs up the inner man, and subjects him to His judgment."[5]

The language of this singular self-disclosure before God in conscience perhaps becomes especially strong in the Reformation and post-Reformation Protestant theologians, but it is not a language that belongs to them alone. Perkins's definition of conscience echoes John Chrysostom, who asks, "Why has God set in the mind of everyone of us such a continuously watchful and sober judge? I mean the conscience. For there is no judge, no judge at all among men as sleepless as our conscience."[6] We can also see something like this theory of conscience in medieval theology in the work of Bernard of Clairvaux who describes conscience variously as an internal testimony and as the voice of God through which a person strives to know herself.[7] More recently, Pope Benedict XVI explains that conscience signifies a person's transparent openness before God; and in this regard he claims to be following John Henry Newman, for whom conscience represents the place within a person in which he or she encounters the self-disclosing demands of God.[8] The reason we can hear similarities here among such an ecumenically wide cast of characters as Chrysostom, Bernard, Calvin, Kuyper, Newman, and Benedict is that this is an idea that belongs to the Christian tradition more broadly. We can find warrants for it in the Hebrew Bible and precedents for it in the New Testament, as well as in the works of patristic theologians and beyond. We will return to this full heritage of thinking about conscience in the final chapter. For the moment my point is simply that what we find in a particular fashion in the Reformation belongs to the Christian tradition more broadly: conscience is a knowledge we have of ourselves as we stand in total transparency before God as God holds each of us singularly accountable before the requirement God lays upon us.

Kant and Kierkegaard preserve this way of thinking about conscience as a person's moral self-awareness in relation to God. But after Kant and largely with Kant in mind, Christian ethicists have become quite suspicious of conscience, and this suspicion leads to the disappearance of conscience from much contemporary theological reflection. Largely by virtue of its association with Kant, in other words, a tradition of thinking about conscience has been dismissed. In this chapter I offer an account of how this dismissal occurred. I begin by rehearsing Alasdair MacIntyre's and Stanley Hauerwas's influential and representative account of the rise of the autonomous individual of modern Western life, the individual who is detached from history, tradition, and community. MacIntyre and Hauerwas, I observe, both hold Kant's moral philosophy as significantly responsible for this unfortunate development. I then turn to Paul Lehmann's and Oliver O'Donovan's accounts of the long devolution of conscience into a license or prop for the

---

5. Kuyper, *Lectures on Calvinism* (Peabody, MA: Hendrickson, 2008), 59.
6. John Chrysostom, *On Wealth and Poverty*, 88.
7. Cf. G. R. Evans, *Bernard of Clairvaux* (New York: Oxford University Press, 2000), 35.
8. Benedict XVI, *On Conscience*, 26.

autonomous individual of modernity MacIntyre and Hauerwas describe. Once again, Kant is held responsible because, according to Lehmann and O'Donovan, he offers a powerful and influential theory of conscience as the knowledge a person has of herself as accountable to a law she makes for herself. Lehmann and O'Donovan, I argue, help us understand why theologians in the twentieth century became anxious about conscience and why they felt the need to rescue conscience. But I conclude that this rescue effort is a pyrrhic victory. I begin with H. Richard Niebuhr and turn, once again, to Stanley Hauerwas and find a trajectory of thinking about self-knowledge, moral identity, and moral accountability that begins as an effort to wrest conscience from its alleged Kantian captivity and ends with conscience quietly vanishing as the work of conscience dissipates in an emphasis on the priority of corporate life and corporate self-understanding. Moral self-awareness is now not an awareness in relation to God, at least not primarily, but an awareness in relation to the community whose practices and habits realize the claim God makes upon us.

MacIntyre and Hauerwas on the Rise of Modernity

Suspicion toward conscience in contemporary Christian ethics can be credited to a suspicion about the role of Kant's moral philosophy in general and his theory of conscience in particular in the rise of the modern moral agent, the ahistorical, autonomous individual. Before I turn to the role theologians such as Paul Lehmann and Oliver O'Donovan assign to Kant's theory of conscience in the rise of this modern, autonomous individual, it is helpful to begin with a brief rehearsal of a popular account of the Kantian origins of modern morality. If we start with our present situation and move backward, then the account—influentially articulated by Alasdair MacIntyre and Stanley Hauerwas—goes like this: Modern Western life is a chaotic din of assertion and counter-assertion about the moral life. These many assertions constitute, in fact, incommensurable moral claims and they present each of us with an arbitrary choice about which claims we will make our own. If we are aware of it, the arbitrariness of this choice might make us uneasy, since it appears to undermine the moral worth of the claims we have made our own. We nonetheless endorse this arrangement because as moderns we hold above all else that we are, or should strive to be, autonomous individuals: we choose for ourselves what will be valuable for us, and we are by ourselves responsible for the choices we have made. To believe that we are autonomous, in other words, is to believe that it is up to each of us individually to fashion our morality. Hauerwas explains that as moderns we think that "moral knowledge is not so much discovered as created through personal choices." Consequently, "the necessary basis of authentic morality is seen as the freedom to choose and the willingness to take responsibility for choices."[9] Our commitment to autonomy, Hauerwas concludes, is a commitment to the idea

---

9. Hauerwas, *Peaceable Kingdom*, 7.

of freedom as "the necessary and sufficient condition of morality."[10] MacIntyre likewise explains that the modern conception of autonomy is a commitment to the idea that each individual is free to "step back from any and every situation in which [she] is involved, from any and every characteristic [she] may possess, and to pass judgment on it from a purely universal and abstract point of view that is totally detached from all social particularity." MacIntyre concludes that "anyone and everyone can be a moral agent since it is in the self and not in social roles or practices that moral agency was to be located."[11]

With this description the account moves back to Kant, "the grand example" of the project of modernity, according to Hauerwas.[12] Kant's major contribution, in this account, is his concern to find the proper test to discern which rules (maxims) are legitimate to give to ourselves as moral agents and which are not; Kant proposes that we find the proper test in the categorical imperative, a procedure of screening principles of action as legitimate or illegitimate depending on whether or not the principle can be willed as a universal law, that is, on whether or not a principle is one that any person at any time, any place, and in any circumstances would be able to will. The categorical imperative, MacIntyre summarizes, allows us to answer the question we pose to any particular principle, "can we or can we not consistently will that everyone should always act on it."[13] When we put this test for screening maxims to further scrutiny, however, MacIntyre is sure that it fails. By abstracting morality from history and tradition Kant places it on such formal ground that he empties it of all content, and consequently it turns out that trivial, nonmoral, and even immoral maxims can pass the test: "'Keep your promises your whole life except one,' 'Persecute all those who hold false religious beliefs,' and 'Always eat mussels on Mondays in March' will all pass Kant's test for all can be consistently universal."[14] The inevitable result of such a system in which each individual prescribes moral laws for himself or herself according to this purely formal procedure is to establish each individual as the normative, creative source of his or her own laws. And so for "most modern people" now, Hauerwas writes, morality "is our individual personal determination of the facts, not a matter of experience, tradition, training, or community." In other words, morality is a creative endeavor from one individual to the next, and this is indeed the case because whether we realize it or not, as moderns we are most likely Kantians.[15]

---

10. Hauerwas, *Peaceable Kingdom*, 9.

11. Alasdair MacIntyre, *After Virtue: A Study in Moral Theory*, third edition (Notre Dame, IN: University of Notre Dame Press, 2007), 31–2.

12. Hauerwas, *Peaceable Kingdom*, 10.

13. Alasdair MacIntyre, *After Virtue*, 45.

14. MacIntyre, *After Virtue*, 46. On a little scrutiny, these examples do not pass Kant's universalization test.

15. Stanley Hauerwas, *Resident Aliens: Life in the Christian Colony* (Nashville, TN: Abingdon Press, 2004), 98.

In this account, then, the characteristic feature of modern life is that "we increasingly feel ourselves compelled to create our own morality" and that this feature has its most direct lineage to Kant's idea that our actions have moral worth only when they stem from laws of our own making.[16] In fairness to MacIntyre, Hauerwas, and others who with anti-modern aims offer this account of modernity, they are more or less following an interpretation of Kant's moral philosophy that has come to prominence under the influence of John Rawls and his disciples. J. B. Schneewind, for example, argues that Kant's method in ethics is "constitutive," which means that it is in our reflection on our motives for action that we find ourselves approving or disapproving the action. We are to act "from the approved motive or set of motives, and the act so motivated is the appropriate action." Schneewind concludes that "there is no other source of rightness or wrongness in actions."[17] In other words, and more explicitly, "we create the moral order in which we live, and supply our own reasons for compliance."[18] The moral order within which we live is an order "we impose on ourselves as individuals."[19] Between MacIntyre, Hauerwas, and Schneewind there is no real difference in how Kant's moral philosophy is interpreted. The difference is that Schneewind and others like him offer this interpretation and embrace its contemporary implications, while MacIntyre, Hauerwas, and others offer this interpretation as a warning and an exhortation to search for ways out of the moral chaos of modern life.

Lehmann and O'Donovan on Modern Morality and the Decline of Conscience

I recount this interpretation of modernity that so heavily credits Kant for shaping modern moral identity because, on the one hand, while it is well-worn I think it still basically holds in contemporary Christian ethics. On the other hand, and more importantly, I recount it because it is the basic interpretation that informs various narratives of the decline and fall of conscience. Conscience becomes suspect, that is, because it is thought significantly to contribute to the rise of the modern moral agent. This suspicion is most clear as Protestant theologians, in an effort over the last few decades to understand why conscience disappeared as a viable element of basic Christian ethics, tell a story that replicates in microcosm the narrative that discovers the origins of the modern moral subject in Kant's moral philosophy. They tell a story, more specifically, that locates in Kant's theory of conscience ideas that later mature and help to establish the modern notion of the autonomous individual. And since conscience in this narrative becomes complicit in the moral

---

16. Hauerwas, *Peaceable Kingdom*, 7.
17. J. B. Schneewind, "Natural Law, Skepticism, and Methods of Ethics," *Journal of the History of Ideas*, vol. 52, no. 2 (April–June 1991), 298.
18. Schneewind, "Natural Law," 302.
19. Schneewind, "Natural Law," 307.

fragmentation we must now overcome, it too becomes a problem we must either discard or attempt to revise.

If we are going to save conscience from ethical irrelevance we have to know where in its history it went wrong. To this end Paul Lehmann offers his narrative of the "decline and fall" of conscience. By "decline," Lehmann means "the fact that the power of conscience to shape behavior both through judgment and through actions has steadily lost persuasiveness and force"; and by "fall," he means the decisive rejection of conscience as "formative of or important for ethical behavior."[20] In the "torturous record" of conscience's decline and fall, Lehmann judges Kant to be the principal architect of its decline and so the figure most responsible for its fall.[21]

Kant's culpability for the decline and fall of conscience follows clearly from the way Kant, in Lehmann's account, synthesizes certain elements of conscience from the prior epochs of its history. Lehmann begins with the classical, Hellenistic conception of conscience as the knowledge a person has with herself about the moral quality of specific past actions; this knowledge is a knowledge, in particular, that a person has with herself that she has transgressed a "fixed order of things," and so it is a knowledge that serves primarily to inflict a person with the pain of remorse.[22] But while conscience is a person's internal connection to a fixed order, this order, according to Lehmann, is opaque to human beings; it is at best inscrutable and at worst seemingly hostile and arbitrary.[23] Conscience acts to inflict a person with pain when she transgresses this order much like my children's tiny hard plastic toys inflict me with pain when I step on them with my bare feet as I make my way in the middle of the night from my bedroom to the kitchen for a glass of water: I cannot see where I am going, and by inflicting me with pain, the toys, strewn about with no apparent order, tell me that I have stepped in the wrong place—though they do not tell me where I should put my foot next. Likewise, conscience does not alert a person to the nature of right and wrong actions generally; it rather simply negates a person when she has crossed a line that remains opaque to her. Just as I am relieved to make it to my kitchen without hurting my foot, so for the person under this classical notion of conscience, it is a joy never to receive a visit from the conscience, never to have occasion to know with herself that she has transgressed the order of things.

According to Lehmann, Thomas Aquinas "domesticates" this "tragic" conception of conscience "as the bearer of ethical negation"; Aquinas does so by situating conscience within "an order of intellectual stability and understanding." Aquinas accomplishes this domestification because he situates conscience within "the promise of man's life as a rational being under grace."[24] For Aquinas, Lehmann

---

20. Paul Lehmann, *Ethics in a Christian Context* (New York: Harper and Row, 1963), 327–8.
21. Lehmann, *Ethics*, 327.
22. Lehmann, *Ethics*, 329.
23. Lehmann, *Ethics*, 329–30.
24. Lehmann, *Ethics*, 332, 336.

explains, conscience is "the bond between law and responsibility," the "liaison" between a good and just order every person by nature knows and discerns within him or herself and the practical implementation of this knowledge.[25] Conscience, no longer a "dark torment of negation and futility,"[26] has become "the link between the internal nature of man and the order in which his life is sustained"; it acts like a "built-in human device for spot checking right from wrong," as an "intrinsic power to distinguish between good and evil."[27] Conscience still accuses a person and brings remorse when she does wrong, but now it also defends and excuses her and lights her on her way. Lehmann does not explicitly endorse this domestification of conscience, but it is clear he thinks it improves upon its classical precedent.

Aquinas is a bright moment in Lehmann's narrative of conscience, but his narrative is nonetheless one of declension because as Kant takes the stage he synthesizes the classical and Thomistic conceptions of conscience in such a way that he undoes whatever victory for conscience Aquinas may have achieved, and he makes easy the work for someone like Freud to divest conscience of any real moral normativity. Lehmann claims that Kant accepts Aquinas's view that conscience is a "faculty of judgment ... concerned with the evaluation of action in accordance with universal moral principles."[28] These principles, however, are for Kant not so much responsive to a moral order that is replicated as a microcosm in the human being and in which the human being participates as much as they are "pure principles of morality" that a person discerns because she is transcendentally free, because she is conscious of herself as "determinable only by laws which she gives to [herself] through reason."[29] Kant then further adds to this view of conscience a strong "astringent," juridical quality reminiscent of the classical view. Conscience functions for Kant, then, "not simply as the intellect or reason in the act of distinguishing good from evil but as a tribunal."[30] Here Lehmann cites Kant's most notable passage on conscience where Kant describes conscience as a "power" within a human being that "follows him like his shadow," and ultimately serves as "the subjective principle of a responsibility of one's deeds before God."[31] Lehmann concludes that even though Kant does not actually go so far as to make the identification, Kant clearly opens the way "for a virtual identification of the voice of conscience as the voice of God."[32] The full picture of Kant's theory of conscience in Lehmann's account, then, is that as free beings we are to act according to laws of our own making and we are to evaluate the rightness or wrongness of our actions with a seemingly divinely sanctioned "moral certainty

---

25. Lehmann, *Ethics*, 330.
26. Lehmann, *Ethics*, 332–3.
27. Lehmann, *Ethics*, 336.
28. Lehmann, *Ethics*, 333.
29. Lehmann, *Ethics*, 334.
30. Lehmann, *Ethics*, 335.
31. Lehmann, *Ethics*, 335.
32. Lehmann, *Ethics*, 335.

in proportion to the inner depth of conscience."[33] Lehmann does not go so far as to conclude that Kant's theory of conscience serves as a warrant for the modern moral agent's "subjective caprice," but that is the clear implication of his narrative.[34] Lehmann concludes by showing how Freud inherits Kant's view of conscience as a purely internal authority evaluating our actions and with relative ease is able to recast it as an oppressive, dehumanizing superego that bears no genuine moral authority and whose influence must be mitigated (though, for civilization's sake not eradicated). Such a conclusion is inevitable, Lehmann suggests, once Kant decisively and influentially removes conscience from a broader context—a context such as we find in Aquinas's theory of conscience—in which a person is able to evaluate her actions in light of a moral order that bears witness to God's gracious actions in history.

Oliver O'Donovan shares Lehmann's opinion that the history of conscience is one of "torturous record." Like Lehmann, O'Donovan tells a story of conscience as one of decline and fall, and like Lehmann, but more explicitly, O'Donovan ties this decline and fall of conscience to the emergence of the free, autonomous, modern moral agent who is in essence independent from "reality."[35] The emergence of a moral agent who conceives of her freedom as autonomy and so as independence from reality is problematic, O'Donovan argues, because we do not live independently from reality but, whether we realize it or not, we live within a moral order that God has restored in Jesus Christ. God's work in history culminates in the resurrection of Christ and the sending of the Holy Spirit who brings "true reality to bear upon the appearances of reality which our world presents us."[36]

We live within a moral order God has made and our freedom is a freedom we exercise in response to it through the "attentiveness of faith." O'Donovan claims that this phrase—derived from Paul's *hypekoe*—identifies "the whole of our response to God from hearing, understanding, and assenting, to willing and doing."[37] By bringing reason and will together under "the attentiveness of faith" O'Donovan stresses that the human being is a reasoning-willing being whose reason and will are to act as a single, unified response to the moral order God has restored in Christ.

---

33. Lehmann, *Ethics*, 336.

34. This is the phrase of Philip Ziegler, who is influenced by Lehmann and who has written on Lehmann's view of conscience with approbation and on Kant's view of conscience with severe criticism. See Ziegler, "A Christian Context for Conscience? Reading Kierkegaard's Works of Love beyond Hegel's Critique of Conscience," *European Journal of Theology*, vol. 15, no. 2 (2006), 93. See also Ziegler, "Doing Conscience Over: The Reformulation of Conscience in Paul Lehmann and Karl Barth," *Toronto Journal of Theology*, vol. 14, no. 2 (1998), 213–38.

35. O'Donovan, *Resurrection*, 114.

36. O'Donovan, *Resurrection*, 104.

37. O'Donovan, *Resurrection*, 110.

Within this picture of reason and will as the single response of the moral agent to the redeemed moral order, O'Donovan briefly presents what role conscience ought to play and from which conscience falls. O'Donovan claims that conscience properly is "self-awareness and especially moral self-awareness. It is the awareness of guilt, an experience that may be portrayed as having a witness to one's acts."[38] Specifically, conscience is "an inner space created within the seat of human agency, the heart,"[39] by which a person's soul is "laid bare."[40] And above all "conscience is our self-opening to the probing interrogation of an encounter with God."[41] By means of the conscience, then, a person, as a reasoning-willing agent, is interrogated about her attentiveness of faith. She is questioned about her responsiveness to the redeemed moral order within which she lives. The authority exists outside of her in the moral order that has been brought under Christ's lordship, and her conscience serves to question her response to that order; significantly, the conscience itself does not bear any legislative moral authority.

Problems begin to arise for conscience when conscience acquires a "directive role." O'Donovan thinks that this acquisition occurs during the patristic era, even as conscience during this era continues to function in its proper role of making the reasoning-willing moral agent morally self-aware of the quality of her faith's attentiveness to God's work in Christ to make all things new. In addition to this role, however, O'Donovan detects in Greek patristic literature a further identification "of conscience as one's instructor."[42] Here O'Donovan finds Chrysostom anticipating Kant, speaking of "two instructors, creation without and conscience within, the latter murmuring suggestions as 'to all that is to be done.'"[43] O'Donovan concludes that conscience here has become "more or less" identifiable with moral reason and has as its context "nothing less than the 'natural law.'"[44] Nonetheless, O'Donovan concedes that there is still enough emphasis in the patristic era on conscience as making a person transparent before God that the conscience is not yet explicitly or exclusively identified with moral reason.

It is in the scholastic era, O'Donovan claims, that the identification of conscience and moral reason, or conscience and "the whole faculty of moral understanding," becomes explicit.[45] We see this identification generally in the scholastic treatment of conscience as the habit that directs a person about how to put into practice the knowledge of "moral first principles" a person knows "a priori."[46] This shift

---

38. Oliver O'Donovan, *The Ways of Judgment* (Grand Rapids, MI: Eerdmans, 2005), 303.

39. O'Donovan, *Ways*, 305.

40. O'Donovan, *Ways*, 304.

41. O'Donovan, *Ways*, 305.

42. O'Donovan, *Ways*, 303.

43. O'Donovan, *Ways*, 304.

44. O'Donovan, *Ways*, 304.

45. O'Donovan, *Ways*, 306. O'Donovan appears to use "moral reason" and "moral understanding" interchangeably.

46. O'Donovan, *Ways*, 306.

in the scholastic era to an explicit identification of conscience with moral reason leads to a deeply problematic moral psychology, O'Donovan argues, that takes as normative a sharp separation of reason and will in the moral agent. This moral psychology is so problematic, according to O'Donovan, because it makes the moral agent accountable not to God and the moral order in which she lives and moves and has her being but to a standard entirely within herself. Whereas in the New Testament and in much patristic literature conscience is an awareness of oneself as accountable to God and a moral order within which a person is a moral agent, here in the scholastic era the identification of conscience and moral reason suggests a shift in the locus of accountability. A person is now no longer a reasoning-willing being accountable through conscience to the moral order, but is rather a moral agent who has a will and is accountable to the content of her conscience as moral reason. O'Donovan sees this most acutely in the scholastic era in Aquinas's account of the errant conscience, specifically, whether an errant conscience creates an obligation and whether it constitutes an acquittal of the moral agent. O'Donovan thinks Aquinas does a valiant job trying to resist a sharp separation, and consequent alienation, of the reason from the will, but the way the question is given to him makes that outcome inevitable. The result is that conscience, appearing here on analogy with "the misguided commands of a ruler or with the accidental weakness of a faculty such as sight or hearing,"[47] now assumes the authority that rightly belongs to the redeemed moral order. The assumption behind Aquinas's questions about the errant conscience is that the conscience carries authority within the moral agent (making the problem of the errant conscience rather troubling) and that the will constitutes the "ontological ground of personal agency, the 'real me' who is the subject of my acts. The will alone," O'Donovan concludes, "is the true moral subject who is 'obliged' or 'excused.'"[48] Consequently, the moral agent becomes essentially a will with a conscience ("or reason") at its disposal.[49] The moral agent is now not so much a reasoning-willing being accountable to God for a faith that is attentive to the moral order as much as a will summoned to attend in freedom to the guidance of conscience as moral reason.

Scholastic moral psychology, according to O'Donovan, with its identification of conscience and moral reason, with its consequent distancing of conscience from the will, and with its emphasis on the free will as the authentic seat of moral agency makes for a very precarious development in moral theology. The task of decisively severing the moral agent from "reality" has yet to be achieved, but, O'Donovan suggests, the scholastics have nicely set that table. If the scholastic moral agent still has a purchase on the redeemed moral order, she is hanging on to it by a thread. The theory of conscience that develops during the Reformation, however, disrupts this precarious decline of conscience and its contribution to

---

47. O'Donovan, *Resurrection*, 116.
48. O'Donovan, *Resurrection*, 116.
49. O'Donovan, *Resurrection*, 116.

the severing of moral agency from reality. During the Reformation, conscience returns to its Pauline and Patristic role as representing a self-disclosing encounter with the judgment of God. But this return, according to O'Donovan, turns out to be a disastrous pyrrhic victory because as the scholastic conception of conscience as moral reason makes a return in the seventeenth and eighteenth centuries, it carries along with it the immediacy of being before God it acquired during the Reformation. Conscience once again acts as an internal moral guide but now with the connotation that it is the voice of God or a divine vice regent in the soul. There are disagreements between rationalists and sentimentalists about the nature of this divinely sanctioned internal guidance, but, O'Donovan argues, there is a more fundamental agreement that characterizes the whole early modern period: "to vindicate freedom as autonomy, that is to say in terms of an authority for action which belonged entirely to the moral agent himself and was not derived from external reality."[50]

The role of conscience in this effort to vindicate freedom as autonomy is nowhere clearer, according to O'Donovan, than in Kant's moral philosophy, where we see "the Western program of agent autonomy" carried "to its height."[51] It is not possible to sustain a sharp separation of reason and will, O'Donovan claims, and in Kant's theory of conscience the two come together again under the heading of "rational will." We see in Kant's theory of conscience as rational will, then, the pinnacle of modern autonomy because, distilling the rationalist and sentimentalist conscience that went before it, Kant's rational will acts as moral reason, as respect for moral law, and as the free, authentic seat of moral agency. Consequently, by means of the rational will the moral agent maintains her "independence from all laws [she] has not legislated for [herself]," and binds herself to "universal principles but without acknowledging any indebtedness to external reality."[52] And so, here in Kant's theory of conscience, the moral agent's decisive separation from reality is complete.

Once the ground is laid to associate conscience with the faculty of moral reason, once conscience begins to acquire a directive aspect, the notion of freedom as autonomy—freedom to be whatever one wants to be—is inevitable. Unlike Lehmann, O'Donovan does not offer this narrative as a prolegomenon to a revised theory of conscience—though through his brief comments we can see what such a theory might look like, and ironically it is not too far from the theory I propose to retrieve from Kant and the theological tradition that follows Kant such as we find in Kierkegaard. This is ironic because O'Donovan's narrative conscience has reached its full decline in Kant's moral philosophy and after Kant, O'Donovan suggests, conscience has become too slippery to retrieve; too many problematic notions now cling to conscience and it appears to be too inextricably tied to the free,

---

50. O'Donovan, *Resurrection*, 119.
51. O'Donovan, *Resurrection*, 119.
52. O'Donovan, *Resurrection*, 119.

autonomous moral agent of modernity to try to salvage now.[53] I think O'Donovan is wrong about this, though, and as I will argue in the final chapter, O'Donovan is a much more affirmative interlocutor of Kant and the trajectory of conscience Kant represents than he might realize.[54]

Lehmann's and O'Donovan's narratives of the decline and fall of conscience share the concern that conscience now serves the purpose of propping up the ahistorical, atomistic, autonomous individual of modern life that MacIntyre and Hauerwas describe. Both also share the view that Kant's moral philosophy and Kant's theory of conscience are foundational in the development of this modern role for conscience. Lehmann especially but O'Donovan as well offers their narratives of conscience as a kind of road map to help us see where we should and should not—but easily could—go in our conceptions of conscience. I have appealed here to Lehmann and O'Donovan because between the two of them we have a leading contemporary moral theologian more or less recapitulating the concern of a leading moral theologian half a century ago. What I think this juxtaposition of their narratives of the decline and fall of conscience suggests is that worries about conscience have changed very little over the past five decades. I have appealed to Lehmann and O'Donovan also because they write at two distinct moments in the recent history of reflection on conscience. Lehmann writes at the end of an era in which almost every major theologian felt compelled to write something about conscience. This compulsion was for the most part born out of a concern like Lehmann's that conscience was in such a bad state that it needed either significant revision or dismissal. Revision appears to have been the majority opinion in the early and middle part of the twentieth century as Emil Brunner, Karl Barth, Dietrich Bonhoeffer, Kenneth Kirk, Paul Tillich, Gerhard Ebeling, H. Richard Niebuhr, Helmut Thielicke among others all attempted to formulate a theory of conscience. Lehmann's attempt to offer a theory of conscience comes

---

53. He claims, for example, that "it is certainly to be regretted that 'conscience' ... appears to the Vatican fathers a suitable category for asserting individual freedom of religious decision" (*Resurrection*, 168). And in his recent *Self, World, and Time: Ethics as Theology* (Grand Rapids, MI: Eerdmans, 2013) he more or less cedes conscience to modernity (36). He does suggest in a footnote in *The Ways of Judgment*, however, that we should perhaps not be "too ready to dispense altogether with the task of reflexive self-examination" that traditionally belongs to conscience (*Ways*, 308). We should not indeed, I argue, and it is by appeal to Kant's theory of conscience that we might begin to reconceive of what that task looks like.

54. But perhaps he does realize this. From *Resurrection and Moral Order* to *Ways of Judgment*, O'Donovan appears to be letting up on his criticism of Kant. In *Ways of Judgment* he offers the same basic account of the history of conscience but where Kant appears at the nadir of this narrative in *Resurrection and Moral Order*, O'Donovan does not mention Kant in *Ways of Judgment*. The description of the nadir is the same just without Kant attached to it. O'Donovan is, moreover, a bit more optimistic in *Ways* that moral theology should still try to make room for conscience.

at the end of this flood of attention to conscience that would soon after turn to a trickle and eventually dry out. O'Donovan's attention to conscience is notable in part simply because he pays attention to it at all.

Revising Conscience Out of Existence: From Niebuhr to Hauerwas

It is not the case, however, that between Lehmann and O'Donovan a self-conscious consensus emerged that it was best to leave conscience alone. Certainly a weariness with the effort to revise conscience appears to have set in, but the dismissal of conscience from contemporary moral theology stems more from those very efforts in the middle of the twentieth century by theologians like Lehmann, Ebeling, and especially H. Richard Niebuhr to revise conscience; in terms of the narrative I have been telling, the mid-century efforts to revise conscience are efforts to rescue conscience from the Kantian constraints that brought conscience to its nadir, to the point where it licenses a theologically untenable conception of individual moral agency. And so, in response to this devolution and its implications, conscience is revised in such a way as to respect the contingent, historical, and fundamentally social character of our existence as human beings. But from H. Richard Niebuhr to Stanley Hauerwas, we can see how once conscience is enlisted in a description of moral agency as socially formed and socially mediated conscience quite naturally vanishes and gives way to attention to social practices and habits and corporate self-understanding.

For H. Richard Niebuhr conscience is an important element of responsible moral agency. By responsibility Niebuhr draws attention to the basic linguistic and social aspects of our being. He writes that "to be engaged in dialogue, to answer questions addressed to us, to defend ourselves against attacks, to reply to injunctions, to meet challenges—this is common human experience. And now we try to think of our actions as having this character, of being responses, answers to actions upon us."[55] Our actions, Niebuhr explains, are always a response to action upon us that we have interpreted. Our actions are always as if they were a part of a conversation and they flow from us out of our interpretation of ourselves as members of the dialogue. We seek to make our actions "fit," Niebuhr writes, into an interpreted "whole as a sentence fits into a paragraph in a book, a note into a chord in a movement in a symphony."[56] Our sense of who we are, our "active practical self-definition," is not derived, therefore, finally from our relation to an abstract moral law or an ideal final end but from our interpretation of the actions upon us, from our interpretation of just what kind of book or symphony we find ourselves in.[57] And so the responsible self's key questions are "To whom or what am I responsible and in what community of interpretation am I myself?"[58]

---

55. H. Richard Niebuhr, *The Responsible Self: An Essay in Christian Moral Philosophy* (New York: Harper and Row, 1963), 56.
   56. Niebuhr, *Responsible Self*, 97.
   57. Niebuhr, *Responsible Self*, 59.
   58. Niebuhr, *Responsible Self*, 68.

We can be confident that a person as a responsible self knows herself "primarily not before an end or a law but before other selves" because of the swelling of attention to the sociality of human nature. We see much more strongly now than we did before, Niebuhr writes, "the social character of all human life."[59] Niebuhr does not want to deny that the self "exists as a rational being in the presence of mores and laws," but he wants to emphasize the centrality of "the fundamentally social character of self-hood." He explains that "to be a self in the presence of other selves is not a derivative experience but primordial."[60] Niebuhr is making both an epistemic and an ontological claim about the self with this emphasis on "primordial" sociality. His claim is that a person not only rightly knows her moral agency in relation to other selves but also knows that her moral agency "exists in that relation."[61] Niebuhr endorses G. H. Mead's claim that "the self, as that which can be an object to itself is *essentially* a social structure ... it arises in social experiences."[62]

Mead's account of the social self and the social conscience are here foundational to Niebuhr's account of conscience. Niebuhr begins with the assumption that conscience is most basically the experience of "an alter in the ego," the experience of transcending ourselves by becoming an object to ourselves much as other people are objects to us since we encounter them and they encounter us as Thou's, as Not-I's. And so in the conscience we see ourselves as an other because we see ourselves through the eyes of an other. And this is necessarily the case because, again, we are primordially social beings; we exist as selves only in the presence of others. As Mead writes, this means that as human beings we come to selfhood by assuming "the generalized attitude of the group"; we do this "in the censor that stands at the door of our imagining and inner conversation, and in the affirmation of the laws and axioms of the universe of discourse. ... Our thinking is an inner conversation in which we may be taking the roles of specific acquaintances over against ourselves, but usually it is with the 'generalized other' that we converse."[63] Niebuhr summarizes Mead's concept of the "generalized other" as "a sort of composite photograph which the self makes of the associates in his society."[64] Niebuhr thinks this is a good place to begin thinking about conscience, but he offers the qualifications that a person does not live in one society but many and so we would do better to speak of multiple generalized others, and, moreover, it is not with whole groups that we interact at any particular moment but with particular individuals. These particular individuals belong, of course, within a broader system of interaction, and so when a person meets this particular alter in her ego

---

59. Niebuhr, *Responsible Self*, 69.

60. Niebuhr, *Responsible Self*, 71.

61. Niebuhr, *Responsible Self*, 71.

62. Quoted in Niebuhr, *Responsible Self*, 72, emphasis mine.

63. Quoted in H. Richard Niebuhr, "The Ego Alter Dialectic and the Conscience," *Journal of Philosophy*, vol. 42, no. 13 (June 21, 1945), 354.

64. Niebuhr, "Ego-Alter," 354.

she meets "something general in the particular."[65] What Niebuhr means is that within a particular culture—be that the culture of the family, the workplace, the religious community, and so on, a person has particular relationships that exhibit constancies and these constancies are intelligible within their particular system of interaction, within their particular culture. The alter in my ego, for example, might at one time be my brother but it is not simply my brother who confronts me but my brother as he represents something general about my family's culture. To say, then, that we meet in our conscience "something general in the particular" is to say that the conscience "represents not so much my awareness of the approvals or disapprovals of other individuals in isolation as of the ethos of my society, that is, of its mode of interpersonal interactions."[66]

The language of interpreting constancies in particular relations within broader systems of interaction and then internalizing these constancies can suggest a degree of activity in the self's construction of his or her moral agency that Niebuhr carefully qualifies. He does think that we do often actively ask ourselves whether or not our actions would meet the approval of a trusted companion, and he acknowledges that we often deceive ourselves in this questioning since we would prefer "to imagine very friendly others."[67] But for the most part, Niebuhr claims, the others whom we confront within ourselves "are aggressive, entering into the inner life unbidden with painful views of itself ... the self does not have the power over them to fashion them in its own image."[68] Our internalization of constancies within systems of interpersonal relations is, in other words, "not simply an affair of our conscious rational mind, but also of the deep memories that are buried within us, of feelings and intuitions that are only partly under our control."[69] Moral feeling is therefore an integral element of the ego-alter dialectic, especially as that part over it which we do not control. I cannot choose when to feel guilty about what I have done or not done. I have no control over when the alter in my ego will confront me with a rebuke and incite my guilt.

The significant assumption I want to highlight here is that for Niebuhr it is in relation to this alter in the ego, in relation to this representation of a social ethos, that a person experiences guilt or assurance in his or her actions. It is only as members of societies, Niebuhr argues that a person "feels pride and shame."[70] "I experience my guilt," he claims, "not as a relation to the law or to an ideal but to my companions. And I experience it not as my relation to timeless beings but as a relation to a continuous interaction that has gone on and will go on through a long time."[71] Niebuhr is here making an important claim about accountability

---

65. Niebuhr, *Responsible Self*, 77.
66. Niebuhr, *Responsible Self*, 79.
67. Niebuhr, "Ego-Alter," 355.
68. Niebuhr, "Ego-Alter," 355.
69. Niebuhr, *Responsible Self*, 63.
70. Niebuhr, "Ego-Alter," 354.
71. Niebuhr, *Responsible Self*, 95.

and it is a claim at the heart of his account of conscience and moral agency. The responsible self knows herself through and acts by means of her interpretation of actions upon her and in anticipation of responses to those actions. Our actions are contributions to an ongoing conversation, an unfolding narrative and we can only act as we interpret how our action fits in the conversation or the story, and a crucial part of this interpretation is anticipating what will come next, what responses it will solicit. "Our action is responsible," Niebuhr writes, "when it is response to action upon us in a continuing discourse or interaction among beings forming a continuing society. ... Personal responsibility implies the continuity of a self with a relatively consistent scheme of interpretations of what it is reacting to," and "it implies continuity in the community of agents to which the response is being made."[72] The conscience of the responsible self, by means of pride and guilt, counsel and judgment, holds a person accountable to the conversation in which the self and the other are engaged. The conversations in which we participate are the various societies we find ourselves in and the others we find within ourselves are the particulars who hold us accountable to whatever conversation we participate in with them.

Niebuhr here makes use of the language of loyalty to a cause, which he borrows from the philosophy of Josiah Royce. He explains that the ego-alter dialectic always occurs in the "presence of a third from which I and thou are distinguished and to which they also respond."[73] Niebuhr gives the example of the "democratic patriot" in the United States who carries on "his dialogue with current companions, but as one who is also in relation to what his companions refer to—representatives of the community such as Washingtons, Jeffersons, Madisons, Lincolns, etc. Responsive to his companions he is also responsive to a transcendent reference *group*." And this reference group, in turn, refers beyond itself toward something that they and their descendants—the contemporary patriot and his companions—stand for.[74] The dialogue between the self and an other, then, is never simply about that self and that other but "is always explicitly or implicitly about something and that something must be a thing with which both social partners are in communications."[75] The responsible self is accountable to this third thing, this cause about which she and her companions converse. Of course in her accountability she is only relatively independent of her companions because it is only in their presence that a person acquires the skills to describe and interpret what the conversation is about. And of course it is always by means of these companions that a person is held accountable to this third thing. "To these fellow members," Niebuhr writes, "I am challenged to be faithful, but not otherwise than in faithfulness to the common cause."[76]

---

72. Niebuhr, *Responsible Self*, 65.
73. Niebuhr, *Responsible Self*, 79.
74. Niebuhr, *Responsible Self*, 85, emphasis mine.
75. Niebuhr, *Responsible Self*, 80.
76. Niebuhr, *Responsible Self*, 86.

A person lives in multiple societies, with many internalized particulars who hold her accountable to something more general. A person has, as it were, a clamor of consciences within, a host of ego-alter dialectics from the many circles in which she lives. These circles, furthermore, are not only not always concentric but are also often at odds with one another. Here a person's active power of choice becomes particularly important. In one ego-alter dialectic I meet an other who approves of an action and before whom I feel a sense of pride and achievement. But about this same action I find another alter in the ego who disapproves and before whom my feelings of guilt may arise. Clearly, there is a tension here and the responsible self must make a kind of meta-ethical choice about which of these consciences she is going to endorse. She finds within herself a conflict in the causes to which her companions hold her accountable. She wants to be loyal to the American cause, for example, and her experience with AmeriCorps has inculcated in her an ego-alter dialectic that holds her accountable to the American cause by holding her accountable to a certain kind of civil service. But she also grew up in a politically conservative, "Tea-Party" family in the American south. And so she encounters within herself a conflict: on the one hand there is the familial ego-alter dialectic in which she encounters the person of her mother or father or a sibling, extolling the virtues of personal responsibility, self-reliance, and small government. On the other hand, there is the AmeriCorps ego-alter dialectic, in which she encounters the person of a coworker or a client holding her accountable to a certain kind of service that goes against the internalized ethos of her family. If she is going to be a responsible, conscientious self, she must make a choice between these two ego-alter dialectics. We can see here that freedom, according to Niebuhr, is not a nontemporal, supersensible causality in a person, nor is it the condition for arbitrary self-creation. Freedom here is the ability to interpret one's life according to "its ultimate historical context."[77] "It seems," Niebuhr explains, "that in so far as the self has one such last other, or last society which constitutes its last resort, after it has been excluded from or has excluded itself from all other companionship, insofar as it has a god, a being on which it is absolutely dependent for its value and on whose judgment it cannot deny without denying itself."[78] A person's freedom consists in her ability to interpret her past and her future according to a highest court of appeal, a highest cause or loyalty. And so while a person has no choice about which alters she will find in her ego, she does have some power—though not absolute power—to choose which ego-alter dialectics she will heed and which she will not, and of those she heeds the extent to which she heeds them and the order she places them relative to each other. A person's freedom is a freedom to find her "center of valuation," the sense of an "ultimate community of interaction," relative to which the others are penultimate or spurious.[79] The responsible self is free not to create the center of value but to discern where it is and to bring her life

77. Niebuhr, *Responsible Self*, 101.
78. Niebuhr, "Ego-Alter," 357.
79. Niebuhr, *Responsible Self*, 124, 109.

into conformity with it. And so in sum, if responsible action is always action in response to the interpretations of what is going on, and if interpretation of what is going on is a social skill—a corollary of our primordial sociality—then the responsible self is a moral agent who discerns the most fundamental alter in her ego, her most fundamental societal membership and who then freely brings her life into accord with it.

Niebuhr's description of the self who discerns the center of value or highest court of appeals among her ego-alter dialectics conveys his belief that the self is not reducible to the nexus of her personal relations. He assumes, that is, the existence of a self that can step back from the nexus of relations. But God comes to the self through these relations and so it is as the responsible self internalizes these external relations that she can discern the presence of the One behind the many and find her "ultimate community of interaction." The self's responses to the various alters in her ego and ultimately to the most fundamental alter in her ego, Niebuhr explains, are "interrelated with the response to God as the ultimate person, the ultimate cause, the center of the universal community."[80] God is the One who sustains the many societies that constitute any person's life, and when a person seeks a final court of appeal which places all her societies "in the one universal society," she places her faith in the one in whom she and her societies live and move and have their being.[81] Niebuhr is somewhat opaque as he makes this point and his reflection on his own experience is helpful. He says of himself, "my relation to God has been ... deeply conditioned by this presence of Jesus Christ in my history and in our history." And so he claims this history conditioned by Christ's presence as his own, as his highest cause: "I identify myself with what I understand to be the cause of Christ ... I have been challenged to make his cause my own."[82] While Niebuhr affirms that each person "exists and moves and has his being in God," and has as his or her most "fundamental relation" the relation to God, he also claims that the historical qualification of that relation is "inescapable."[83] The primordially social self, that is, cannot "rise above those specific relations to God in which" he or she "has been placed."[84] Rather, God comes to a person in and through these relations. In this account Jesus Christ is not so much a "representative of a society so much as the spiritual organizer of a community."[85] The Christian, then, is one who finds her relation to God, her center of value most fundamentally in the "cause of Christ," which is to say, by identifying above all with those internalized particular others she finds within herself who

80. Niebuhr, *Responsible Self*, 86.
81. Niebuhr, *Responsible Self*, 123–4.
82. Niebuhr, *Responsible Self*, 43.
83. Niebuhr, *Responsible Self*, 44. Here, as we will see in the next chapter, is a crucial difference between Niebuhr and Kant, who refuses to concede to what we might call Niebuhr's bottom-up approach to conscience.
84. Niebuhr, *Responsible Self*, 45.
85. Niebuhr, "Ego-Alter," 354.

represent the ethos of the society that carries that cause. It is in this cause that the Christian finds her fundamental relation to God and so it is in this cause that she is able to place the ultimate meaning of the many societies in which she lives. And it is only by transgressing the norms of this cause, norms she knows and feels through the presence of the particular companions she finds within herself, that she feels the guilt that threatens the very core of her being and summons her deepest repentance.

For Niebuhr, in sum, conscience is the internalization of a social ethos, and God is at work as the One behind the many societies that make up life on earth. The contingencies of every human life determine for each person the interpretive social contexts for his or her agency, and it is within these societies that a person seeks to discern the One that helps her best grasp the whole, the one that informs her understanding of the many, and the One which she cannot deny without denying herself.

Between Niebuhr and Hauerwas: MacIntyre's Narrative Self

It is not surprising that Stanley Hauerwas offers an account of moral agency with clear resemblances to Niebuhr's ethics of responsibility. Hauerwas's intellectual formation was deeply imbued with Niebuhr's influence and he credits his initial concern with agency to his study of Niebuhr with James Gustafson (himself a student of Niebuhr).[86] What is noteworthy, however, is that while Hauerwas can sound so much like Niebuhr in his description of moral agency and action, he never entertains a theory of conscience. The reason for this is not that Hauerwas explicitly rejects Niebuhr's theory of conscience or the notion of conscience in general, but rather that by developing further an account like Niebuhr's of the social formation of moral agency and the social mediation of self-knowledge Hauerwas illustrates that conscience is at best superfluous and at worst counterproductive in such an account.

Hauerwas's work on moral agency comes at the end of a trajectory that has Niebuhr's theory of conscience at its outset. An important moment in this trajectory especially for Hauerwas's work is Alasdair MacIntyre's account of the "narrative concept of selfhood." Hauerwas himself claims that MacIntyre's work builds on Niebuhr's contribution in the "rediscovery of narrative."[87] MacIntyre's case for a "narrative concept of selfhood" is, somewhat like Niebuhr's account of the social formation of conscience, in contrast to the Kantian-inspired modern individualism that tells us to believe that we are what we choose to be and that tells

---

86. See Stanley Hauerwas, "Agency: Going Forward by Looking Back," in *Christian Ethics: Problems and Prospects*, ed. Lisa Cahill and James Childress (Cleveland, OH: Pilgrim Press, 1996), 185-6.

87. See Hauerwas and Jones (eds.), *Why Narrative? Readings in Narrative Theology* (Eugene, OR: Wipf and Stock, 1997), 5, 8-9.

us that we can always "put in question ... the merely contingent social features" of our existence.[88] To think in this modern individualistic mode, MacIntyre argues, can only "deform" our "present relationships" because we are, each of us, "in key part what" we inherit, "a specific past that is present in some degree in" our present. We find ourselves, he continues, "part of a history and that is generally to say, whether [we] like it or not, whether [we] recognize it or not," we are each "bearers of a tradition."[89] "We approach all our own circumstances," in other words, "as bearers of a particular social identity."[90] Individual personal identity is therefore derivative from the story of a particular community. The self, that is, "has to find its moral identity in and through its membership in communities." "We enter human society," he continues, "with one or more imputed characters—roles into which we have been drafted."[91]

We come into being, MacIntyre claims, in the midst of a particular history, a narrative or drama, and within this narrative we are given a particular role to play. Like Niebuhr, MacIntyre depicts the narrative quality of our moral agency and identity in terms of a conversation, which MacIntyre claims is "an enacted dramatic narrative" and is "the form of human transactions in general."[92] It is as though we have been thrust into the middle of an ongoing conversation, and our task as moral agents is to learn the conversation's distinct language and to find our particular voice, to discover the roles we are given to inhabit. "What is good for me," MacIntyre argues, "has to be the good for one who inhabits these roles. ... These [roles] constitute the given of my life, my moral starting point."[93] What we have to do, then, is to learn our given role so that we can join in the conversation, so that we can "be able to understand how others respond to us and how our responses to them are apt to be constructed."[94] Like Niebuhr, then, MacIntyre grounds moral agency in interpretation—interpretation of where one is and what is going on—and like Niebuhr he describes proper moral action as action that fits with the interpretation.

What we will find as we take up our role and join in the conversation is that we are participants in a tradition, a "historically extended, socially embodied argument ... about the goods that constitute that tradition,"[95] and it is only as we participate in this particular argument that we can "search for the good" that is universal for human beings as such.[96] But, like Niebuhr, MacIntyre cautions that in

---

88. MacIntyre, "The Virtues, the Unity of a Human Life, and the Concept of a Tradition," in *Why Narrative*, 105; with Kant in view, 106.
89. MacIntyre, "The Virtues," 105.
90. MacIntyre, "The Virtues," 105.
91. MacIntyre, "The Virtues," 101.
92. MacIntyre, "The Virtues," 96.
93. MacIntyre, "The Virtues," 105.
94. MacIntyre, "The Virtues," 101.
95. MacIntyre, "The Virtues," 107.
96. MacIntyre, "The Virtues," 106.

this search we never leave behind our contingent social locations or our particular given roles. With our conversation partners—our fellow bearers of a particular tradition—we embark on a quest that is "not at all a search for something already adequately characterized, as miners search for gold or geologists for oil." We better understand our quest as a constantly evolving "education both as to the character of that which is sought and in self-knowledge."[97] It is as our particular conversation unfolds that we discern more clearly what it is we are talking about and who we are as participants in the conversation.

Our moral identity is constituted by the conversation we find ourselves in, and, MacIntyre argues, it is as participants in the conversation that we are ultimately accountable as moral agents. We possess "*only the resources of psychological continuity*," MacIntyre claims, which is to say we cannot create our moral identity but we can give an account of the unity of the life given to us to live. MacIntyre affirms both that "I am what I may justifiably be taken by others to be" and that "I am the subject of a history that is my own and no one else's."[98] I cannot find my identity but I must take ownership of the role given to me and I do so by being able to give an intelligible account of my own life. We "are never more (and sometimes less) than the coauthors of our own narratives,"[99] but we are each accountable to "respond to the imputation of strict identity."[100] We are each to be like literary critics who can adequately interpret the story we find ourselves in and who can account for the character in the story we have been given to play. And, likewise, we are to hold others accountable to give their own intelligible interpretations of the story and of their lives in it. In his narrative account of the self, then, MacIntyre claims that we know ourselves rightly only in our accountability to others. It is within a particular tradition that others give to us our moral identity, but we become responsible participants within that tradition as we become capable to give an account to our companions of who we know ourselves to be.

The Disappearance of Conscience: Hauerwas on Corporate Self-Awareness

Stanley Hauerwas's account of moral agency, accountability, and self-knowledge builds on Niebuhr's account of responsibility and MacIntyre's account of the narrative self. Hauerwas does not, of course, describe his moral theology as an ethics of responsibility, but in his account of moral agency he stresses the importance of action that is fitting, coherent, and intelligible. Like Niebuhr Hauerwas's primary question is not "what must I do," but "what is going on," and so like Niebuhr and MacIntyre he argues that moral agency requires interpretation if action is to be coherent, intelligible, and fitting. Like Niebuhr and MacIntyre,

---

97. MacIntyre, "The Virtues," 104.
98. MacIntyre, "The Virtues," 103, emphasis mine.
99. MacIntyre, "The Virtues," 99.
100. MacIntyre, "The Virtues," 102.

furthermore, Hauerwas emphasizes the indispensable centrality of social life, of community to train a person to interpret what is going on and to act accordingly. Hauerwas is not, of course, interested in a general ethic or a general anthropology but in the church and what it means for the church to live as the church in the world. But while this ecclesial emphasis sets him apart from Niebuhr, his account of interpretation and intelligible action remains close to Niebuhr's ethics of responsibility. He writes, "We can only act in the world we can envision and we can envision the world rightly only as we are trained to see. We do not come to see merely by looking but must develop the disciplined skills through initiation into that community that attempts to live faithful to the story."[101] It is in the community, in life with others, that a person discerns certain constancies of actions, habits and practices that disclose a vision of how the world is and that provide a precondition for fitting or intelligible action.

But why, for Hauerwas, is it the case that action requires interpretation and that interpretation requires community? Action requires interpretation, he claims with Niebuhr and MacIntyre, because we are irreducibly contingent, historical beings. Our existence, he writes, is *"historically determined,"* and so "we should not be surprised to discover that our moralities are historical; they require a qualifier. We are unable to stand outside our histories in midair."[102] We are, in other words, "narrative determined creatures," and we cannot act until we discern the narrative we are in. "It is in our nature to be historic," and so our action is coherent only as we act in accord with the history that determines us; "we are," in short, "beings whose life requires narrative display."[103]

Perhaps it goes without saying, but the affirmation that we are irreducibly historical, narrative beings is an affirmation also of our primordial sociality because historical traditions represent constancies in the life of a people over time; any given history or tradition constitutes the life of a particular people and that particular people mediate their tradition through their life together. A moral agent, therefore, is one who is able to place her action within a history, which is to say, "within a community of language users."[104] To say that we are historical beings, then, is to say with Niebuhr and MacIntyre that our moral agency has been given to us by others. And here Hauerwas endorses MacIntyre's claim that "I am in key part what I inherit, a specific past that is present to some degree in my present. I find myself part of a history and that is generally to say whether I like it or not, whether I recognize it or not, one of the bearers of a tradition."[105]

An important corollary of this commitment to our basic historicity and sociality is that, for Hauerwas as for Niebuhr and MacIntyre, the norms by which we live our lives intelligibly within a given history are social norms. Moral norms are

---

101. Hauerwas, *Peaceable Kingdom*, 29.
102. Hauerwas, *Peaceable Kingdom*, 29, emphasis mine.
103. Hauerwas, *Peaceable Kingdom*, 35.
104. Hauerwas, *Peaceable Kingdom*, 42.
105. Hauerwas, *Peaceable Kingdom*, 45.

"dependent on a particular people's history," that is, because "the very nature and structure of ethics is determined by the particularities of a community's history and convictions."[106] Hauerwas's claim here is similar to Niebuhr's that our action is intelligible not only as it is informed by the history that determines us but also as it anticipates responses from those with whom we share that history. We can see this in what Hauerwas says about a community's prohibitions. The prohibitions that determine the kinds of actions available to us if we are going to continue to act as bearers of that tradition are socially determined prohibitions. "Prohibitions," Hauerwas explains, "are the markers of the outer limits of the communal self-understandings. In short, they tell us if we do this or no longer disapprove of that we will no longer be living out the *tradition* that originally formed us."[107] This is not to say, Hauerwas claims, that community creates its norms arbitrarily; it is to say, however, that moral norms emerge in and are realized through the community's practices and habits, and as the community reflects on these practices and habits in light of its "ongoing experience."[108] It is within this ongoing reflection on its own life that a community comes to a greater self-understanding and sees more clearly what actions do and do not correspond to that self-understanding. We are accountable to the community's cause, in other words, and I think Hauerwas could here say with Niebuhr, "I experience my guilt not as a relation to the law or to an ideal but to my companions. And I experience it not as my relation to timeless beings but as a relation to a continuous interaction that has gone on and will go on through a long time."[109]

For Niebuhr the social mediation of moral agency and moral norms created the problem of competing ego-alter dialectics, a problem we resolve, he argues, by finding a highest court of appeal, a kind of supreme conscience among the many consciences. The problem emerged, in part, because Niebuhr is intent to describe moral agency in general and moral agency in general occurs across several communities. A person always plays many roles. Hauerwas is not naïve or insensitive to this point, but his concern is with the inner life and mission of the Christian community and with what it means to conceive of agency within that community. Hauerwas here could turn to conscience as the moral agent's internalization of the Christian community's moral norms. He might say that the Christian is one who makes these norms his or her highest court of appeal. And this would be consistent with his account of freedom as a freedom to embrace our history, as a freedom to claim our lives as our own by learning to tell the story that above all others determines our lives.[110] When we so freely act, we find that the community's self-understanding takes root in us affecting our subjective state, disciplining not only our moral reason but also our moral feeling so that whether

---

106. Hauerwas, *Peaceable Kingdom*, 2, 1.
107. Hauerwas, *Peaceable Kingdom*, 119, emphasis mine.
108. Hauerwas, *Peaceable Kingdom*, 119.
109. Niebuhr, *Responsible Self*, 95.
110. Hauerwas, *Peaceable Kingdom*, 8, 26.

we like it or not contentment and assurance, guilt and shame will accompany our actions depending on the conformity or lack of conformity of our actions to the community's self-understanding.

So why does Hauerwas not turn here, as Niebuhr does, to a description of conscience? He very well could along the lines I suggested, and I think it would appear, accordingly, quite similar to Niebuhr's ego-alter dialectic. But I suspect for that very reason Hauerwas does not entertain a theory of conscience. By assimilating the processes of social formation to the ego-alter dialectic, Niebuhr converts these processes into objects for the responsible *self* to evaluate as she looks within herself. There are hints of a similar dynamic in Hauerwas's account of agency. Hauerwas too appears to assume the existence of a self who exists with a degree of independence from narrative, history, or tradition and who makes use of these to claim her life as her own. But Hauerwas is aware of this and he worries about the ways he might unwittingly assume "an ahistorical view of the self, a transcendental self somewhere always behind my character."[111] Unlike Niebuhr, Hauerwas clearly rejects this notion of the self. Niebuhr's ego-alter dialectic offers an image of the individual moral agent who turns within herself and discerns the claims made upon her by the various ego-alter dialectics and who then steps back from these claims, transcending them, in order to adjudicate among them. Hauerwas denies that a person can step back in this way.

For Hauerwas we are contingent beings fully determined by our history; our history gives us our character and "we are our character."[112] Why, then, should a person turn within herself? This is the question Hauerwas's account of the social formation of moral agency and self-knowledge presents. It is not that the individual's subjective state is unimportant—for an ethics of character like Hauerwas's that would be an absurd claim. But the locus of deliberation and discernment should not be located within the individual but without, in the community. If we are our character and if our community determines our character, then self-examination and self-knowledge are properly social tasks. This is Hauerwas's point that casuistry is not about adjudicating "difficult cases of conscience," but rather that it is "the process by which a tradition tests whether its practices are consistent ... or inconsistent in light of its basic habits and convictions or whether these convictions require new practices and behavior."[113] Through its habits and practices and its reflection on those habits and practices the community discerns what it means to act according to its tradition; the individual, then, should look not within herself but to those habits and practices, and she should then bring her life into conformity with those habits and practices. Hauerwas of course leaves some space for personal self-examination but this is a practice the individual undertakes chiefly to ensure her life is in concert with the narrative of the people of God where she finds her life.[114]

111. Hauerwas, *Peaceable Kingdom*, 39.
112. Hauerwas, *Peaceable Kingdom*, 39.
113. Hauerwas, *Peaceable Kingdom*, 120.
114. Hauerwas, *Peaceable Kingdom*, 131.

Like Niebuhr, then, Hauerwas makes the claim that God is present to us through our nexus of relationships, our histories, narratives, traditions. Unlike Niebuhr but like MacIntyre, Hauerwas is uncomfortable with any notion of selfhood or moral agency independent of history and tradition, and unlike Niebuhr, Hauerwas makes a strong claim for the church as the tradition that mediates God's presence. Niebuhr wants to affirm both the individual's direct, "fundamental relation to God," and the social mediation of that relation, and it's not entirely clear how he maintains both affirmations. Hauerwas is clearer. He claims we must be careful not to assume "our relationship with God has an immediacy that makes the journey of the self with God irrelevant."[115] That journey, he is clear, is our history, and our history, again, is the life of our community. Our freedom is a freedom to be who God calls us to be, Hauerwas writes, and, demonstrating the influence of MacIntyre, he argues that we not only know who God calls us to be but we can also become who God calls us to be only as we "become part of the people who carry the story of Jesus." God is present to us in Jesus Christ, that is, in the life of the people who carry that story. And so God's summons to us to be who God calls us to be is a summons heard and realized through the life of that people.[116] To speak of conscience might risk averting our attention away from the social location where we live and move and have our being. It is better to focus on social deliberation, better to look outward to the life of the people who make God's life present to us; it is better to engage in those practices than it is to turn within ourselves to discern the claim God is making upon us.[117] The task, for Hauerwas, is not to look within oneself but to let the particular, contingent, historical community that carries the story of Jesus speak through oneself.[118]

Summary and Conclusion

Through the course of this chapter I have presented two major challenges to the theory of conscience I propose to retrieve from Kant and Kierkegaard. There is, first, the challenge that this theory of conscience valorizes the modern, autonomous individual. To think of conscience along the lines Kant thinks about conscience, that is, encourages us to think we are whoever we choose to be, that we are accountable to a law we give to ourselves simply because it is the law we, as autonomous moral agents, have chosen for ourselves. In the next chapter I will offer an interpretation of Kant's theory of conscience in which it becomes clear that this

---

115. Hauerwas, *Peaceable Kingdom*, 27.
116. Hauerwas, *Peaceable Kingdom*, 46.
117. This commitment becomes even clearer later as Hauerwas claims that "the community called the church is constitutive of the gospel proclamation." See Stanley Hauerwas, *With Grain of the Universe: The Church's Witness and Natural Theology* (Grand Rapids, MI: Baker Academic, 2001), 145.
118. See here also Hauerwas's later essay, "Agency: Going Forward by Looking Back," 189.

first challenge rests on a severe misinterpretation of Kant's practical philosophy and moral theology in general and his theory of conscience in particular. I will argue that, for Kant, conscience is the knowledge we have of ourselves in our relation to God as God holds us accountable to a law that is necessary and binding for all rational beings. Kierkegaard stands in a line with Kant in this regard; he also offers a theory of conscience as our moral self-awareness in relation to God. Kierkegaard differs from Kant inasmuch as he understands the relation to God in much more personal and particular terms. But both present theories of conscience that resist the inadequate dichotomy we are presented with in much Christian ethics today: either an atomistic, self-asserting, autonomous individual or a communitarian, narrative determined self. Belonging to neither pole of this dichotomy, Kant's and Kierkegaard's theory of conscience depicts the individual as singularly accountable before God for the quality of his or her life, and they depict this accountability as ultimately distinct from any accountability before human communities.

There is indeed, I will argue, a strong emphasis on the individual in Kant's and Kierkegaard's theory of conscience. The testimony of a person's conscience is the testimony that the individual person has about herself in her relation to God. Correlatively, it is in the testimony of a person's conscience that she finds herself singularly and irreplaceably accountable to God. Kant and Kierkegaard each make a case, I will argue, for what Oliver O'Donovan describes as "the spiritual liberty of the individual" relative to the community, a liberty grounded in "the fact that [the individual] is immediately addressed by God."[119] Whatever may be the claim a community makes on a person, a person knows herself in her conscience as ultimately singularly accountable before God about the conformity of her life to the claim God makes upon it. The individual held up by Kant's and Kierkegaard's theory of conscience is not, then, the atomistic, autonomous individual of much modern ethical theory or the emotive self so prevalent in popular culture, but rather the single individual accountable not to herself but to the God who claims her and who holds her accountable to a way of life she does not posit for herself but that she is free to claim as her own.

The second challenge to the theory of conscience I propose to retrieve comes in the assertion that the moral claims that bind us come to us in and through our lives with others, and so we know ourselves rightly only as we learn to see ourselves through the lens of the communities that constitute our moral identity. As we will see, Kant and Kierkegaard each offer an objection to this assertion on the grounds that it confuses what should be, ultimately, distinct: the transcendent claim of God and the empirical, contingent claim of the group. But for the moment, it is sufficient to recall that this challenge arises largely as an effort to wrest conscience from its alleged Kantian captivity. And so we can see already that this challenge is a myopic challenge, overly informed by a misinterpretation of and

---

119. O'Donovan, *Resurrection*, 168. This is true for Kant and Kierkegaard, though for each, as we will see, in a distinct way.

consequent overreaction to Kant. Consequently, this challenge never sufficiently confronts the heritage of thinking about conscience—the heritage Kant and Kierkegaard preserve—as an individual's moral self-awareness in relation to God. Kant and Kierkegaard, I will argue in the final chapter, stand in a line I identify as stretching back to the Psalms, running through the Synoptic Gospels, Pauline and Petrine epistles, patristic theologians and beyond. Kant and Kierkegaard stand in this line as they affirm that self-knowledge is a central facet of our moral and spiritual formation, and that because we always stand totally transparent before God as God judges us we only rightly know ourselves when we know ourselves with God as God holds us accountable to the claim God makes on us. With this tradition of thinking about conscience Kant and Kierkegaard affirm that moral and spiritual formation require that we become transparent to ourselves—that we fight self-deception and become honest with ourselves about who we are—and we become transparent to ourselves when we begin to see ourselves with the eyes of the one from whom nothing is hidden. We have to see ourselves with those eyes, know ourselves in that knowledge, if we are to discern the path between who know ourselves to be and who we know we ought to be. This heritage has been dismissed without the hearing it deserves. Where better to make its case than to begin where it is thought to be most problematic.

Chapter 2

SELF-KNOWLEDGE AND THE APPROXIMATION OF DIVINE JUDGMENT: CONSCIENCE IN THE PRACTICAL PHILOSOPHY AND MORAL THEOLOGY OF IMMANUEL KANT

Introduction

Moral theologians in the twentieth century became suspicious of conscience largely because of its association with Immanuel Kant, who allegedly articulates a theory of conscience with no regard for history, community, or tradition, and in which we know and judge ourselves before a moral law we create for ourselves. Conscience after Kant and primarily because of Kant, in this account, becomes a means to self-consistency, or, in the banal language of popular culture, a means to be true to oneself. From H. Richard Niebuhr to Stanley Hauerwas we find a trajectory of thinking about self-knowledge, moral identity, and moral accountability that begins as an effort to wrest conscience from its alleged Kantian captivity by situating conscience within commitments to the irreducible contingency, the primordial sociality, and the narrative quality of our lives as human beings. This trajectory ends, I have argued, with conscience quietly vanishing as the work of conscience dissipates in an emphasis on the priority of corporate life and corporate self-understanding. In this chapter I will challenge this trajectory by offering a different interpretation of Kant's theory of conscience. I will argue that for Kant conscience is the knowledge we have of ourselves in our relation to God as God judges us and holds us accountable to the moral law. I realize this appears to be a bold claim, and establishing its veracity is probably the single most important thing this book can do to revitalize theological interest in conscience as moral self-awareness before God. And in this vein, I conclude in this chapter that the dismissal of conscience from Christian ethics significantly relies on a severe misinterpretation of Kant's theory of conscience and that this dismissal has resulted in an omission in Christian ethics of an important biblical and theological witness that the Kantian theory of conscience captures well: that God knows each individual and that each individual is singularly accountable before God.

Conscience as Tribunal

We have a duty, Kant claims, to assess the morality of our actions. We ought to consider not simply the legality of our actions but, more fundamentally, whether our actions have genuine moral worth. Kant's basic assumption is that a person of good morals, a person whose actions conform to what is morally right, is not necessarily a morally good person.[1] Action that conforms to morality can be righteous or unrighteous,[2] and a life devoid of illegality may still lack actions with genuine morality at their core.[3] And so we have a duty to assess the worth of our actions not just by whether or not they formally conform to what is right but by the morality that undergirds or informs them in their intent. We must assess the incentives of our actions,[4] that is, and this assessment, Kant claims, is the business of conscience.[5]

When we exercise our conscience and assess the morality of our actions, Kant explains that we should think of ourselves in a kind of juridical setting. To say that we "exercise" our conscience might not be quite right, however, because while Kant emphasizes our active role to assess the morality of our actions, he also describes our relation to the juridical setting of conscience in passive terms. We find ourselves, he claims, before a tribunal, at the bar in a courtroom, where we are judged. "Every human being has a conscience," Kant explains, "and finds himself observed, threatened, and in general kept in awe (respect coupled with fear) by an internal judge." He continues,

> This authority, watching over the law in him is not something that he himself (voluntarily) *makes*, but something incorporated into his being. It follows him like his shadow when he plans to escape. He can indeed stun himself or put himself to sleep by pleasures and distractions, but he cannot help coming to

---

1. *Religion*, 6:31.
2. *Lectures*, 129.
3. *Metaphysics of Morals*, 6:392.
4. *Metaphysics of Morals*, 6:393. Kant's concern seemingly is as much if not more with our evaluation of actions that conform to duty than our evaluation of actions that do not. We know what we ought to do, he insists, and when we act contrary to what we know we should do, then of course the thought of duty for its own sake will not be at the base of our action. If I see someone who needs my help and I know I am capable to offer my help but I do not in fact help, then of course my action must have as its maxim something other than the thought of duty. If I do offer my help, however, this does not necessarily mean I helped for the right reason. My maxim could have been, help people when you can only if you get something in return. In this case, the right action was done for an "unrighteous" reason.
5. As Jens Timmerman rightly observes, conscience is for Kant "subordinate to practical reason." It is "the consciousness of the moral quality of one's actions," not the source of moral norms in the way practical reason is. For this reason, Timmerman writes, conscience is absent from the *Groundwork* since there Kant commits to "finding and establishing the supreme principal of morality" (Jens Timmerman, "Kant on Conscience, 'Indirect' Duty, and Moral Error," *International Philosophical Quarterly*, vol. 46, no. 3 (September 2006), 295–6).

himself or waking up from time to time; and when he does, he hears at once its fearful voice. He can at most in extreme depravity bring himself to heed it no longer, but he still cannot help hearing its voice.[6]

Kant here clearly depicts conscience as something within us over whose operation we have no control. It clearly belongs to our nature since it is "incorporated" into our being. And yet conscience is not something a person actively conjures up. Conscience asserts itself within us, Kant claims, whether we like it or not. And the impression is that we will not like it. The control we have with respect to conscience, then, concerns whether or not we will listen to it and heed its verdict.

We might not like to hear the testimony of conscience since it might inflict us with a feeling of guilt. Conscience is not itself moral feeling, Kant explains, but rather practical reason holding a person accountable before the moral law.[7] But the verdict of conscience seeks to "affect moral feeling" in us, and so we heed or ignore the conscience first by heeding or ignoring the feelings of guilt or assurance conscience means to evoke.[8] When we do heed these feelings what we find is that our conscience has made a judgment about the moral worth of an action we have done, are doing, or are about to do. We have no choice about whether or not we will have a conscience; it is there monitoring us, stalking us, chasing us, but we can become deaf to it. We can ignore the feelings it means to evoke, and in this way we can "hurt or injure" our conscience in the sense that we can make ourselves insensitive to its verdict.[9] We can think of conscience as something that is capable of becoming weakened, so that eventually, Kant quips, "a man becomes as used to his vices as to tobacco smoke."[10] So conscience appears to be, for Kant, something we exercise only as we listen to it, as we choose to hear its voice as it passes its verdict on the morality of our actions.

When we listen to our conscience Kant explains that we experience a division within ourselves. We are like a defendant on trial, accused by a prosecutor, "for whom there would be no place unless there were also a law within us," and defended by an advocate who "brings forth many arguments in our defense and whose pleas the prosecutor in his turn endeavors to refute."[11] All of this is "peculiar," Kant writes, because while the "business" of conscience is a business

---

6. *Metaphysics of Morals*, 6:438.
7. *Metaphysics of Morals*, 6:400.
8. *Metaphysics of Morals*, 6:401.
9. *Lectures*, 133. We can see how conscience itself is not, according to Kant, moral feeling since moral feeling is something we can deaden. Conscience pronounces a verdict that wants me to feel guilty but I may ignore the feeling and, consequently, ignore the verdict. But if I keep ignoring the feeling, the feeling eventually will weaken and perhaps vanish altogether. But conscience itself, Kant insists, will continue to pass its verdict whether I feel badly about my action or not.
10. *Lectures*, 134.
11. *Lectures*, 132.

we have with ourselves, we are "constrained" by our reason "to carry" it out "as at the bidding of another person."[12] Conscience is a tribunal, and it makes no sense, Kant explains, to identify a person with his conscience where he finds himself prosecuted; when the defendant and the prosecutor are one and the same, the prosecutor has no chance to win, and so it is necessary to understand conscience as a tribunal convened by an other, a judge, who hears the prosecution and the defense and then pronounces a verdict on the morality of the person's action.[13] We should think of this other, Kant concludes, as "an actual person or a merely ideal person that reason creates for itself."[14]

Kant is telling us how we should think about the nature and function of our conscience. He is offering an analogy for how we should think of what is going on when we pass judgment on ourselves. It is useful, he suggests, to think of our conscience—to think of our experience of finding ourselves judged—as having this juridical quality, of being like a judgment passed on us by an actual or ideal person other than ourselves. Kant claims we should think of ourselves as judged by an other, but he also claims that conscience is our business with ourselves. The other who judges us in our conscience is, moreover, an other our "reason *creates* for itself." Kant further qualifies the idea of this reason-created actual or ideal other, claiming that "I, the prosecutor and yet the accused as well, am the same human being." Because each person is *noumenally* free and so "subject to a law he gives himself," it is useful for the "*sensible being* endowed with reason" to regard himself or herself as divided in these various courtroom roles and to hear the judge's verdict as if it were the verdict of someone other.[15]

Conscience and Autonomy

The impression these claims might create is that Kant's theory of conscience is of a piece with the standard interpretation of Kant's notion of autonomy, an interpretation which can be characterized as having to do with "making an absolute value of choice for its own sake, so that autonomous acts are wherever one acts to express oneself as such, with no special regard for any content, let alone law that the act might serve."[16] Recall MacIntyre's and Hauerwas's objection to modern morality, taking its bearing from Kant, they claim, as expressing a basic commitment to individual autonomy as the personal freedom to fashion our morality as we see fit and to hold ourselves accountable to the choices we have made. As free autonomous beings, that is, we hold ourselves accountable to a law

---

12. *Metaphysics of Morals*, 6:438.
13. *Metaphysics of Morals*, 6:438.
14. *Metaphysics of Morals*, 6:438.
15. *Metaphysics of Morals*, 6:438. Emphasis added.
16. This is Karl Ameriks's helpful summary of this line of interpretation. Karl Ameriks, "Vindicating Autonomy," in *Kant on Moral Autonomy*, 53.

we create for ourselves. Kant's claim that conscience is our business with ourselves as moral agents who give a law to ourselves seems, then, to lend itself nicely to an interpretation like Paul Lehmann's or Oliver O'Donovan's who see Kant's theory of conscience as epitomizing the modern moral ethos MacIntyre and Hauerwas describe. Kant's theory of conscience, they claim, becomes the prevailing theory and gives the modern moral subject a license to view herself as accountable not to a tradition, a community, a particular history, or to an objective moral order, but to herself as her own lawgiver. Kant gives us, on this reading, a theory of conscience that helps us understand the experience of moral judgment as the experience of holding ourselves accountable to the way of life we happen to have chosen. As H. Richard Niebuhr argues, Kant reduces the phenomenon of conscience entirely to an "as if." Kant's account of the "experience of conscience" is merely "like being judged by another person." Niebuhr explains that for Kant conscience is like being judged by another person but only because a person in her "isolated reason" invents "another person" so that in her moral reason she can be "consistent" with herself.[17]

There is no doubt some truth in this line of interpretation. Kant is indeed arguing that it is psychologically useful to think of the experience of conscience *as if* being judged by an other. But Kant does not recommend interpreting the judgment of conscience on the analogy of the judgment of an other because he thinks the analogy is a helpful way to describe the process in which we hold ourselves accountable to a law we make for ourselves. This cannot be the point of Kant's analogy because Kant does not think we are the authors of the law in the sense that we create it. Kant's formula of autonomy, the third formulation of the categorical imperative, is the claim that "the will is not *merely* subject to the law, but subject to it in such a way that it must be viewed as *also* giving the law to itself."[18] The "merely" and "also" in this formula by themselves should give pause to any interpretation of it that affirms "we create the moral order in which we live and supply our own motives for compliance."[19] The formulation by itself intimates that the moral law is something necessary for rational beings as beings of practical reason, whether or not the human rational being recognizes this necessity. We are not "merely" subject to the law, but we are indeed subject to it. Outside this formulation of autonomy Kant frequently describes our relation to the moral law as a relation to a law that necessarily holds for rational beings as such and not simply for human beings as rational beings. He writes, "by what right could we bring into unlimited respect, as a universal precept for every rational nature what is perhaps valid only under the contingent conditions of humanity."[20] He claims, likewise, that "unless we want to deny the concept of morality any truth ... we cannot dispute that its law is so extensive in its import

17. Niebuhr, *The Responsible Self*, 75.
18. *Groundwork*, 4:431, emphasis mine.
19. Schneewind, "Natural Law," 302.
20. *Groundwork*, 4:408.

that it must hold not only for human beings but also for all rational beings as such."[21] Kant means, in particular, that our will, as practical reason, cognizes a law that a "perfectly good will," a will like the will of God, also cognizes. He writes that a "divine will," like the human will, must "equally stand under objective laws of the good."[22] As rational beings we know the law as the "fact" of our reason.[23] We know the law is true and we know it is binding on us because we know it as binding on all rational beings, beings like us who are rational creatures, beings of reason and of sensible inclination, as well as for a being like God, a being we conceive of as a rational being without sensible inclinations. Our practical reason, in other words, "cognizes" what is "practically necessary," what is not contingent but universal; our practical reason has access to what is valid not only for beings like us but for a being like God.[24] The difference between us and a being like God, who is not a creature of sense and need like us and therefore lacks incentives arising from a sensuous nature, is that God knows no "ought." We cognize the moral law as a synthetic a priori, as a categorical imperative, while "no imperative holds for the divine will ... the 'ought' is out of place here because [divine] volition is of itself necessarily in accord with the law."[25] As rational beings, like God, we are under "objective laws of volition;" but our relation to these laws as rational *creatures* is a relation characterized by "imperatives," "formulae expressing the relation of objective laws of volition in general to the subjective imperfection of the will" of sensible beings like us.[26] Kant is not claiming here that our cognizance of the moral law as something binding, necessary, and absolute for us as rational beings is at the same time a cognizance of a supreme moral lawgiver. His point, rather, is to emphasize the absolute, necessary, unconditional nature of the law that we as rational beings have the capacity to discern. And if God is a rational being, then God, like us, discerns the law, but unlike us God wills necessarily in accord with it. The moral law is necessary; neither we, nor God, Kant argues, create the law. And so when Kant affirms our autonomy as self-legislating beings we should not miss by focusing on the "self" of "self-legislating" Kant's concern for law. "Simple hermeneutical charity," Karl Ameriks writes, "dictates that one consider starting with the obvious fact that what most impresses Kant is the singularity and absolute necessity of moral lawfulness."[27]

Kant is also clear that we are not the authors of the law in the sense of being the creators of the law when he gives his account of our membership in the kingdom of ends. The kingdom of ends is, Kant claims, the "very fruitful concept" that

---

21. *Groundwork*, 4:408.
22. *Groundwork*, 4:414.
23. *Practical Reason*, 5:31.
24. *Groundwork*, 4:412.
25. *Groundwork*, 4:414.
26. *Groundwork*, 4:414.
27. Ameriks, "Vindicating Autonomy," 67.

brings together the three different formulations of the categorical imperative.[28] We are to imagine ourselves, Kant explains, as self-legislating, and so as autonomous members of a kingdom. As self-legislating members of this kingdom, we ought to will only what could consistently be willed by anyone else in the kingdom, as though our maxim could stand morally in the kingdom on analogy with the laws of nature. We should, furthermore, imagine ourselves in a kingdom where we should will only what any other member of the kingdom could also will because we respect the dignity of each member of the kingdom as a self-legislating, end-setting being. As members of this kingdom, finally, we should imagine ourselves as living in it under a head or sovereign. He writes that the kingdom of ends has two kinds of members: self-legislating members who are subject to the kingdom's laws as well as a "sovereign" who is "not subject to the will of any other," and who is "a completely independent being, without needs and with unlimited resources adequate to his will."[29]

By stressing that the king is not subject to the will of an other, Kant implies that the other members of the kingdom should see themselves as subjects to the will of another, namely to the will of the king. Unlike the king, we do not will perfectly in accord with the law; the king's necessary willing in accord with the law is for us, who do not will necessarily in accord with the law, a kind of promulgation of the law. Kant explains that

> a law that binds us a priori and unconditionally by our own reason can also be expressed as proceeding from the will of a supreme lawgiver, that is, one who has only rights and no duties (hence from a divine will); but this signifies only the idea of a moral being whose will is a law for everyone without his being thought as the author of the law.[30]

The king's will, as a will perfectly in accord with the law, can be thought of as a law for us; in other words, the king's will can be thought of as that which binds us and summons our obedience. We recognize our duties because we know the moral law but we should recognize our "true duties ... as *at the same time*" as the commands of "the supreme lawgiver of an ethical community."[31] In the kingdom we are subjects to a law, a law perfectly recapitulated in the will of the king, and a law that summons our assent. The point is that the law is not something we create but something we know as necessary and, accordingly, something we encounter as if it were promulgated to us. And so immediately following the description of the king of the kingdom of ends Kant goes on to explain that "morality consists, *then*, in the reference of all action to the lawgiving by which alone a kingdom of ends is

---

28. I am indebted here to John Hare, *God and Morality* (Boston, MA: Wiley Blackwell, 2009), 145–56.
29. *Groundwork*, 4:434.
30. *Metaphysics of Morals*, 6:227.
31. *Religion*, 6:99.

possible. This lawgiving must, *however*, be found in every rational being himself and be able to arise from his will."[32] Kant is insisting that we are autonomous, self-legislating beings in as much as we are free to put ourselves under the law. "The lawgiver," Kant explains in his ethics lectures simultaneous with the writing of the *Groundwork*, "is not the author of the law, rather he is the author of the obligation of the law."[33] Our freedom as rational beings is a freedom to recognize the law, to appreciate, to endorse it.[34] And so the autonomous agent can legislate the law to himself or herself, but as "the author ... of the obligation in accordance with the law, but not always the author of the law" in itself, which is necessary. We can think of ourselves as makers of the law in itself only with regard to "positive (contingent) and chosen law."[35] But the moral law we know as the fact of our reason is, again, a law we know as necessary, unconditional, and absolute. Even in our conception of a supreme lawgiver, Kant suggests, we are not to think of a being who creates the law; even for this being, and so that much more for us, we should think of the law as something not created but acknowledged; even for this being, and so, again, that much more for us, we should think of the authorship of the law as an authorship of the obligation of the law. Kant is telling us, in short, how we should think of our relation to the moral law. He makes this relation especially vivid through the analogy of a supreme lawgiver who does not create the law but, rather, who we can think of as creating the obligation of the law. We can imagine our relation to the law, Kant claims, "as expressed" as a relation of obligation to the holy will of the supreme lawgiver. Because we know the law as a categorical imperative we can imagine our obligation to the law as if it proceeds from the will of this being, who knows no "ought," and we can imagine our accountability to the law as an accountability to this holy being.[36]

Consequently, when Kant tells us we should understand the experience of being judged in our conscience as like being judged by an other, he tells us we should think of this other as a being like God. Kant does not leave unqualified how we should think about the actual or ideal other who judges us in our conscience. If he failed to qualify how we should think of this other and claimed instead, as Niebuhr suggests, that reason creates an other, simply considered, then it might be easier to interpret Kant's description of conscience as an explanation of how we hold ourselves accountable to law we make for ourselves.[37] But Kant does

---

32. *Groundwork*, 4:434, emphasis mine.

33. Kant, "Moral Mrongovius II," 29:633–634. Cf. Hare, *God's Call*, 95.

34. This is characteristic of Hare. See, for example, *God's Call: Moral Realism, God's Commands, and Human Autonomy* (Grand Rapids, MI: Eerdmans, 2001), 87–88.

35. *Metaphysics of Morals* 6:227.

36. See Hare's helpful explanation of this relation of accountability (*God and Morality*, 142–3).

37. The sparse literature on Kant's theory of conscience neglects this important vertical dimension. Jens Timmerman, for example, in order to make the point that Kant's theory of conscience is juridical and self-reflexive, notes in passing that Kant here "follows the New

qualify how we should think about this other. He tells us that we ought to see "the authorized judge of conscience" as a "scrutinizer of hearts," as one able to "impose all obligation." And this other, he continues, "must be, or be thought as, a person in relation to whom all duties whatsoever are to be regarded as his commands." Kant concludes, "since such a moral being must also have all power (in heaven and on earth) in order to give effect to his laws (as is necessarily required for the office of judge), and since such an omnipotent being is called God, conscience must be thought of as the subjective principle of being accountable to God for all one's deeds." God, Kant concludes, "in fact ... is always contained in the moral self-awareness of conscience."[38]

Kant's "as if," then, is not abstract in the way Niebuhr suggests. We do not just invent any other for the sake of being consistent with ourselves. Kant tells us we should think of ourselves in the experience of being judged in our conscience as if we are being judged by God. But he does not say that the voice of our conscience is the voice of God, and he denies that the experience of being judged in conscience gives us license to know theoretically that God exists. Kant's primary concern is, again, that the moral law is absolute, necessary, and unconditional. We are not its authors any more than God is its author. We know ourselves under this law, furthermore, as beings under a categorical imperative and we can conceive of a holy will under the law but not under a categorical imperative since such a will wills necessarily in accord with this law. We can think of our duties as coming to us from our knowledge of the law and "at the same time" as coming from a "supreme lawgiver," Kant claims, and we should think of that supreme lawgiver as "one who knows the heart," who sees our fundamental disposition, and judges "the worth of [our] actions."[39] And so Kant suggests that we ought to think of ourselves in the experience of judgment as accountable to a being who wills necessarily in accord with the law and who can see the conformity of our hearts to the law.

We should understand the judgment of conscience as if it were the judgment of a divine being, a supreme lawgiver, Kant argues, for the very reason that we are tempted to treat our conscience somewhat like the way Niebuhr himself recommends we should treat it, as a judge that judges according to contingent, empirical standards.[40] We would like to judge ourselves, Kant claims, by empirical

---

Testament and German Protestant tradition." But Timmerman then, strikingly, ignores the reference Kant makes in almost every discussion of conscience to God as the seer and judge of hearts (Timmerman, 295). See also, Allen Wood's *Kantian Ethics* (New York: Cambridge University Press, 2008), where the neglect of God in Kant's theory of conscience is especially apparent in the discussion of conscience as an "inner court" (85ff).

38. *Metaphysics of Morals*, 6:438; cf. *Religion*, 6:99.

39. *Religion*, 6:99.

40. Niebuhr, of course, thinks what is transcendent comes mediated through the contingent, empirical norms. Conscience as the internalization of social norms does not, for Niebuhr, disclose only what is empirical. But Kant would still object that to affirm the empirical, contingent mediation of what is unconditioned and necessary obscures the grasp

standards, by moral norms contingent on particular times and places. We would like to judge ourselves from the vantage of our sensibility. When our vice is common to a class, Kant writes, we are all too prone to take it as virtue.[41] But if we judge ourselves according to contingent factors, Kant claims, then it is as if we have convened our own tribunal and appointed our own prosecutor, whose case, again, would have no chance really to be heard. And we know we cannot really do this. We are aware, Kant insists, of a law that is not contingent upon empirical factors, that is universal and unconditioned, and so in order to hold ourselves accountable to this law, in order to judge whether or not in our actions we are putting ourselves under the law's obligation, it is good that we think of ourselves as accountable before a "lawgiver" whose law is universally binding.[42] We ought to see ourselves in our conscience as accountable to a nonarbitrary, noncontingent, nonempirical, necessary standard, and we can see ourselves accountable in this way no more vividly than when we imagine a holy being whose holy will endorses (but does not create) the law with such perfect necessity that it is as if our accountability is to that being.

Conscience and the Approximation of Divine Judgment

But we are not, Kant qualifies, "entitled" by the experience of conscience, "to assume such a supreme being actually exists outside" ourselves.[43] We do not have to believe in God to hear the voice of conscience, even if we assent to the judgment of conscience as judgment before a necessary moral law, and even if we accept the analogy that the judgment of conscience is like being judged by a supreme lawgiver who wills necessarily in accord with the moral law. To see ourselves accountable in our conscience to a "holy being" is a particularly helpful way to see ourselves as accountable to "morally lawgiving reason," to a standard that holds for all rational beings as such and so only for that reason for beings like us who are

---

practical reason has on what is necessary. This is an underlying point in Kant's essay, "What Is Enlightenment."

41. *Religion*, 6:33.

42. *Metaphysics of Morals*, 6:439. As Allen Wood observes, Kant makes a distinction between conscience as a "voice ... of society," that is, of "art and education," and conscience as "self-judgment based on genuine rational principles" available to all beings of practical reason. It is not that Kant denies, Wood argues, that society is able to help a person hear the voice of conscience in this latter sense; but as Wood rightly notes, for Kant "if conscience reflects *only* what society and upbringing have instilled in him, it has no rational validity." Wood concludes that "to hold that human beings never have any conscience except this one [the voice of society] would be in effect, to deny that they are moral agents at all and it would follow that none of them could be held morally responsible for anything" (Wood, *Kantian Ethics*, 186).

43. *Metaphysics of Morals*, 6:439.

not only creatures of sensible inclinations but also beings of practical reason.[44] But even taking Kant's ideal other here as a psychologically useful analogy still resists the implications of Niebuhr's claim about Kant's "as if." We do not, Kant suggests, see ourselves accountable to a generic other before whom we are accountable to ourselves as self-legislating beings. We think of ourselves "as if" accountable to God because in our conscience we find ourselves accountable to a law that holds for all rational beings, including our idea of a holy being who wills necessarily in accord with the law.

While the experience of being judged in our conscience does not by itself entitle us to assume that God exists outside ourselves, Kant does think we have grounds to believe that God exists and that God sees our hearts and judges us. In the preface to the first edition of *Religion within the Boundaries of Mere Reason* Kant claims that "morality thus leads to religion and through religion it [morality] extends itself to the idea of a mighty moral lawgiver outside the human being, in whose will the final end (of the creation of the world) is what can and at the same time ought to be the final human end."[45] Kant's argument that morality extends itself to religion and through religion to God begins with his insistence that we are not the kinds of beings who can be indifferent to the ends of our actions. We live according to two kinds of purposiveness, that of freedom and that of nature, and our morality, as creatures of this composition, needs both.[46] If human beings lived only according to the purposiveness of freedom, then we could think of the human being as one who acted rightly from no incentive other than the moral law, and who would have no need of the idea of God searching the heart and holding each person accountable.[47] In this regard, Kant claims, morality can stand alone without religion.[48] But we are not the kinds of beings who can think of our morality alone in that way. We are creatures who live also according to the purposiveness of nature and so beings who have a "natural need;" our conception of morality cannot ignore this need without at the same time hindering "our moral resolve."[49] Kant is clear that this natural need cannot be the determining ground of our action. The law alone "contains the formal condition of the use of freedom."[50] Action that has moral worth has the moral law as its chief determining ground. And yet, Kant explains, for beings of natural need, who live according to a natural purposiveness, "an end proceeds from morality just the same," and consequently, "it cannot be a matter of indifference to reason how to answer the question, What is the result of this right conduct of ours."[51] Our incentive for action should be the

---

44. *Metaphysics of Morals*, 6:439.
45. *Religion*, 6:6.
46. *Religion*, 6:5.
47. *Religion*, 6:3.
48. *Religion*, 6:3.
49. *Religion*, 6:5.
50. *Religion*, 6:5.
51. *Religion*, 6:5.

moral law but we must still concern ourselves with what we are trying to achieve in our action. And so our moral reason leads us inexorably to "the idea of the highest good in the world," the idea of the union or the harmony "of all such ends as we ought to have (duty) with everything which is conditioned upon ends we have and which conforms to duty (happiness proportioned to [duty's] observance)."[52] When our action has moral worth we act for the sake of the moral law as our sufficient incentive, but we must also ask what we intend to bring about and Kant is here claiming that our moral reason leads, as we ask this question, to the idea of a system in which our action from duty harmonizes with our natural need for happiness. We cannot conceive of a morality that does not take these two kinds of purposiveness into consideration and so we are led by our moral reason to the idea of a system, a kingdom, or a realm in which they cohere. "This idea" of the highest good, Kant explains, "meets our natural need, which would otherwise be a hindrance to moral resolve, to think for all our doings and non doings taken as a whole some sort of final end which reason can justify."[53] If, then, we are going to be the moral beings we find ourselves called to be by the "fact of reason," by the presence of the moral law within us,[54] then we have to believe in the possibility of a world in which our two kinds of purposiveness harmonize. The possibility of such a good enables us to believe that to act with the moral law as our chief incentive is not inconsistent with our need to be happy.

But even as our reason leads us to this idea of a highest good, we are also aware that it is beyond our power to bring it about. The belief, required by our morality, in the possibility of the highest good, therefore leads us also to another belief required by our morality, that there is a "higher, moral, most holy, and omnipotent being who alone can unite the two elements of [the highest] good."[55] Our morality, in other words, requires us to believe in the possibility of the "final end which reason can justify," the idea of the highest good, and we can believe in the possibility of the highest good only if we also believe in the possibility of a being who is king both of the kingdom of ends and of the kingdom of nature, a holy omnipotent being who is able to bring into harmony our actions done for the sake of duty ("the ends we ought to have") and our "natural need" ("happiness proportioned to [duty's] observance"). If we are to live as our practical reason calls us to live, then, "we *must* assume" the existence of God.[56]

We are justified on moral grounds, Kant affirms, to believe that God exists. And this means, Kant explains, that there are certain attributes of God our practical reason leads us to believe. We are "driven to believe" in God as the "moral ruler" of the world, and our concern is who this ruler is for us as moral beings, as beings under the moral law. We cannot know who this God is in God's essence: "our

---

52. *Religion*, 6:5.
53. *Religion*, 6:5.
54. *Practical Reason*, 5:31.
55. *Religion*, 6:5.
56. *Religion*, 6:5, emphasis mine.

concern," Kant writes, "is not so much what he is in himself (his nature) but what he is for us as moral beings." Outside of this constraint of who God is for us as moral beings "we can cognize nothing about him," but within it we can indeed cognize something.[57] What we are "driven to believe" about God, Kant explains, follows from the affirmation every human being has the capacity to make through practical reason: that we are to lead good lives in accord with the moral law; that we find a respect for the moral law woven into the fabric of our being; and, consequently, that we can have hope that, however demanding, we can make this respect manifest in our actions; and to this end we must scrutinize ourselves "as if summoned to accounts before a judge." Kant concludes that "reason, heart, and conscience all teach this and drive us to it."[58] We cannot expect to know more than this, Kant concludes, since more would exceed what is universal.[59] What God is for us as moral beings, Kant claims, is constrained by this affirmation. But within the limits of this affirmation we are driven to believe in God as the giver of the moral law, as a good and holy ruler, and as the highest judge of human conduct.[60]

On the one hand, then, Kant claims we should interpret our experience of moral self-judgment, our business with ourselves as we pass judgment on the morality of our actions, on the analogy of being judged by "a being called God." On the other hand, Kant claims that as moral beings we can and should believe that there is a God who sees our hearts and who judges us. On the one hand Kant claims conscience is the experience of being judged by another person our own practical reason "creates for itself," while on the other hand he claims "conscience is the representative of the divine judgment seat; it weighs our dispositions and actions in the scale of a law which is holy and pure; we cannot deceive it, and lastly we cannot escape it, because, like the divine omnipresence it is always with us."[61] These claims are not contradictory. We can hold them together, and I think for the full picture of Kant's theory of conscience we have to do just that. He is not saying that on the one hand conscience is our own voice, and that on the other it is the voice of God. He is saying we should judge ourselves *as if* we were accountable to a perfectly good will that wills necessarily in accord with the law, and that we should believe a being of such a good will actually exists and does in fact judge us, each of us. I conclude that conscience is, according to Kant, "the subjective principle of being accountable to God for all one's deeds,"[62] because it is through our conscience that we strive to judge ourselves according to God's actual judgment of us. The judgment of our conscience is our endorsement of what we take to be God's judgment of us. It is through our conscience that we search ourselves in an effort to know ourselves as we are known by the one who searches the heart and

57. *Religion*, 6:139.
58. *Religion*, 6:144–5.
59. *Religion*, 6:144–5.
60. *Religion*, 6:139.
61. *Lectures*, 133.
62. *Metaphysics of Morals*, 6:438.

sees the moral quality of our deeds.[63] In other words, when Kant says conscience is the principle of our accountability to God, he means it.

Conscience as Means to Knowledge of the Heart

Conscience is, according to Kant, where we judge the moral worth of our actions by discerning the incentive behind them. And we make this judgment in our conscience on the analogy of the judgment of the supreme lawgiver who scrutinizes our hearts and sees clearly the incentive behind our actions. I have argued that because we are, according to Kant, justified in believing in the existence of God as this lawgiver and just judge, we should interpret the judgment of our conscience as an approximation of God's judgment. I want to turn now to the role Kant assigns to conscience in his broader moral theology, and I will argue that conscience is, according to Kant, the means through which we approximate God's judgment of our hearts. Kant likes Jesus's analogy that a tree is known by its fruits because he believes that the moral worth of our actions discloses the moral quality of the source of our actions, the heart.[64] And so while conscience deals directly with the fruit of our lives, it has an important role, according to Kant, as we seek to discern the quality of our hearts. It is no coincidence that Kant immediately follows his discussion of conscience in *The Metaphysics of Morals* with the claim that "the first command of all duties to oneself" is the command to "know (scrutinize, fathom) yourself." He counsels, in other words, "know your heart—whether it is good or evil, whether the source of your actions is pure or impure."[65] By juxtaposing a theory of conscience and a reflection on this command to know the heart, Kant conveys that while conscience itself is not immediately or directly knowledge of the heart, it is the means through which we can fulfill this duty to know our hearts.

Kant's assumption, first of all, is that there is a "source" of all our actions. The name he gives to this source is, variously, "the heart," the will, "the first subjective ground of the adoption of maxims."[66] Kant's next assumption is that the heart is either "good or evil," "pure or impure."[67] And Kant is clear that this fundamental spring of our action "can only be a single one."[68] Kant is making here a basic claim about how the free will works. Antecedent to the exercise of freedom, Kant explains, there must be a "subjective first ground" which is itself "a deed of freedom." His point is that the will, if it wills freely, first must determine its ground, its rule or maxim through which it then adopts "this or that" particular maxim.[69] If, in other

---

63. *Religion*, 6:99.
64. *Religion*, 6:45.
65. *Metaphysics of Morals*, 6:441.
66. *Religion*, 6:25.
67. *Metaphysics of Morals*, 6:441.
68. *Religion*, 6:25.
69. *Religion*, 6:22

words, all actions proceed from particular maxims, and if behind our actions there must be either a good or evil maxim, then, in order to will at all, the will must first determine the first ground by which it will decide about these maxims.

Kant then goes on to explain what he means when he claims that the human being is "by nature evil."[70] Kant claims human beings have three basic predispositions and he divides these predispositions into two categories. There is, on the one hand, a predisposition to the good, which Kant calls the "predisposition to personality," the "predisposition to respect for the moral law as of itself a sufficient incentive to the power of choice."[71] There is, on the other hand, a predisposition to self-love, a predisposition Kant divides between the "predisposition to animality" in which we find our desire for self-preservation, the propagation of the species, and for life with others, and the "predisposition to humanity" in which we find ourselves inclined "to give worth in the opinion of others."[72] As part of the basic composition of our nature as human beings all the predispositions are good. But these predispositions belong in a certain order, and it is on account of this order that the heart is either good or evil. Morality requires that we act above all from the predisposition to the good, out of "respect for the moral law as of itself a sufficient incentive to the power of choice." Morality requires, that is, that we rank the predisposition to the good over the predisposition to self-love. There is no spectrum of possibilities here. Either we act from our predisposition to the good or we subordinate the predisposition to the good to the predisposition to self-love. Kant's assumption is that there is a basic orientation in a person's heart regarding these predispositions. It is in the heart that a person fundamentally places either the predisposition to the good first, or subordinates the predisposition to the good to the predisposition to self-love. The incentive behind particular actions derives from the adopted order of incentives in a person's heart. Conscience, according to Kant, passes its verdict on the particular actions and, as I will explain, helps us delve further to discern the quality of the heart.

The difficulty is that, as Kant repeatedly claims, both the incentive behind any particular action and the depths of the heart are opaque. We can never absolutely be sure that we have acted with the right incentive. "Even by the most strenuous self-examination," Kant claims, seemingly undermining his theory of conscience, we cannot get "entirely behind our covert incentives, since when moral worth is at issue, what counts is not actions which one sees but those inner principles one does not see."[73] Kant makes a similar claim about the heart: "The depths of the human heart are unfathomable." And since the heart is unfathomable, none of us can know if the incentive behind any particular action "proceeds entirely from the law or whether there are not many other sensible impulses contributing to [the incentive] that look to one's advantage (or to avoid what is detrimental)."[74]

---

70. *Religion*, 6:21.
71. *Religion*, 6:27–28.
72. *Religion*, 6:26–27.
73. *Groundwork*, 4:407.
74. *Metaphysics of Morals*, 6:447.

A possible criticism of Kant is that when his insistence on the opacity of our incentives for acting and on the opacity of the disposition of our hearts combines with his insistence that morality requires a pure heart the outcome is a moral agent paralyzed by anxiety. Jennifer Herdt rightly observes that Kant is "deeply concerned with the character of the agent" and not simply concerned with the rightness of actions.[75] She also rightly observes that for Kant "we cannot know with certainty whether [an] action was determined by respect for the moral law," and that our determining reasons for action "always remain opaque," even to ourselves.[76] But given the affirmation that moral actions originate from a pure heart and the affirmation that the purity of the heart is opaque to us, Herdt argues that Kant leaves us in a position where we cannot know whether or not our moral striving reflects a "morally good disposition" or "glittering vice."[77] A person may strive to do the right thing for the right reasons but she can never know whether she is sincere in her efforts or if she is a hypocrite. Herdt concludes that "it is ultimately unclear how," if we are Kantians, "we can avoid getting bogged down in anxiety over the state of our fundamental disposition."[78]

Kant's theory of conscience can answer this criticism. Herdt's analysis of Kant's moral theology is accurate and has more nuance and subtlety than most treatments of Kant in contemporary Christian ethics, but she misinterprets Kant's claim that our incentives for acting and the depths of hearts are "inscrutable." Where Herdt sees a moral agent "bogged down" in paralyzing self-examination over the purity of the heart, Kant sees a moral agent calmly, occasionally assessing his or her heart on the basis of what can reasonably be assumed about the heart by virtue of the reliable judgment of conscience on particular actions. When Kant claims that the "*depths*" of the heart are inscrutable, and that we cannot get "*entirely* behind our covert incentives," he clearly suggests that something of the heart is open to our scrutiny and that we can get at least somewhat behind our covert incentives (emphasis mine). His theory of conscience is in fact unintelligible if he thinks we can know nothing about our incentives for acting. And his stress on the inscrutability of our hearts must be taken alongside his affirmation that "the beginning of all human wisdom is to know (scrutinize, fathom)" the heart.[79] Given that this affirmation immediately follows his discussion of conscience, it appears, then, that Kant sees no contradiction in the assertion that it is the business of conscience to help us scrutinize what he also claims is, at least to us, inscrutable. How does he hold these claims together?

Kant is clear that we cannot scrutinize ourselves the way he thinks we should believe God scrutinizes us. If we thought the voice of our conscience were actually

---

75. Jennifer Herdt, *Putting on Virtue: The Legacy of the Splendid Vices* (Chicago, IL: University of Chicago Press, 2009), 324–5.
76. Herdt, *Putting on Virtue*, 326.
77. Herdt, *Putting on Virtue*, 326.
78. Herdt, *Putting on Virtue*, 337.
79. *Metaphysics of Morals*, 6:441.

God's voice and that we could see our hearts the way God sees our hearts, Kant would accuse us of being deluded and would deny that anyone can have a special, personal relation to God.[80] Here Herdt is right that for Kant, "since everything we experience is by definition phenomenal," we cannot, therefore, in Kant's strict sense of knowing, "know whether our fundamental disposition is good or evil."[81] We see the appearances of our actions in time, but we see neither the particular incentives behind them nor the fundamental disposition behind these incentives. "Like freedom in general," Herdt notes, the fundamental disposition is for Kant "noumenal, not accessible to experience because it escapes the causal determination of the Newtonian phenomenal realm."[82] Kant therefore explains that we can certainly recognize our unlawful actions as unlawful, but, he clearly states, "we cannot observe maxims, we cannot do so unproblematically even within ourselves."[83] Our maxims and their fundamental ground, the heart, are not, then, just really difficult to know. Kant is clear that they are impossible to know. And so when Kant tells us that the first command of all duties is to do that which we can affirm only God can do, namely to scrutinize ourselves, he must have in mind a scrutinizing or a fathoming that is not, like God's, direct and definite, but that is, rather, indirect and approximate. When we evaluate in our conscience the morality of our actions and when we seek to know our own hearts, we strive for an approximate, indirect knowledge of that which God knows with perfect clarity.

There is a kind of two-step procedure in the movement from the judgment of actions to an assessment of the heart that Kant leaves implicit in *The Metaphysics of Morals* and makes explicit in *Religion within the Boundaries of Mere Reason*. The first step is the proper or direct business of conscience, the business of judging the morality of particular actions. Conscience judges the action based on the incentive behind it, and though through the conscience we do not "get entirely behind our convert incentives," Kant suggests our conscience nevertheless discerns our incentives clearly enough to pass its verdict. When Kant says that the incentives behind our actions are covert or inscrutable, he evidently means something more like translucent than entirely opaque.[84] Kant assumes that in each particular action our conscience renders a verdict that is basically reliable if not absolutely certain. Kant's close association of conscience and sincerity at the end of

---

80. *Religion*, 6:201. This is not to say Kant denies an individual's singular status before God as an individual accountable before God for the moral quality of his or her life. That Kant denies a "special" familiarity with God does not also entail, that is, a denial an individual's distinct moral relation to God with respect to God as the one whom the individual should believe promulgates the moral law and before whom each individual is truly morally accountable. We will take this theme up again briefly at the start of the final chapter.

81. Herdt, *Putting on Virtue*, 334.

82. Herdt, *Putting on Virtue*, 332.

83. *Religion*, 6:20.

84. I take this way of putting it from a very helpful conversation with Karl Ameriks.

Religion helps to illustrate this point. I may know and profess that it is right to do something—helping an elderly man or woman with arms full of groceries to cross the street, for example—and I know it is right to act in this way simply because I know it to be the right thing to do, regardless of my desires. And by virtue of my conscience, Kant argues, I can be sincere: I can and must be truthful with myself about whether or not I have acted in the way I know I ought to act.[85] Discernment of our incentives for acting, Kant insists, is possible "at least to some extent."[86] Even children, he claims, "are capable of discovering even the slightest taint of admixture of spurious incentives" and can discern when an action "loses all moral worth."[87] We cannot see any maxim directly, but Kant is clear that we can trust the verdict of our conscience about whether or not our action has moral worth. There is no need for an anxious paralysis of action out of fear of hypocrisy. He assumes, on the contrary, that we can listen to our conscience and then proceed "on our way."[88]

The first step to fulfill the duty to know our hearts is to listen to the verdict of our conscience about the morality of our action. From this first step, Kant explains, we can make a consequent inference about the heart from which our maxims originate. A person can, in other words, "extract his disposition from the deed."[89] We can "estimate our disposition not directly but only according to our deeds."[90] Kant denies only the possibility of a direct knowledge of our disposition, not knowledge of our disposition altogether. Kant's affirmation is like Paul's claim that we see through a glass darkly; we should not miss that though the glass is dark, we can nonetheless see. In the case of an evil heart, for example, Kant claims "*it must be possible* to assume from a number of … evil actions, or even from a single one, an underlying evil maxim."[91] The work of conscience is assumed in this claim by the confident, matter-of-fact description of the actions as evil. There is no angst here about the hidden incentives and the possibility of hypocrisy. If the fruit is rotten we will discern it well enough and after so many rotten fruits we can start to make a reasonable inference about the tree.[92] The work of conscience, again, is to make the localized judgment on the particular action and it is from this judgment, Kant claims, that we can move a step further and "extract" or "estimate"

---

85. *Religion*, 6:189–93; cf. "On the Miscarriage of all Philosophical Trials in Theodicy," 8:268.

86. *Religion*, 6:77.

87. *Religion*, 6:48.

88. *Lectures*, 135.

89. *Religion*, 6:77.

90. *Religion*, 6:76.

91. *Religion*, 6:21, emphasis mine.

92. I take Kant's emphasis to be on making a judgment from a series of actions as having primacy here. It might be possible that a person can extract her disposition from a single deed but Kant must mean such a person who could act over the course of time in such and such an immoral way might "even from a single" action be able to discern the immoral heart.

our basic disposition. And so while "we cannot see through" to our hearts, we can still reasonably "infer it from the consequence it has on the conduct of our lives."[93] Here, again, the work of conscience is assumed to have occurred in the evaluation of our life conduct, and now it is possible to move to a further inference about what that evaluation means about who we are most deeply in our hearts.

We are not, then, completely in the dark about ourselves. We cannot see ourselves as God sees us but because we have a conscience that offers a reliable verdict on the morality of our actions, we can make a reasonable inference about the stable disposition of our hearts. It is in this way that we seek an indirect, approximate knowledge of ourselves. Kant's counsel is for a modest self-examination. He cautions us not to think we can know with certainty the incentives behind our actions or that we can know with certainty the ultimate disposition from which our actions derive. But he also encourages us that we can listen to our conscience, acquire a rough and reliable discernment about the quality of our actions, and that we can follow the trail of our actions down to a reliable estimation of our hearts.

We can press further and ask why it is so important for Kant that we have a duty to know our hearts. Here it is significant that while Kant describes the experience of conscience in passive language, Kant describes the act of following the verdicts of our conscience to a reliable estimation of our hearts in active language. Conscience passes its verdict whether we like it or not; it is within us making its judgments and all we can do is listen to it or ignore it. But examining ourselves upon the verdicts of our conscience is something we must actively choose to do. Unlike the involuntary activity of conscience, the act of knowing our own hearts is voluntary. There is no need for a command to have a conscience, Kant claims, but we are commanded to know ourselves.[94]

Conscience as Antidote to Self-Deception

We have a duty to search and know our own hearts, first of all, because, according to Kant we have a natural propensity to deceive ourselves. After all, Kant depicts us in flight from the voice of our conscience. We are so prone to ignore it that it needs to stalk us, to chase us like our own shadows. The human heart, Kant explains, is not very trustworthy; we are prone to self-deception, especially when it comes to our most basic moral disposition. And this is especially the case when our actions are, by and large, morally good.[95] We are prone to lie to ourselves about

---

93. *Religion*, 6:71.

94. Kant insists that a human being has no choice but to have a conscience; it is not a social construct or something a person can work to develop. It is simply part of what it means to be a rational creature of sense and need. And so it makes no sense to say a person has a duty to have a conscience. Knowledge of the heart, on the other hand, is something we have a duty to provide for ourselves (*Metaphysics of Morals*, 6:400, 6:441).

95. *Religion*, 6:138.

why we do what we do.[96] Even our apparently best actions might have some less-than-admirable incentive behind them but the better the appearance, the easier it is to hide the incentive from ourselves. One significant means to self-deception, Kant argues, is social life. We might think as civilized people, as people brought up under certain civilized mores, that we are better off morally speaking than the uncivilized peoples in a "state of nature" where we can witness all kinds of egregious behavior. But, Kant cautions that we are quite adept at using our civilized, cultured life to hide "many ... vices ... under the appearance of virtue."[97] In our life together, uncivilized and civilized alike, we will "mutually corrupt each other's moral dispositions and make one another evil."[98] Social life has this corrupting influence, Kant explains, because we desensitize each other to vice as vice; our customs can make what we know to be vicious appear to be normal. Consequently, we count someone "as good," Kant argues, "when his evil is common to a class."[99] In civilization we impose conditions of life on each other that we take to be virtuous but that in reality inculcate evil in us.[100] And in turn we use social life to persuade ourselves and others that our vicious behavior actually is virtuous.

Kant's belief that social life can corrupt us and can be a means through which we deceive ourselves about our corruption clearly resists the trajectory I explored at length in Chapter 1, the trajectory from H. Richard Niebuhr to Stanley Hauerwas that emphasizes the social formation of moral identity and that prioritizes the social location of accountability and self-knowledge. We should pause here for a moment to examine further Kant's claim about the social origins of self-deception and to compare it to Niebuhr's and Hauerwas's claims. Kant is not claiming that the moral life is an atomistic affair for the individual removed from others; he is not claiming that we do not need others as we strive to be morally good. He thinks, in fact, as we will see later, that we do very much need others. A certain kind of social life, Kant argues, is necessary in our striving to be morally good and it is beneficial in our ability to hear and heed the voice of our conscience. But he worries, as he writes in his essay on enlightenment, about our proclivity to "self-incurred minority."[101] He worries that we have a proclivity to allow others to determine for us what is right and that we will take as morally normative, consequently, the "private," contingent demands laid upon us by those we happen to meet in the course of our lives.[102] Kant insists, as we have seen, that morality is not confined to the contingencies of our lives, and he insists, furthermore, that if we are to be moral it is up to each one of us to recognize what is right and to act accordingly. And so he worries, finally, about the injury done to the public good and the possibilities of injustice

---

96. *Religion*, 6:43.
97. *Religion*, 6:33.
98. *Religion*, 6:93.
99. *Religion*, 6:33.
100. Cf. Hare, *God and Morality*, 170.
101. "Enlightenment," 8:35.
102. "Enlightenment," 8:36.

when such "self-incurred minority" rules the day.[103] A clear inference of Kant's thought here, in other words, is that when a community makes a demand on us that is immoral, we have the capacity, a capacity we must exercise, to discern the immorality and to resist it.

Presumably, Niebuhr and Hauerwas think something similar: Niebuhr thinks we have the ability to value one ego-alter dialectic over another, and Hauerwas thinks the formation of identity in the life of the church enables us to resist the various and insidious influences of the modern liberal cultures surrounding us. But, Kant might ask, why choose this ego-alter dialectic or why choose this community and not that one? Or, to put this question in terms of conscience, why take this ego-alter dialectic or this particular community as a normative source of accountability? For both Niebuhr and Hauerwas the answer is that the individual discerns God's summons behind a particular ego-alter dialectic or in the life of a particular community. But the question remains as to how this discernment is possible. How am I able to discern in this ego-alter dialectic or this community my final source of accountability? Since Niebuhr equates conscience with the phenomenon of the ego-alter dialectic (and so allows for more than one conscience), he cannot appeal to conscience to answer the question. And ultimately Niebuhr's answer is a vague appeal to a person's freedom to find her "center of valuation" without explaining exactly how this discovery is possible.[104] Hauerwas appeals to the church's ability to offer a narration, a narration of its own history and of the history of its rival communities, that is better than the narration offered by its rival communities.[105] But both the church Hauerwas means to identify and what counts as a "better" narration are notoriously vague in Hauerwas's writing, frustrating even his friendly interlocutors.[106] Hauerwas's criteria for what counts as a better narration seem to come from within the life of the Christian community as it mediates the narrative of God's work in history.[107] The argument is circular and, in the end, problematic: Our grasp on what counts as a better narrative is mediated to us through the community that witnesses in its life to that narrative. My reason for taking this particular community as my ultimate source of accountability appears, then, to be a reason that comes from the criteria given to me by this particular community. Hauerwas wrongly credits Kant as the chief architect of the modern moral subject, the moral subject who holds herself accountable to certain moral norms simply because they are the norms she has given to herself. But it is hard to see how the same relativism Hauerwas identifies and rejects in this interpretation of Kant does not appear again in his

---

103. "Enlightenment," 8:36.

104. Niebuhr, *The Responsible Self*, 124, 129. Cf. Wood, *Kantian Ethics*, 186.

105. Hauerwas, *A Better Hope: Resources for a Church Confronting Capitalism, Democracy, and Postmodernity* (Grand Rapids, MI: Brazos Press, 2000), 35–46.

106. See Richard Hays, *The Moral Vision of the New Testament: A Contemporary Introduction to New Testament Ethics* (New York: HarperCollins, 1996), 264–6.

107. Hauerwas, *A Better Hope*, 37.

own account of community.[108] The Christian community holds itself accountable to particular moral norms because these are the norms that are mediated through and emergent in its own narrative-shaped life.[109] It is this relativistic implication that is problematic, not so much the argument's circularity. I make a gesture at the end of this chapter that what is problematic is also the assumption that this argument dismisses, an assumption deeply rooted in the Christian tradition and that we see here in a fashion in Kant's thought, namely that God sees each individual's heart and holds each individual singularly accountable for the life they live before God. I return to this argument and extend it in the final chapter.

Kant's claim, a claim he knew and that we know history confirms all too well, is that communities, Christian communities included, can be overbearing, malicious, and unjust. We belong to many different communities and we need a way to discern which communities bear genuine moral authority and which do not. Kant argues that the individual must have some kind of access to something beyond the claims of the community so that the individual can enter into the life of one community that calls into question the life of another community she considers unjust. And so for the sake of the public good, for the sake of life in community with others, Kant thinks there must be some locus of accountability that is distinct from the various internalizations of external social norms, distinct from the various corporate self-understandings of particular communities. For Kant it is through practical reason that human beings grasp moral norms that are universal and necessarily binding, and it is through the conscience that human beings hold themselves accountable to these norms as if they were given by God and not by contingent, temporal standards. As we will see, Kierkegaard echoes Kant's claim that our accountability to God ultimately is distinct from our accountability to any community, and he echoes the claim, consequently, that our moral self-awareness cannot be reducible to the claim any community makes upon us. Kierkegaard departs from Kant by replacing Kant's emphasis on practical reason with an emphasis on the personal presence of God. This is, of course, a significant theological difference, but nonetheless, both Kant and Kierkegaard think that there is a singularity in our moral self-awareness before God, and that to confuse our accountability to God with our accountability to a community risks disastrous self-deception.

In short, Kant thinks we are prone to self-deception, and to this end we use each other to hide from ourselves. But social life is not the only means at our disposal to deceive ourselves. We also use actions that are ostensibly good in order to deceive ourselves; we are never more deceived about ourselves, Kant insists, than when we do those things that make us appear good in the eyes of others.[110] From

---

108. Cf. Despland, "Can Conscience Be Hypocritical," 368. From the Kantian vantage, according to Despland, the kind of commitment Hauerwas displays here "can easily dissolve into sociology" and be "menaced by relativism."

109. Hare has made a similar argument, clearly with Hauerwas and MacIntyre in view. See, especially, *Why Bother Being Good*, 173–93.

110. *Religion*, 6:68.

"love of humankind," Kant explains, "I am willing to admit that even most of our actions are in conformity with duty; but if we look more closely at the intentions and aspirations in them, we everywhere come upon the dear self, which is always turning up."[111] Our reasons for acting in conformity with duty are often chiefly not from duty. The "dear self" has incentives other than duty and prior to duty behind its actions that conform to duty.[112] "How many people," Kant asks, "have lived long and guiltless lives" who are really just fortunate "in having escaped so many temptations."[113] The distinction implicit here is between a morally good person and a person of good morals.[114] A person of good morals avoids actions that are illegal and patently immoral (and so open to public shaming) but he or she may act in this way from a basically immoral disposition, from a heart motivated by self-love. According to Kant, such a person uses his or her good morals to hide an immoral heart from others and from himself or herself.

Imagine a parent—I am a father of children around kindergarten age, so let's say a father of children around kindergarten age. He and his wife recognize that parents have an obligation to do their best to educate their children and it is time to think about where to send their oldest child to kindergarten. They know that the choice for kindergarten is important by itself but also that it can have implications for the broader trajectory of the child's education at least through high school. The father is not so sure about the public high school in town. Even though it is where he went to school and he thought he received a good education, he has friends whose opinion he trusts who tell him the school is not what it used to be. He and his wife decide after much thought that they really should consider the good private school. But like all good private schools nowadays the school is expensive and it is hard to enroll your child if you enroll them too late. Kindergarten is, in fact, a good time to start. They review their finances and decide to start their child in the school's kindergarten in the Fall. Time goes by and while the father wishes their budget were not so tight, he is happy with their choice as their child seems to be thriving. From time to time as he thinks about the choice and as he thinks about the work he does to help send the child to the school, he has a sense that in this choice and in his work he does what is right for his child. But from time to time he is aware, sometimes faintly and sometimes more clearly, of ulterior motives. He is aware that he values the choice to send their child to this school not simply because it is best for the child but because the school is prestigious and he enjoys the prestige he thinks he and his family acquire by association. He is aware also that he values their choice because he thinks the school will give his child a "leg up" on other children. He values, in other words, that he and his own will be better off than other people and their children. Finally, he considers the sacrifices he and his wife make in order to send their child to the school and he realizes he values

---

111. *Groundwork*, 4:407.
112. *Groundwork*, 4:407.
113. *Metaphysics of Morals*, 6:393.
114. *Religion*, 6:31.

the choice because it makes him think well of himself and he occasionally hopes that in the long run his child will appreciate and love him more for it.

In these ulterior motives we find what Kant calls "the dear self," the self who, under the cover of right actions, can deceive himself about his impure motives. The deception begins by ignoring the conscience. In the case of this father, in Kant's view, his conscience will pass a negative judgment on him for acting according to these incentives. He can then either heed the verdict of his conscience and acknowledge the impurity of his actions, or he can ignore it. If he persists in ignoring it, then, according to Kant, conscience will begin to lose its power. The unconscientious person becomes less sensitive to the vice as a vice and can even begin to think of the vice as a virtue. Recall Kant's claim that when vice is common to a class we are prone to deceive ourselves and take it as virtue.[115] Kant is clear that for a person like this father the conscience will pass its verdict on the vice and that he, like everyone else, cannot avoid hearing it. But he learns to ignore it and even begins to think that it is a fault in his nature that he occasionally has a sense it is wrong, for example, to want his child to be better than other children. He has become convinced that giving his child a competitive edge is just what good fathers should do. He comes to think, furthermore, that expecting respect, love, and appreciation is just what good parents should reasonably expect from their sacrifices and hard work. Kant is clear that a person can become quite habituated in the act of ignoring the conscience, even as the conscience continues to pass its verdict. But we should note, as Jens Timmerman explains, for Kant "it is no more than a *facon de parler* ... when we say that someone 'has a no conscience,' for (strictly speaking) it is impossible for an agent to lack conscience. Rather such a person has a conscience but 'pays no heed to its verdict.'"[116] Likewise, as Michael Despland writes, Kant assumes that for every rational being "the cure of self-knowledge is always at hand" because the conscience "drives home bits of self-knowledge to the most insidious heart. To be a hypocrite," in other words, "we need to work at it, and a hypocrite will always be reminded of what he is."[117] Even a very morally callous person will "from time to time" hear the voice of conscience and will have some awareness that in his or her actions something is amiss. The persistence of conscience underscores Kant's assumption that self-deception is self-incurred. The person who makes a habit of ignoring the conscience will not willingly choose, consequently, to engage in an act of self-examination in which he or she asks: why do I keep doing what I am doing for reasons I know to be impure? If a judgment about the heart derives from a review of the judgment of conscience on particular actions over time, then to ignore these particular judgments necessarily entails ignoring a voluntary judgment on the heart. The occasional flickering of conscience may cause the person to think of this question but he or she is as likely to engage it as

---

115. Cf. *Lectures*, 134.
116. Timmerman, "Kant on Conscience," 297, 304. Cf. *Lectures*, 130.
117. Despland, "Can Conscience Be Hypocritical," 366.

a repeat offending plagiarizer is likely to volunteer to go before a school's honor council and confess—I am a cheater.

We are prone to self-deception, Kant claims, but we are also not helpless against it. Because we have a conscience we can basically discern well enough when we have acted according to the "dear self's" incentives and we can endorse the verdict of our conscience that these incentives are impure. If, to return to the father, the father is conscientious, then when he acts for the wrong reason and his conscience accuses him, he will not ignore his conscience but will heed its judgment, and he will acknowledge that while what he does conforms to what he knows he should do, he frequently does what he does for his child for reasons he knows to be impure. And after acknowledging this judgment often enough, he moves a step further and asks himself why he continues to catch himself in this impurity. He will have to conclude, according to Kant, that there seems to be something impure at the source of his actions.

Conscience and "Moral Repentance"

Voluntary conscientious self-examination is so important, Kant thinks, because it helps us fight self-deception and we need to fight self-deception, in turn, because we need to know if we have had the change of heart necessary to live the moral life we know we should live. Conscientious self-examination aims at what Kant calls "moral repentance."[118] The heart is "difficult to fathom," but we must strive after such "moral cognition," Kant claims, because it is only when we know if an "evil will" is "actually present" that we can then "remove the obstacle within."[119] It is only as we hear the verdict of our conscience over time and make a reliable inference about our heart that we can make a radical change of heart.[120] We cannot hope for moral improvement if we try to fix this failure here, that failure there, and so on. Kant insists that we must go straight to the source of our actions, reliably discern whether it is good or evil, and if it is evil we have to change it. When we ignore our conscience and, consequently, neglect to examine ourselves, we deceive ourselves and hinder our ability to change our fundamental disposition.[121] The moral life requires a decisive starting point, a singular decision to reverse "the supreme ground of his maxims by which he was an evil human being" and thereby become "a subject receptive to the good."[122] If we want to be moral, Kant tells us, we must first repent, turning from our fundamentally impure motive for all our actions toward a pure one. We must change the impure, disordered source of all our impure, disordered maxims. But we will not repent if we first do not strive

118. *Lectures*, 131.
119. *Metaphysics of Morals*, 6:441.
120. *Religion*, 6:68.
121. *Religion*, 6:38.
122. *Religion*, 6:47.

to know our hearts, and we strive to know our hearts when we first listen to our conscience.

Conscience plays an important role, then, in what Kant calls the "revolution of the will" from a state of "radical evil." The problem we find ourselves in as moral agents, according to Kant, is that before we have any experience of our freedom we have already perverted the order of our predispositions. Evil is innate in us, Kant claims, in the sense that "it is posited as the ground antecedent to every use of freedom given in experience (from the earliest youth as far back as birth) and is thus represented as present in the moment of birth."[123] We are "by nature evil," then, in the sense that from our birth, our "cognition" of our "experience" is that our hearts are evil.[124] Kant explains that our propensity to evil originates from our freedom, but what is peculiar is that "the concept of a propensity" concerns "a subjective determining ground that precedes every deed, and hence is not itself a deed."[125] And yet, mysteriously, this corruption of our hearts is a fault that belongs to each of us. It is our own "intelligible deed," by which Kant means that it is a deed "cognizable through reason alone apart from any temporal condition," through which we adopt in the supreme ground of all our maxims a perversion of the right order of predispositions.[126] Outside of our temporal experience we are responsible for ranking in our hearts the predisposition to self-love above the predisposition to the good. And so we can say, according to Kant, that evil is innate in human nature but also something for which we are each accountable. That this radical evil is universal is evident enough, Kant claims, just by paying attention to everyday human experience.[127] According to Kant, then, a conscientious person who seeks to fulfill the duty to know the heart will inevitably discover herself in a dire situation. It is as conscience is roused to judgment that we see the need for a revolution of our hearts.[128] What is necessary is not mere reform, Kant insists, but revolution. The ultimate determining ground of our will is fixed in a corrupted state; but we also can only conceive of this ultimate determining ground as our choice, as something for which we are responsible. And so we also must believe that we are able to change it. Our conscience helps us to see we need a radical change, that each of us must become a "new creature;" we must, that is, go through a change of heart.[129] And this is the revolution, the singular choice by which a person reverses the corrupt spring at the root of all particular actions.[130]

But how, we should ask, is this reversal, this revolutionary change, possible? Conscience leads a person to the point that he or she becomes aware that this

---

123. *Religion*, 6:31.
124. *Religion*, 6:32.
125. *Religion*, 6:31.
126. *Religion*, 6:31–32.
127. *Religion*, 6:33; cf. 6:34–35.
128. *Religion*, 6:69.
129. *Religion*, 6:47.
130. *Religion*, 6:47.

conversion of the will is necessary, but many interpreters of Kant claim that Kant's conception of the corruption of the will, of the will in a state of radical evil, is more than his conception of conversion can bear. Kant's would-be convert, so the criticism runs, is in too deep a ditch to climb out. The problem is that Kant claims that we must be able, on our own, to change our disposition,[131] but also that we are so mired in radical evil that we are unable to do so.[132] With these two claims Kant leaves us, John Hare explains, with an unresolved antinomy, "with the apparent conclusion that the revolution of the will is both possible (because obligatory) and impossible (because the ground of our maxims is corrupt)."[133] To resolve this dilemma, Gordon Michalson rightly observes, Kant "begs his own question by simply assuming that this transformation has occurred."[134]

I do not want to deny that this antinomy is a real problem for Kant's moral theology. But we should observe that it is not a problem that arises from his theory of conscience, nor is it a problem his theory of conscience is able to resolve. It is, nonetheless, a problem *for* his theory of conscience, because if the situation is as Kant suggests, then when a person turns to her conscience she will find herself in a dilemma she is both responsible to resolve and powerless to do so. And it is hard to imagine that a person can live with such a testimony; it is hard to imagine, that is, that a person would continue to heed the testimony of her conscience if this is how she is disclosed to herself by it.

To avoid discouraging the conscientious person in this way, Kant needs to affirm that we are not the kinds of creatures who are made to bridge on our own the gap between who we are and who we ought to be. He cannot have, as Michalson aptly puts it, "a theory of radical evil [that] appears to force him in an Augustinian direction," and at the same time a "conception of grace that reintroduces an obviously Pelagian element based on human effort and merit."[135] This unbridgeable gap appears for Kant's conscientious person as a gap presented by the pure religion of reason, the translation of historical faith into pure moral concepts universally accessible through practical reason and therefore universally binding. It is only the faith of the pure religion of reason that is for Kant, as Hare notes, "without qualification necessary for salvation,"[136] since historical faith makes contingent claims that cannot be universally morally binding.[137] But, as we

---

131. *Religion*, 6:44.

132. *Religion*, 6:143. For helpful discussions of this conundrum in Kant's moral theology, see Wolterstorff, "Conundrums in Kant's Religion," in *Kant's Philosophy of Religion Reconsidered*, ed. Philip Rossi and Michael Wren (Bloomington: Indiana University Press, 1991), 48; Hare, *The Moral Gap*, 60; Herdt, *Putting on Virtue*, 337.

133. Hare, *The Moral Gap*, 61.

134. Gordon Michalson, *Fallen Freedom: Kant on Radical Evil and Moral Regeneration* (New York: Cambridge University Press, 1990), 94.

135. Michalson, *Fallen Freedom*, 97.

136. Hare, *The Moral Gap*, 67.

137. *Religion*, 103.

can see, the pure religion of reason leaves Kant with an "incoherence in practical reason," and so we should be "skeptical," Hare concludes, "about whether Kant did in fact find a pure rational religion which is all that would be necessary for saving faith."[138] But I think we can follow Hare who finds resources within Kant's thought to see how the dilemma could be resolved. The key is that Kant wants not only to translate historical faith into pure moral concepts in which he subtracts "from the traditional understanding of God's work any mediating role for anything that is not already human."[139] Kant also wants to find the consistency between historical faith—or special revelation—and the pure religion of reason. Kant's mistake is to give absolute and unqualified priority to the pure religion of reason. But his other project in which he looks for consistency between revelation and reason allows us to find coherence between historical faith and the pure religion of reason. And so here, as Hare explains, "if our ordinary notion of the moral life leaves us with a problem for which the resources of the pure religion of reason are inadequate," we can then "go on to explore [special revelation]" to solve it. In this case we can affirm special revelation as an indispensable resource.[140] In other words, if the pure religion of reason is inadequate on its own to resolve the dilemma the conscientious person finds herself facing, then it must be consistent with reason to admit that we are fundamentally in need of assistance. And here, when Kant is not translating special revelation, he feels the need to acknowledge our need for "heavenly influences," "supernatural assistance," "cooperation from above."[141] Hare explains, then, that on one hand Kant admits that some notion of grace is necessary "if we are to hold ourselves accountable to the moral law."[142] There is nothing inconsistent about this with reason since reason on its own reaches an unsolvable dilemma. Kant's failure—a failure Hare notes represents a basic inconsistency within Kant's thought—is to assume also, on the other hand, that the pure religion of reason will be sufficient in itself.[143] If this is the case, then Kant's conscientious person is stuck, left paralyzed before an impossible dilemma. But there are resources within Kant's thought to see how this person might be conscientious without getting stuck in this way. When she comes to the point where she finds herself before a gap she cannot bridge on her own, she also has good reason to believe that she will have help from beyond herself to bridge it.

I said that the dilemma of this moral gap does not arise from Kant's theory of conscience. Kant's theory of conscience is not responsible for this dilemma, but the dilemma is nonetheless a problem for Kant's theory of conscience, a problem his conscientious person will confront. And we can see how the dilemma might be resolved from within Kant's thought by expanding Kant's appeal to divine

---

138. Hare, *The Moral Gap*, 67.
139. Hare, *The Moral Gap*, 65.
140. Hare, *The Moral Gap*, 68.
141. *Religion*, 6:88, 178, 52.
142. Hare, *God's Call*, 91.
143. Hare, *God's Call*, 91.

assistance and by chastening the priority he gives to the pure religion of reason. We can see, at least, that the resolution of the dilemma the conscientious person faces comes in Kant's thought—even as it stands in tension with other elements of his thought—from the direction of divine grace.

Conscience and Perseverance

Conscience helps lead us to the revolution of the will necessary to live the moral life; it is, according to Kant, like a spur toward "moral repentance." Conscience brings us to the dilemma of the revolution of the will. We have seen how this dilemma exposes a deep tension in Kant's thought, but also how there are resources within Kant's thought to resolve this tension. Once we see how this tension can be resolved, we can move to the role Kant gives to conscience after the revolution of the will. Conscience, that is, is not only a spur toward repentance. We need to believe we can live as moral beings, that we can live "in accordance with"—that is, respond appropriately to—the verdict of conscience.[144] And to this end we need, Kant claims, confidence that our lives are anchored the good disposition, confidence we can find as we survey our lives after we have undergone the revolution of the will.[145] Having attempted to "break with evil," to change our hearts, we now listen to the voice of our conscience over time, assess our lives, and try to discern if our actions are congruent with the change. If they are, and, again, Kant assumes we will basically know if they are, then we can be confident that our heart is in fact good and that we can persevere. If finding such confidence is not possible—if our fundamental disposition were categorically inscrutable—then, Kant claims, perseverance in a good disposition would likewise not be possible.[146] The dynamic of Kant's account of conscientious self-examination, moral repentance, and perseverance in the moral life is like the practices of a person who resolves to go on a diet and succeeds in the resolution. He goes in for a routine check-up and his doctor tells him that health complications are around the corner if he does not lose weight. And so he resolves to be healthy. He knows if he checks the scale every day he will be discouraged since the progress will appear too slight, but he also knows it is important to check in. If he sees that he can do what he set out to do, then he will be encouraged to persevere. Likewise, Kant claims that when our good moral resolve shows in our actions over the course of time, and when we discern no backsliding, we can rest assured in the genuineness of our resolution to become a subject receptive to the good.[147]

To persevere in the moral life, then, we need to be able to believe our hearts our good, which, for Kant, is the same as believing we have become "well-pleasing"

---

144. *Lectures*, 131.
145. *Religion*, 6:68.
146. *Religion*, 6:68.
147. *Religion*, 6:71.

to "the accuser" or "judge within," that is, to our conscience, and analogously that we have become "well-pleasing to God."[148] But if we are to be well-pleasing before our own conscience and before God who wills perfectly in accord with the moral law and who sees our hearts, then we must be holy. Holiness is what our moral repentance seeks to establish.[149] And yet, Kant concedes that despite the revolution of the will there remains in that person's actions a "deficiency which is in principle inseparable from the existence of a temporal being." Consequently, the person who fundamentally changes his disposition still is "never able to become quite fully what he has in mind."[150] The disposition has undergone the requisite change and yet such a person's actions remain "at each instant" deficient.[151] Robert Adams helpfully explains that Kant can maintain that a person's disposition is holy and reject the possibility of "any sinless period of time" in a person's life because Kant accepts "something like Luther's doctrine that the regenerate person is *simul justus et peccator* (at the same time righteous and sinner)."[152] Adams explains that what this means for Kant is that once a person undergoes the revolutionary change her "temporal existence is grounded in both timeless dispositions." Before the revolution of the fundamental disposition a person acts only from an evil heart; after the revolution, an evil heart and a good heart exist simultaneously.[153] Prior to the change of heart a person's heart, and consequently all of his or her actions, are in a state of radical evil. After the change of heart there is a conflict between the good and evil heart. In order to explain how we can trust whether or not we find ourselves in this post-revolutionary state, Kant appeals to the idea of progress, to the idea of an advance in goodness wherein a person over time can discern her good disposition gaining "the upper hand over the evil principle formerly dominant."[154] However this progress works in Kant's account, from what we have seen of his theory of conscience, Kant is clear that through our conscience we have a reliable assessment of our action, and so through our conscience we have a reliable means to assess whether or not the good disposition is in fact gaining the upper hand over the evil disposition. We can discern well enough whether or not in our actions we are living increasingly in accord with the law for the sake of the law.

But there is still a dilemma: perseverance in the moral life requires that we be able to affirm that we are well-pleasing in the eyes of our conscience and, by analogy, to God. And to be able to make this affirmation we need to be able to affirm

---

148. *Religion*, 6:76–77.
149. Cf. *Religion*, 6:47.
150. *Religion*, 6:67n.
151. *Religion*, 6:67.
152. Adams, "Introduction," in Immanuel Kant, *Religion Within the Bounds of Reason Alone and Other Writings*, edited by Allen Wood and George di Giovanni (New York: Cambridge University Press, 1998), xviii.
153. Adams, "Introduction," xx.
154. *Religion*, 6:73.

that our hearts are unqualifiedly good. Kant's idea of progress, however, assumes a persistence of imperfection throughout our lives, a fact that calls our moral goodness into question since appearances suggest from time to time a qualification in what is supposed to be true of us as good moral agents unqualifiedly. How, then, can we have confidence that we can persevere in the moral life as morally well-pleasing before God and before the demands of practical reason? And how can we avoid getting "bogged down" in this question? To answer these questions Kant, once again, appeals to the existence of God as the one who sees our hearts. We cannot see our hearts, but we can discern the moral worth of our actions and we can reliably discern whether or not, after having made a decision to be subjects fundamentally receptive to the good, good actions are becoming more prevalent in our lives. We must believe, Kant argues, that God, who searches the heart, sees this progression of our lives toward a final victory of the good principle, a final victory of the good heart and that God sees this progress as a "perfected whole," so that whenever we die can have confidence that we die well-pleasing to God.[155] We begin, then, with our conscience where we approximate God's judgment of our action. And we move from this reliable, approximate judgment to a deeper judgment of our hearts as the source of our actions. This deeper judgment is, like the judgment of conscience, an endorsement, an endorsement we make with justified hope, that God sees our hearts and judges us to be morally well-pleasing. And so while, according to Kant, in our experience we know ourselves as not yet what we resolved to be, we can persevere in the moral life because we have good reason to believe that we can with God judge ourselves to be already morally well-pleasing.

We need to be able to believe we are morally well-pleasing to God if we are going to persevere in the moral life, and we can believe this as we heed the voice of our conscience and make a conjecture about our hearts. But it is noteworthy that for Kant, to be "well-pleasing to God" has to do, as Robert Adams explains, "only [with] an internal or monadic property of the self." It has nothing to do with a special, familiar relationship to God "that is the goal of spiritual aspiration."[156] Likewise, John Hare finds in Kant no sense that our obedience to the moral law is "a route to union with God." For Kant, Hare observes, "obedience or respect for the law remains as our end, together with the happiness proportionate to it."[157] Kierkegaard, like Kant, thinks that the knowledge we have of ourselves in conscience is a knowledge of ourselves in relation to God that aims to help us live in conformity to what it means to be well-pleasing to God. But unlike Kant, Kierkegaard thinks that it is for the sake of our union with God that our conscience discloses us to ourselves before God. Until we come to the final end where we rest transparently with God in our relationship to God we are, according to Kierkegaard, restless. Perhaps, then, Kant's conscientious person remains restless, though Kant would surely deny this, since this conscientious person is moving

---

155. *Religion*, 6:67. Again, note the singularity of self-awareness before God.
156. Adams, "Introduction," xxiv.
157. Hare, *God's Call*, 90.

toward victory, toward a perfect harmony of respect for the moral law and the happiness proportionate to it. We might object to Kant's theological assumptions here, but I think we can do so without also seriously objecting to his theory of conscience.

To summarize, for Kant the knowledge we have of our hearts is an approximate knowledge we have of ourselves in our relation to God, who we believe promulgates the law to us and who sees our hearts' conformity to the law. It is no coincidence, moreover, that Kant almost never discusses conscience at any length before he makes reference to the one who sees or reads the heart.[158] Just as the judgment of conscience is an approximation of God's judgment of our actions, so the consequent inference we make about our hearts by means of our conscience is an approximation of the knowledge God has of our hearts. It should be clear by this point, furthermore, that only by a severe misinterpretation can Kant's theory of conscience be interpreted as an endorsement of the modern autonomous individual who knows herself as the source of her morality and as accountable to a law she makes for herself. For Kant, a person strives to know herself in her conscience and by means of conscience with God and before God; and she knows herself as accountable to a law she gives to herself in the sense that she recognizes and makes her own a law that is necessary and universal and that she believes she encounters as a law God as Supreme lawgiver promulgates to her. Kant's translation of special revelation into the pure religion of reason and his elision of any sense that our highest end is to find rest in God raise possible serious problems *for* his conscientious person, but, as we noted, these are not problems that arise *from* his theory of conscience; they are not problems his theory of conscience creates.

Conscience and Community

There remains a concern that Kant's theory of conscience is excessively individualistic and that it is implausible in its insensitivity to the positive role of particular, tradition-bearing communities for a person's moral formation. And admittedly, while Kant does think, as we will see, that a good society can help us to hear and heed our conscience, this concession to the positive role of sociality in his theory of conscience is a rather thin one. His theory of conscience is indeed individualistic because he thinks each individual knows himself or herself as singularly accountable before God to the moral law and that this accountability is distinct from accountability to other people. But in this regard Kant's theory of conscience is in concert with a Scriptural witness that God searches, knows, judges, and holds accountable each individual. Consider Peter's claim that God "judges each man's work impartially," Paul's declaration that God is the one "who searches hearts" and discloses our secrets, Jesus's repetition in the Sermon on the

---

158. Cf. *Lectures*, 133; "On the Miscarriage of all Philosophical Trials," 8:270. *Religion*, 6:189; *Metaphysics of Morals*, 4:439.

Mount that the Father "sees in secret" each of us, and, finally, the affirmation we find in Hebrews that no "creature is hidden from [God's] sight, but all are naked and exposed to the eyes of him to whom we must give account."[159] The singular, individualistic strain of these passages (as in Kant's thought) is clear. Kant is not, furthermore, without good company in the Christian tradition in stressing the individual's singular accountability before God. It is in this spirit that Augustine famously declares to God, "You were more inward than my most inward parts and higher than the highest element within me."[160] I make quick reference to these passages from Scripture and the Christian tradition, passages we will return to in the final chapter, simply to say that Kant's focus on the individual standing before God accountable to a claim she believes God makes upon her does not herald the advent of the modern autonomous individual; rather his focus stands in an important trajectory of reflection on the individual's singular accountability to God, a trajectory that runs from Scripture through the Christian tradition Kant inherits.

The individualism of Kant's theory of conscience carries solid biblical and theological credentials. Kant's theory of conscience is not, furthermore, excessively individualistic. Kant does not think we can pursue the moral life alone. We need, he claims, a virtuous society.[161] John Hare explains that Kant believes "that because we make one another evil, there has to be a radically changed society if there are to be morally good people."[162] Because we are corrupted by our social life, as we have already seen Kant affirms, our pursuit of virtue requires our concerted efforts to establish a society that seeks the dominion of virtue. "In addition to prescribing laws to each individual human being," Kant writes, "morally legislative reason also unfurls a banner of virtue as a rallying point for all those who love the good, that they may congregate under it and thus at the very start gain the upper hand over evil and its untiring attacks."[163] Our moral striving, according to Kant, requires the presence of others to help us on our way, or as the author of the epistle to the Hebrews explains, it requires us to encourage each other and to "spur one another on toward love and good deeds."[164] We are just not the kinds of creatures, according to Kant, who can do without this fellowship if we are to live the lives we know we should live. And Kant thinks, moreover, that a proper ecclesiastical faith is indispensable for us to help us understand what a society under the dominion of virtue should look like.[165]

---

159. 1 Pet. 1:17; Rom. 8:27; Mt. 6:4, 6, 18 (the singular reference is unmistakable); Heb. 4:12-13.
160. Augustine, *Confessions*, 3.6.11, p. 43.
161. *Religion*, 6:94.
162. Hare, *God and Morality*, 170.
163. *Religion*, 6:94.
164. Hebrews 10:24-25.
165. Cf. *Religion*, 6:105.

The significance for Kant's theory of conscience of his affirmation of community concerns the formation of conscience. Kant does not think, strictly speaking, that conscience is something we form. We have a conscience as part of our nature as rational beings. What is malleable is our ability to hear and heed the voice of our conscience, and we have already seen that social life can have a negative influence on us in this regard. And so while Kant disagrees with those "who have argued that conscience is a work of art and education, and that it judges and sentences by a force of habit," he concedes that conscience is something we can "hurt or injure," and he concedes that the intrinsically social activities of "art and education" can help bring conscience to "fruition."[166] I take it, then, that one of the tasks of the congregation united under the banner of virtue is to help each individual hear the voice of his or her conscience more clearly and to act accordingly.[167]

Summary and Conclusion

In conclusion, we can affirm, according to Kant, that we strive to know ourselves rightly when we strive to know ourselves in our relation to God who, as the supreme moral lawgiver, holds us accountable to the demands of practical reason. Conscience is the knowledge we have of ourselves as we approximate God's judgment of our actions. And conscience is the means we have to approximate God's judgment of our hearts. Conscience, according to Kant, serves to help us stave off self-deception, to lead us to moral repentance, and to encourage us as we persevere in the moral life. Kant's theory of conscience is not, moreover, a driving factor in a notion of autonomy that valorizes choice for its own sake. His theory of conscience is not a way to describe how an autonomous agent (so understood) remains consistent with herself about the choices she arbitrarily has made. Such a notion of autonomy and consequent notion of conscience, I have argued, are foreign to Kant's practical philosophy and moral theology. Kant's theory of conscience, rather, is better understood as belonging in a trajectory from the Pauline epistles, to the Patristic era, and into the Reformation in which conscience is the locus of a person's "self-opening to the probing interrogation and challenge of an encounter with God."[168] If I am right in my reading of Kant's theory of conscience, then we must call into question any account of the decline and fall of conscience in which Kant is the principal villain. Kant's theory of conscience is not a problem to overcome but a resource that can help us think about how we know ourselves as moral agents singularly accountable before God to the claim God makes upon us.

---

166. *Lectures*, 133.
167. *Lectures*, 133.
168. O'Donovan, *Ways*, 305.

Chapter 3

SELF-KNOWLEDGE AND THE ENORMOUS WEIGHT OF GOD: CONSCIENCE IN SØREN KIERKEGAARD'S SECOND AUTHORSHIP

Introduction: Conscience in Kierkegaard's Second Authorship

In the previous chapter I argued that for Kant, if we are going to live the moral life we have to strive for knowledge of ourselves. And we strive to know ourselves when by means of our conscience we approximate the judgment God makes of us before the moral law. We can say, in other words, that for Kant conscience concerns the knowledge we have of ourselves in relation to God as God makes a claim on us. I will argue in this chapter that Kierkegaard shares with Kant in this heritage of thinking about conscience. Like Kant, Kierkegaard thinks that self-knowledge is a central facet of the moral life; and like Kant, Kierkegaard thinks that self-knowledge is a knowledge in relation to God and that this knowledge is the business of conscience.

Kierkegaard does not, however, like Kant make a distinction between conscience as the knowledge a person has of herself in her actions and conscience as the means, thereby, to acquire a conjectural knowledge of the heart. The knowledge of the moral law, the knowledge of conscience, and the knowledge of the heart are indeed interdependent in Kant's thought but nonetheless distinct. In his theory of conscience, Kierkegaard unites what Kant distinguishes. Knowledge of the claim made upon us, knowledge of our actions' moral quality, and knowledge of ourselves are all forms of knowledge that belong to a person's self-disclosing encounter with God in conscience. Furthermore, in distinction from Kant, Kierkegaard insists that the claim God makes upon each person is unique in each person's special relationship to God. The knowledge we have of *ourselves* in relation to God as God claims us and the knowledge of *the claim* God makes upon us are, for Kierkegaard, ultimately indistinguishable. By bringing the objective and subjective so closely together, Kierkegaard's theory of conscience, in its own way, opens itself to the same questions we asked of Kant's theory of conscience: does it ultimately give license to an autonomous moral agent who values freedom for its own sake? Does it encourage, even if unwittingly, an individual to know herself as accountable to a law simply because it is the law she has given to herself? In this vein, Karl Barth once criticized Kierkegaard's work generally for encouraging a "subjectivity that as such [regards] itself as the truth."[1] And so we will have to consider whether or not this is also true of Kierkegaard's theory of conscience in particular.

Defining Conscience

When Søren Kierkegaard turns in the second part of his authorship to a direct communication on the nature of Christian existence, conscience becomes a central theme.[2] This claim might appear dubious since Kierkegaard evidently has a great deal to say about "the crowd," the "single individual," and the "God-relation," and very little to say about conscience.[3] And the "crowd," the "single individual," and the "God-relation" are indeed fundamental in Kierkegaard's thought. A good summary of Kierkegaard's aim in his "second authorship" is that he wants to help his reader become a Christian by helping her break away from the crowd, acquire a singular relation to God, and become the single individual God created her to

---

1. Karl Barth, "A Thank-You and a Bow—Kierkegaard's Reveille," in *Fragments Grave and Gay* (San Francisco, CA: HarperCollins, 1971), 99.

2. I am focusing, in other words, on the major works from Kierkegaard's "second authorship," the authorship from 1847 to 1851 in which Kierkegaard offers in his own name and relatively straightforwardly an account of Christian existence, as distinct from the aesthetic and ethical-religious modes of existence Kierkegaard examines in the pseudonymous literature that concludes with *Concluding Unscientific Postscript*. The works from this period I consider are *Two Ages* (1846) (an important transitional book), *Upbuilding Discourses in Various Spirits* (1847), *Works of Love* (1847), *Christian Discourses* (1848), *The Sickness unto Death* (1849), *Practice in Christianity* (1850), *For Self-Examination* (1851), *Judge for Yourself!* (1851), and Kierkegaard's *Discourses at the Communion on Fridays*, a work that comprises discourses spanning this whole period. Kierkegaard's attention to conscience is constant throughout these works in a way he simply was not in his earlier pseudonymous authorship.

3. It might appear dubious also in light of the overwhelming silence on the topic of conscience in the secondary literature on Kierkegaard. There are, however, suggestive hints here and there. See, for example, Louis Mackey, *Points of View: Readings of Kierkegaard* (Gainseville: University of Florida Press, 1986), 31–3; Steven Evans, *Faith beyond Reason: A Kierkegaardian Approach* (Grand Rapids, MI: Eerdmans, 1986), 124; Sylvia Walsh, *Living Christianly: Kierkegaard's Dialectic of Christian Existence* (University Park: Pennsylvania University Press, 1997), 33–4; Marilyn Piety, *Ways of Knowing: Kierkegaard's Pluralist Epistemology* (Waco, TX: Baylor University Press, 2010), 32; Murray Rae, *Kierkegaard and Theology* (New York: T&T Clark, 2010), 151, 174; George Pattison, *Kierkegaard and the Theology of the Nineteenth Century: The Paradox and the Point of Contact* (New York: Cambridge University Press, 2013), 49–52; Zachman and Ziegler are exceptional as the only two scholars who devote more than a few pages to Kierkegaard's understanding of conscience. See Zachman, *Reconsidering John Calvin*, 137–51; and Ziegler, "A Christian Context for Conscience."

be. But consider what he has to say about conscience in relation to the crowd, the single individual, and the relation to God: the "sum and substance of public life is actually from first to last to lack a conscience";[4] "What does it mean to be and to will to be the single individual? It means to have and to will to have a conscience";[5] "the relationship between the individual and God, the God-relationship is the conscience."[6] What these claims make clear is that conscience is one of the basic filters in Kierkegaard's thought. It is a central concern for Kierkegaard in every major theological topic he addresses.

Conscience is central for Kierkegaard, but it is not necessarily clear what he means by conscience. Given the unsystematic, occasional, and dialectical nature of his writings, Kierkegaard rarely describes conscience the same way twice. While one definition of conscience never contradicts another, the content of his definitions shifts and takes on different nuances with different contexts. To understand Kierkegaard's theory of conscience, then, it is necessary to examine the nature and function of conscience across the breadth of his second authorship. There he defines conscience sometimes in terms of "the eternal," and claims that conscience is "the eternal" in every person's consciousness;[7] conscience, he writes, is a "voice" that acts within every person's inner being as, what he calls, the "accounting of eternity."[8] In this sense of accountability Kierkegaard also defines conscience as an inner "confidant" that opposes or counterbalances a person's temporal drives and inclinations;[9] and it is also what he calls the "preacher of repentance" assigned to each of us that questions us about the conformity of our lives to what we read in God's Word.[10] Finally, and most significantly, he defines conscience as the transparency a person has to herself before God.[11] It is in this sense that he defines conscience even more broadly, as we have seen, as a person's relation to God.[12] The conscience is the relation to God, he explains, because it is in the conscience that God "looks at a person" and summons a person "in everything" to look back to God.[13]

With regard to conscience, Kierkegaard's chief concern as an author during his "second authorship" is to help awaken his reader's conscience; he wants to help lead his reader toward his or her own distinct self-disclosing encounter with God in conscience. Kierkegaard is not concerned, however, that his reader understands what precisely the conscience is. But despite the lack of a consistent, systematic

---

4. *JP*, 3:320.
5. *JFY*, 91.
6. *WL*, 143.
7. *UDVS*, 125.
8. *UDVS*, 128.
9. *DCF*, 138.
10. *CD*, 192.
11. *SUD*, 124.
12. *WL*, 138.
13. *WL*, 385.

presentation of conscience in Kierkegaard's works, we can come to a preliminary definition that will bear out over the course of the chapter. We can infer that for Kierkegaard conscience is a person's distinct, singular moral self-awareness in relation to God. What he means, for example, when he says that conscience is a person's relation to God in which God and a person are looking at each other is that conscience is the knowledge every person shares with God—however conscious a person is of this knowledge—about who he or she is and about who he or she ought to be. Kierkegaard conceives of conscience in this way because, as we will see, he derives his theory of conscience from the omnipresence and omniscience of God,[14] dogmatic categories whose significance for Kierkegaard is existential: that God is omnipresent means that God is present to a person right now and at every moment of her life and is more intimate to her than she is to herself; correlatively, that God is omniscient means that God knows a person right now and at every moment of her life infinitely more than she knows herself. And ultimately, that God is omnipresent and omniscient means for Kierkegaard that God summons a person right now and at every moment of her life to commune with God by resting transparently in God's presence to her, and sharing transparently in God's knowledge of her. It is by virtue of this summons, finally, that Kierkegaard claims that everyone has a conscience but that everyone must also will to have a conscience.

What is central for Kierkegaard's theory of conscience is not an atomistic, autonomous, promethean subject. What is central for him and his theory of conscience is the omnipresent and omniscient watchful presence of God. Kierkegaard's theory of conscience here resists the charge of sanctioning the modern autonomous individual in much the same way Kant's theory of conscience resists the charge. Recall the discussion in the previous chapter about the "as if" in Kant's theory of conscience. I raised H. Richard Niebuhr's objection to Kant's theory of conscience that for Kant the "experience of conscience" is merely "like being judged by another person." According to Niebuhr, Kant suggests that conscience is a matter of the free autonomous individual knowing herself before a law she makes for herself. In order to hold herself accountable to this law she creates a generic Other; it is "as if" in her conscience she were accountable to this Other, Niebuhr suggests, but this Other is finally a fiction, created by the autonomous individual to help her be consistent with herself. But, as I argued, Kant thinks we should imagine ourselves not simply "as if" before a generic Other. We judge ourselves in our conscience "as if" before God. And we think of ourselves in this way, Kant believes, because in our conscience we hold ourselves accountable to a law that is absolute and necessary, holding as much for us as for God. We think of ourselves "as if" before God, furthermore, because we should believe, Kant insists, that God exists as the Supreme Lawgiver and judge who sees our hearts. The experience of being judged in conscience "as if" by God is an approximation we make in our conscience of the reality of God's judgment of us. The "as if" corresponds to

---

14. Cf. Ziegler, "A Christian Context," 99.

what we must believe is really true. Kant's theory of conscience does not give us license to value freedom for its own sake or to think of ourselves as accountable to ourselves as creator of the moral law. We know ourselves rightly, Kant claims, when we know ourselves in relation to God.

Like Kant, Kierkegaard does not value freedom for its own sake. A person is not simply accountable to herself, accountable to be consistent with herself, as a being of freedom. A person's moral self-awareness, according to Kierkegaard, is an awareness in relation to God; it is an awareness, as such, of one's accountability before God. As we will see, Kierkegaard's theory of conscience does make the affirmation that we are accountable to ourselves, but only as each of us has a self that God gives to us and gives to us for the sake of our relation to God. The chief difference between Kant and Kierkegaard is that while Kant affirms we know ourselves in relation to God, we know ourselves in relation to God for the sake of our continued obedience to the moral law (and not for any kind of special relationship to God); we know ourselves in relation to God as the Supreme Lawgiver who holds us accountable to the dictates of our practical reason for the sake of living in greater conformity to them. For Kierkegaard the relation to God is everything. We know ourselves in relation to God for the sake of our relation to God. Conscience is a sharing with God in God's knowledge of us as beings created by God and for God.

The claim that conscience is a personal sharing with God in God's knowledge of us might suggest that conscience is something exclusive for Kierkegaard in a way that it is not for Kant, since for Kant every person knows the moral law and can know himself or herself in relation to God before the moral law. But for Kierkegaard since conscience is strictly a knowledge in relation to God for the sake of that relation, and since not everyone appears to have this relation, it might appear that only some people have a conscience.[15] And in a certain semantic sense it is true for Kierkegaard that only some people have a conscience, but one of his central presuppositions is that conscience is a basic, constituent feature of being a human being. He presupposes that everyone has a conscience because he presupposes that everyone has a relation to God. It is also true, however, that every person must awaken the conscience, and if conscience remains asleep then it is just as well to speak of such a person as not having a conscience.[16] Kierkegaard explains that conscience is something everyone has but must also "will to have."[17] Everyone has a conscience but there is also nothing so difficult to acquire: "every human being has a conscience—yet there is no accomplishment ... which requires such an extensive and rigorous schooling as is required before one can genuinely

---

15. The world, he claims, does not believe in God (*JP*, 2:223).

16. Since, however, the God-relation and, therefore, conscience are ineradicable, and since it is only true that a person does not have a conscience in a semantic sense, Kierkegaard will also describe the state of not willing to have a conscience as positively having a "bad conscience." Cf. *UDVS*, 127.

17. *JFY*, 91.

be said to have a conscience."[18] And so even though everyone has a conscience, Kierkegaard claims that in a person's last judgment he or she will be asked, "have you or have you not had a conscience."[19]

Understanding Conscience from Its Absence: The Crowd

The fact that Kierkegaard can imagine an examination of a person about whether or not she has had a conscience clearly means that he assumes it is possible for a person to live as if she did not have a conscience. Kierkegaard sees this possibility fully realized in the life of the "crowd," a favorite foil throughout his writings that appears under a variety of names such as "the public" and "the herd."[20] In the crowd, he writes, people say to one another, "'Lets be part of a group,' for if we are part of a group it means good-night to conscience. We cannot be two or three, a Miller Brothers and Company around a conscience."[21] Since, then, Kierkegaard roundly equates the crowd with the lack of conscience, when he identifies certain qualities the crowd lacks, it is possible to infer that these qualities disclose something significant about the conscience. An examination of Kierkegaard's description of the crowd can therefore help to identify certain key features of his theory of conscience.

How, then, does the crowd live and what does the crowd's life disclose about conscience? What is first apparent about the crowd is that it is a place of such

---

18. *JP*, 1:320. Likewise, he explains, every person has a conscience but everyone nonetheless must become "equipped ... with a conscience" (*JP*, 1:321).

19. *JP*, 1:321.

20. I should stabilize Kierkegaard's language on the "crowd" (*mængden*) before we move further because Kierkegaard makes a distinction between the "crowd" and "community." As Julia Watkin explains, "the crowd (*Mængden*) or 'public' (*Publikum*)" is Kierkegaard's name for "groups of people forming irresponsible pressure groups." Watkin finds in Kierkegaard's journals of 1850 a careful distinction between such pressure groups and a genuine, normatively healthy community. "The crowd consists simply of people en masse, physical numbers, in which the group is formed by the unthinking and the irresponsible. A community, on the other hand, consists of a group of individuals in which each individual is attempting to live according to an ethical-religious ideality. The validity of the entire group [the community] is thus maintained when all are striving to do this. The individuals guarantee the group's status as an authentic community, just as the thoughtless crowd does the opposite" (Julia Watkin, *Historical Dictionary of Kierkegaard's Philosophy* (Lanham, MD: Scarecrow Press, 2001), 59). The point I am making at the moment is that the pressure the "crowd" exerts on the individual is a pressure to silence the conscience. Shortly, we will see how the awakening of conscience aims at the flourishing of "authentic community," in which individuals help each other hear the voice of their own conscience and live accordingly.

21. *JP*, 2:417.

constant striving after "earthly and worldly distinction"²² that its life constitutes a collective effort to live "totally in the momentary."²³ To live as part of the crowd, he writes, is to seek rest in "the breast of temporality in the cradle of finitude."²⁴ The crowd is the embodiment of the "demand of the times,"²⁵ which is to say it is an embodiment of pure inconstancy, temporality, and finitude, a "something" now that will become "something else" later.²⁶ The crowd's life marches in step with the undulating forces of "all earthly and worldly difference," and so he likens the crowd to a "herd" of animals in which each animal lives moment by moment according to what the others are doing.²⁷ And in this way the person in the crowd acts as a "mirror" that "intercepts the world."²⁸ Such a person has no "innermost being" because it "has been consumed … in the service of nothingness," in all "his hankering after loftiness" he loses his innermost being and so, consequently, "ceases to be a human being" because he "has himself become what was coveted."²⁹ What happens in the crowd is that individuals become like mirrors for each other in an endless hall of mirrors in which each person "intercepts" from another person some fleeting temporal standard and then reflects it back to another person who then repeats this cycle, so that each person becomes a dubious "something" in a collection of dubious selves. Kierkegaard concludes that underneath its life the crowd is "a revelation of emptiness."³⁰

The person who lives without a conscience in the crowd lives an empty life because she lives without inwardness,³¹ by which Kierkegaard means, she lives without having acquired any transparency to herself about who she is and why she does what she does. At the same time, however, Kierkegaard claims that individuals in the crowd have some awareness or intuition that something is not right. It seems that conscience from time to time willy-nilly breaks through a person's emptiness. Kierkegaard is not expansive about this, but he suggests that individuals in the crowd have some faint knowledge that "the moment of silence would make the emptiness plain."³² Consequently, they are, however faintly, self-conscious that they choose to live in the crowd without a conscience. "The truth of the matter," Kierkegaard writes, "is this":

> All of us human beings are more or less intoxicated. But we are like a drunk man who is not completely drunk so that he has lost his consciousness—no, he

22. *EUD*, 301.
23. *CD*, 78.
24. *EUD*, 316.
25. *LR*, 11.
26. *EUD*, 313.
27. *LR*, 66.
28. *EUD*, 308.
29. *CD*, 59.
30. *LR*, 92.
31. *LR*, 60; cf. Evans, *Faith beyond Reason*, 94.
32. *LR*, 87.

is definitely conscious that he is a little drunk and for that very reason is careful to conceal it ... if possible, from himself. ... We have a suspicion of ourselves; we gradually become conscious that we are not really sober. But then sagacity and sensibleness and level-headedness come to our aid and with their help we obtain something to sustain us—the finite. ... But if the unconditioned unconditionally were to *catch sight of us—yet we avoid this glance*, and that is why we conceal ourselves in finitude and among the infinitudes in the same way as Adam hid among the trees.[33]

Every person has a conscience because every person has a relationship with God in which God is watching, and try as she might a person cannot avoid from time to time becoming conscious of this watchful presence; try as she might, a person cannot eradicate her conscience, her awareness of herself before this presence. For this reason Kierkegaard likens life without a conscience to life with a "bad conscience."[34] This is the earlier point that to say a person lacks a conscience is true only semantically because conscience is something basic in a human being that ultimately is inextirpable. And so try as she might, Kierkegaard assumes, a person is simply incapable as a human being of living "totally ... in the momentary."[35] The person in the crowd sleepwalks through life but it is a "semi-somnolent" sleepwalking.[36] It is on account of this "semi-somnolent" state of people in the crowd that Kierkegaard describes the crowd's life as a "double-minded" life. In one mind, a person in the crowd has a faint awareness of who she is and how she should live, because she has a faint awareness of the watchful presence that claims her in particular; but with another mind she is conscious of the crowd.[37] A person tolerates this confusion only so long before she has to be rid of it. The most fitting description of the crowd, Kierkegaard concludes, is that it is a hiding place. The person in the crowd has in her "innermost being a secret anxiety about and wariness of the truth, a fear of getting to know too much"; the person who goes to the crowd, then, "hides from the truth as Adam hid among the trees."[38] Every person has an inextirpable awareness of a truth that is deeper than the crowd's life and every person in the crowd has, however faintly, an inextirpable awareness that life in the crowd constitutes an evasion of this truth.

Of course, when Adam hid among the trees with his "bad conscience" he hid from God. Therefore, the sum and substance of the crowd's life, the sum and substance of life without a conscience (or life with a bad conscience), consists

---

33. *JFY*, 113, emphasis mine.
34. *UDVS*, 128.
35. *CD*, 78.
36. *LR*, 87.
37. *UDVS*, 37.
38. *CD*, 170; cf. *UDVS*, 128, where Kierkegaard claims that Adam hides with his "bad conscience."

in hiding from God. In particular, Kierkegaard explains, a person hides in the crowd from "God's inspection" of her "as a single individual."[39] The crowd, then, is the absence of conscience because the crowd is a place of hiding from God's inspection of a person as a single individual. If we inverse this negative equation then we can make the positive inference that willing to have a conscience consists essentially in stepping out from hiding, acquiring inwardness, and embracing this singular inspection. The life of the crowd, in sum, discloses that conscience is a knowledge of oneself in one's singular relation to God. And so Kierkegaard claims that "to have and to will to have a conscience" is "to be and to will be a single individual."[40]

Defining the "Single Individual"

The "single individual" is a keystone idea in Kierkegaard's moral theology and his theory of conscience, and so it is important that we understand how he defines "the single individual." Unsurprisingly, since Kierkegaard binds the definition of the single individual to the definition of conscience, his definition of the single individual, like his definition of conscience, is not always clear. But as with conscience, we can infer well enough what Kierkegaard primarily has in mind. The key is in the enigmatic phrasing, "to be and to will to be a single individual." His point is that each person is a single individual but that each person must also choose to live accordingly. Every person is a single individual because every person is an individual in relation to God. The single individual is the individual in a distinct relation to God. What God sees when God looks at the crowd is not the crowd but each person as an individual created by God for a singular relationship with God. But, as we have seen in this discussion of "the crowd," a person can hide from God and ignore this singular relationship. A person can try to forget that she is a "single individual." And so while every person is created by God as a single individual, as an individual summoned for a relationship to God, every person must also choose to step out of the crowd and to live into this relationship. It is worth noting, again, that Kierkegaard's valorization of the individual here clearly resists the charge that Kierkegaard's individual is an atomistic, self-enclosed subject. The valorization of the "single individual" is not a celebration of freedom for its own sake, or "subjectivity that as such regards itself as the truth." Kierkegaard emphatically draws our attention with his concept of the "single individual" to the singular relationship each person has to God.

Kierkegaard's concern is to reverse what he thought had become normative in his day, the belief that the community is the prior category and that the individual

---

39. *UDVS*, 128. Cf. Ferreira, *Kierkegaard* (Boston, MA: Wiley Blackwell, 2008), 122–3; Bruce Kirmse, *Kierkegaard and Golden Age Denmark* (Bloomington: Indiana University Press, 1990), 290.

40. *JFY*, 91.

emerges secondarily.[41] He insists on the contrary that the single individual has the priority. And since to be a single individual is to have and to will to have a conscience, conscience does not emerge from but is the precondition for genuine community. Where there is genuine community there is a collection of individuals who each individually will to have a conscience. Before there can be any healthy relationships between persons, "eternity" must first seize each person "by the strong arms of conscience."[42] Only then can a person turn to life with others. Kierkegaard is quite clear, then, that conscience is distinct from the community and must be isolated from the community. Only then, he concludes, is there any possibility of genuine sociality.[43] His polemic against the crowd is therefore not a polemic against social life as such, but against the kind of social life hostile to the single individual who wills to have a conscience. His basic axiom is that "the 'single individual' is higher than the 'race.'"[44] Consequently, "not until the single individual has established an ethical stance despite the whole world, not until then can there be any question of genuinely uniting."[45] The crowd reverses this order and people therefore become deaf to their conscience, and to a certain unconscious degree encourage others to do the same. Kierkegaard thinks that the only way out of this desperate condition is for an individual to break away from the crowd and to isolate the voice of her conscience from the crowd's extraneous voices and influences.[46]

I have stressed that Kierkegaard's emphasis on the "single individual" does not sanction the individual of modern ethical theory, the autonomous individual detached from history, tradition, and community that MacIntyre, Hauerwas, and others worry about. But Kierkegaard's emphasis on the individual and the priority of the individual conscience to social norms likely remains implausible to many readers. I need to address two charges that suggest Kierkegaard's theory of conscience is implausible. The first is the charge that Kierkegaard's emphasis on the individual and the priority of the individual conscience to social norms creates an isolationist, misanthropic ethic; Kierkegaard's theory of conscience, this charge runs, encourages a disregard for social life and concrete, flesh and blood others. The second charge is that Kierkegaard's theory of conscience appears implausible

---

41. *JP*, 2:224. Kirmse and Rae both nicely address Kierkegaard's concern with the individual and society though neither does so with reference to conscience. See Kirmse, *Golden Age*, 259–486; Rae, *Kierkegaard and Theology*, 87–8.

42. *UDVS*, 133.

43. Cf. Kirmse, *Golden Age*, 290.

44. *JP*, 2:224. See note 321.

45. *LR*, 106. One of the great strengths of Jamie Ferreira's work is its relentless defense of the claim that Kierkegaard's ideal of interiority does not constitute an ethic "that distances people from one another or" that fosters "an egocentric concern with one's responsibility to oneself" (Ferreira, *Love's Grateful Striving*, 87).

46. *JP*, 1:321.

in its insensitivity to the reality of the social formation of moral identity. We will examine the first charge now and the second charge later.

Does Kierkegaard's emphasis on the individual and the priority of the individual conscience, especially as this emphasis appears in the context of his strong polemic against the crowd, encourage a misanthropic, isolationist wariness of human relationships? Does he emphasize the single individual breaking away from the crowd to listen to her conscience, in other words, to such an extent that his theory of conscience has no way to affirm the good of social life?[47] Kierkegaard certainly can sound guilty of offering unfortunate answers to these questions. Any "alliance" between people, even (especially) between intimate friends, he writes, can lead to double-mindedness; a person's most intimate friendships, that is, can encourage a person to filter herself into the crowd.[48] Better than the most intimate friendship, Kierkegaard strikingly claims, is a "sense of shame before one who is dead."[49] So for the single individual, there is the crowd on the one hand, the dead on the other, and the choice is clear. The dead, invisible and inaudible, cannot be brought into a double-minded alliance.[50] Other people can be used to hide, but we cannot hide with the dead.

To will to have a conscience is to be a single individual, and to be a single individual a person has to step out from the crowd and consider herself before one who is dead. And she does this because before one who is dead, Kierkegaard insists, a person is exposed for who he or she is and there can be no persuading the dead to the contrary.[51] The reason for this is that the dead, unlike the living, are "transfigured" and therefore cannot be changed or persuaded by the promptings of the crowd's double-mindedness.[52] By "transfigured" I think Kierkegaard means something like "glorified." He is imagining individuals firmly established in their singularity, who perfectly will to be single individuals before God. They cannot be cajoled or shaken, and in their presence the double-minded person is confronted with a standard that she knows claims her as well but that she, unlike the transfigured dead, tries to evade. By virtue of their own singularity, then, the dead help to draw a person out of the crowd and to will to be a single individual. The dead do not disclose a person to herself in her most fundamental moral identity, but they do disclose a person to herself as one who evades this identity. A person's conscience is not a moral awareness before those who are dead, that is, but the dead do help awaken a person's conscience.

---

47. Showing how Kierkegaard is defensible against such charges is very much the concern of Jamie Ferreira throughout *Loves Grateful Striving*. See especially, 5–6; 188–90; 209–10.
48. *UDVS*, 55, 131.
49. *UDVS*, 55.
50. *UDVS*, 55.
51. *UDVS*, 55.
52. *USVS*, 54–5.

The dead help a person become a single individual, while earthly, real-life relationships apparently do not. Even a close friend "can perhaps be favorable toward you, perhaps also too unfavorable." And it is all too easy, Kierkegaard claims, for a person to worry about how favorable or unfavorable he or she appears to others. This worry tempts us to desire that favor as "the most important thing."[53] The intimate friend can be persuaded that one is in fact just as one appears to be even if this is a lie. And the approval of that friend helps a person avoid accountability before God as a single individual.

Consequently, Kierkegaard encourages us to be single individuals through an imaginative engagement with those who are living as if they too already are dead. What this means is that Kierkegaard is suggesting we engage with the people we meet as though they were their glorified selves, as if they were transfigured. We are to engage with every person we meet as if we were engaging with an individual unshakably established in his or her singular relationship to God. If we do not engage with people as if they were already transfigured, we will, instead, succumb to temptation and employ that person in the service of double-mindedness. Kierkegaard assures us, "that temptation will not disappear until you associate with him as with one who is dead."[54] The only way for a person to live as a single individual, then, is to acknowledge the singularity of every person she meets. Kierkegaard's emphasis on the single individual and the priority of the single individual's conscience leads, in other words, to an emphasis on respecting others in their own singularity and distinctness. The awareness of oneself as a single individual, he insists, should transform living relationships. Kierkegaard therefore repeatedly asks, "Are you living in such a way that this awareness can acquire the time and stillness and liberty of action to penetrate your life relationships?"[55] Awareness of oneself as a single individual before God, then, should not lead to a misanthropic withdrawal from life,[56] but rather will include awareness of one's responsibility before those who are dead, an awareness that will, in turn, "support and transfigure and illuminate [one's] conduct in the relationships of life."[57] To know oneself before one who is dead can teach the single individual, Kierkegaard claims, to become "more humble, more humanly involved with every human being."[58]

Kierkegaard's single individual is not a misanthrope, but a person who takes the others she meets seriously, who is engaged with others in a way that honors the deepest ground of their dignity as human beings. The only way to take others seriously, in fact, is to live as a single individual, because when you live as a

---

53. *UDVS*, 54–5.
54. *UDVS*, 55.
55. *UDVS*, 137.
56. *UDVS*, 137.
57. *UDVS*, 137.
58. *UDVS*, 138.

single individual you are living in the awareness that you and the individuals you meet exist primarily in and for a singular relationship to God. It is only in this awareness, Kierkegaard insists, that genuine sociality can thrive, because it is only in this awareness that "petty diversities are forgotten."[59] Eternity's requirement, Kierkegaard claims, is the same for all human beings.[60] Social life in the crowd is demoralizing, Kierkegaard thinks, because in the crowd each person's singularity disappears. But when the single individual tries to imagine the others she meets as transfigured, she is trying to imagine them in their singularity, in their genuine distinctness before God. When the single individual imagines the other before her as first an other before God she embraces that other as an other genuinely diverse from her. When the single individual embraces the other in this way, she keeps always before her eyes both her own singularity and the singularity of all human beings before God.[61]

An integral aspect of living as a single individual, then, is to be able to acknowledge the singularity of every person. But Kierkegaard's concern is not only to affirm each person's singularity. His claim is also that genuine sociality is possible only through such an affirmation. He emphasizes, in other words, both the genuine diversity of single individuals and the unity all people share as creatures in the image of God. When Kierkegaard emphasizes the image of God, he stresses worship as the activity that is to unite all human beings. To be a human being in the image of God, that is, is to be a "worshipper."[62] The creation of each person as a single individual in relation to God makes for a necessary diversity, but this diversity finds in worship a more fundamental unity. Kierkegaard therefore writes that in "whatever" a person does "he must absolutely not forget—to worship."[63] And so while there are as many distinct individuals created for a distinct relation to God as there are human beings in the world, to be created in God's image is to be created for only one thing and that is to worship. This is what Kierkegaard means when he writes that "the unanimity of the singled out is the band playing well orchestrated music."[64] Here, then, is Kierkegaard's answer to the charge that his emphasis on the single individual and the priority of the individual conscience creates an excessively individualistic and misanthropic ethic. The final aim of life as a single individual is to sing in worship before her creator, but to do so by joining with all the other single individuals, and with their glorious diversity to harmonize in one symphonic chorus.

---

59. *UDVS*, 138.
60. *USVS*, 81.
61. Cf. *UDVS*, 138, 139.
62. *UDVS*, 193.
63. *UDVS*, 194.
64. *LR*, 55.

Isolating the Relationship of Conscience

But before joining this chorus, the single individual first must will to have a conscience, and the single individual wills to have a conscience when she finds stillness and solitude. If you want to hear the voice of your conscience, he explains, "there must be stillness around you, while you concentrate your attention completely on inwardness."[65] This is the only way to have a conscience because "without stillness, conscience doesn't exist at all." And so if you want to have a conscience—if you would not only have but also will to have a conscience—then you must "endure" this stillness. Otherwise you choose "a nature echo from the crowd, a confused collective scream, a general opinion in which one, out of cowardice, fearing for oneself, is not alone."[66] Without stillness and "tranquility," Kierkegaard claims, it is "impossible to gain any deeper knowledge of oneself" or to gain "the transparency that is necessary for understanding oneself."[67] If, in sum, a person wills to have a conscience, then she must remove herself from the noise all around her, find stillness, and "concentrate."

Kierkegaard thinks a person acquires self-knowledge and transparency in stillness not simply because other voices have become silent but above all because in stillness God's voice becomes audible. When a person removes herself from the crowd and pays attention to herself, when she pays attention to herself and focuses "completely on inwardness," then she "discovers in the deeper sense that God is."[68] In the stillness where conscience exists, a person begins to hear "God's voice."[69] For this reason Kierkegaard writes in such a style that he hopes will prompt his reader to find a quiet and solitary place where she can read slowly and aloud.[70] And if she follows this prompt, he claims, she will find herself alone "before God," speaking with herself and to herself in the presence of God.[71]

It is the "presence of God," Kierkegaard insists, that "changes everything."[72] God is, of course, always present to everyone, but it is only when you know that God is present to you that you then become more deeply conscious of yourself and of the task, he claims, "before God of paying attention to yourself."[73] The idea is that once you become conscious that someone is paying attention to you, you become self-conscious, and the more important the person who is paying attention to you, the more self-conscious you become and the more you sense a need to look to yourself. That much more, Kierkegaard claims, with the intimate, caring watchfulness of

---

65. *WL*, 329.
66. *TUD*, 11–12.
67. *UDVS*, 68.
68. *WL*, 361.
69. *TUD*, 11; cf. Evans, *Faith beyond Reason*, 124.
70. Cf. *UDVS*, 5; *FSE*, 3; *JP*, 5:370.
71. *UDVS*, 124.
72. *UDVS*, 125.
73. *UDVS*, 125.

God. "The person sitting in the showcase," he writes, "is not as embarrassed as every human being is in his transparency before God. This," he concludes, "is the relationship of conscience."[74] Through the conscience, in other words, a person becomes aware of herself because she is aware of herself in her relationship to God. In stillness and solitude, then, we come into God's presence, and become conscious in a deeper sense that "God is" and that God is looking at us; this makes us deeply conscious of ourselves and immediately cognizant that if God is taking an interest in us, we should take care to look to ourselves as well.

We rightly look to ourselves, Kierkegaard explains, when "in everything [we] ... look at [God]." Kierkegaard claims both that when we discover that God is looking at us we are to look to ourselves, and that when we discover God is looking at us we are to look back to God. Kierkegaard's point is that we only really look at ourselves and know ourselves rightly when we know ourselves as we are reflected in the eyes of God. Kierkegaard will refer to the "relationship of conscience," then, because he conceives of conscience as a knowledge-in-relation, and specifically as a knowledge-in-relation to God. It is in the conscience, in other words, that we look to God and begin to see ourselves as God sees us. In conscience we look to ourselves but we look to ourselves rightly only when we look to God.[75]

Kierkegaard knows that acquiring solitude and stillness at a remove from the crowd so that we can look at to God is a difficult task that almost no one attempts.[76] The crowd is quite capable to alter perceptions and to dictate a person's self-understanding. When others "come between you and God," he writes, they mediate the relation to God and when others mediate your relation to God "you are easily deceived ... you then get a fraudulent criterion, the criterion of human comparison."[77] If the crowd represents a semi-somnolent state, this means not only that there is a faint awareness among those in the crowd that they are hiding from God but also that there is a sleepiness to this reality, that individuals in the crowd also have forgotten themselves. Breaking away from the crowd to the place of stillness where conscience exists therefore constitutes a difficult task. To do this will seem to a person risky because it will go against the sense of herself as a responsible human being that she appropriates from the crowd's "fraudulent criterion." But a person will only hear her conscience when she fights this self-deception and breaks from the crowd.

We have already answered the charge that Kierkegaard's theory of conscience is misanthropic. Kierkegaard's understanding of the single individual and his emphasis on the priority of the individual conscience to the community aims at a genuine sociality. But his worry about the crowd's ability to deceive a person about who he or she is, and his counsel that the first thing to do is to get away from everyone compel us to consider the charge that Kierkegaard's theory of conscience

---

74. *SUD*, 124.
75. Cf. *WL*, 383.
76. Cf. *SUD*, 28.
77. *DCF*, 103.

is implausible because of its insensitivity to the social formation of moral identity. Kierkegaard here clearly shares Kant's concern about the social sources of self-deception. Kierkegaard presses his concern more forcefully than Kant does, but the idea is the same: social life can corrupt us and can be a means through which we deceive ourselves about our corruption. This concern about the corrupting influence of social life allowed us to consider how Kant's theory of conscience resists the trajectory from Niebuhr to Hauerwas that emphasizes the social formation of moral identity and that prioritizes the social location of accountability and self-knowledge. Kierkegaard's response to this charge is very much like the response Kant's theory of conscience offers. Like Kant, Kierkegaard is not condemning social life as such; we have already seen how Kierkegaard affirms an ideal type of social life that respects the genuine diversity of each individual and looks toward the union of all the single individuals in one chorus of praise to God. But, again, like Kant, Kierkegaard worries about what Kant calls "self-incurred minority," about our tendency to allow others to tell us who we are and to determine for us what is right. Kierkegaard is also not oblivious that we internalize social mores, that our subjective state has this kind of malleability. I think this is what he means when he sarcastically remarks that "what ... most people call conscience is not conscience but moods, stomach reflexes, vagrant impulses, etc.—the conscience of a bailiff."[78] There are many claims swirling around within us, and the challenge is to separate the spurious claims from the claim God makes upon us. The point Kierkegaard makes negatively in his polemic against the crowd is that a person's moral identity is not reducible to the nexus of her relations and that each person has as his or her highest relation the relation to God. And he insists that this relationship is absolutely distinct from every empirical and contingent relation in one's life. He insists with Kant, that is, that morality is not confined to the contingencies of our lives. For Kant, it is through practical reason that human beings grasp moral norms that are universal and necessarily binding, and it is through the conscience that human beings hold themselves accountable to these norms as if they were given by God. For Kierkegaard, it is through the relationship to God in conscience that a person both knows the claim God makes upon her, and knows herself in her accountability before this claim. Kant and Kierkegaard think that to confuse our accountability to God with our accountability to a community risks a disastrous self-deception. Kierkegaard affirms with Kant that there has to be a means to call a community's life into question; and given Kierkegaard's affirmation of a certain kind of sociality, we can say that the single individual calls a community's life into question ultimately for the sake of that community.

It is important, furthermore, not to read into Kierkegaard's polemic against the crowd the idea that moral discernment is from beginning to end an isolated, individual affair. It is hard to imagine what Kierkegaard thinks he is doing as an author if this is what he thinks. Inasmuch as Kierkegaard's theory of conscience concerns the individual and God, it is primarily a solitary affair and it is finally a

---

78. *JP*, 1:321.

solitary affair, but Kierkegaard affirms that we need help. To be clear, Kierkegaard does not go out of his way to stress this point. When he talks about finding help to discern the voice of conscience, he discusses, as we will see, not other people, but nature and hardships. His polemic against the crowd and his worries about the ways the crowd can deceive us are so severe that it is hard to imagine that Kierkegaard gives us much reason to trust our human relationships to help us discern the voice of our conscience. But given his affirmation of a certain kind of social life and given the trust he thinks we as his readers should have in him as our guide to help us awaken our conscience, I think there is clearly a space in his thought to offer an affirmation—however chastened—that other people can help us awaken our conscience. His discussion of imagining ourselves before those who are dead, for example, bears a kind of resemblance to Niebuhr's "ego-alter" dialectic. Like Niebuhr, Kierkegaard affirms that we should imagine ourselves in relation to others that we have encountered in our lives, and like Niebuhr he affirms that these others help us discern the claim God makes upon us. They do this negatively, in Kierkegaard's account, because they disclose us to ourselves as people hiding from God's claim upon us. But this is still help from others. The crucial difference between Kierkegaard and Niebuhr is that Kierkegaard, like Kant, denies that the claim God makes upon us is constituted in and through our relationship to these others. Like Kant, Kierkegaard cannot affirm Niebuhr's claim that the social self is unable to "rise above those specific relations to God in which" he or she "has been placed."[79] The claim God makes upon us is a categorically distinct claim, a claim God makes directly upon each individual. But Kierkegaard clearly thinks each individual needs help to discern this claim; when she does discern it, the point is that she stands alone before God. She stands alone before God, but again, in such a way that all her earthly relationships are permeated by her relationship to God as a single individual. The danger is not sociality as such, other people as such, but the crowd, the temptation to allow others to make an ultimate, determinative claim on our lives. He insists that we cannot live rightly for others when we allow them to claim our lives in this way.

And so against this danger of crowd, Kierkegaard's most basic exhortation here is that a person must "tear" herself loose.[80] Kierkegaard describes the move away from others toward the relation of conscience in stillness and solitude as a "leap" individuals must make "by themselves."[81] A person comes to a decisive, "dangerous moment," a moment in which she can choose to collect herself, "withdraw from the surroundings and become alone before God."[82] Kierkegaard depicts this moment of decision as a struggle between what he calls the "first" and "deeper" self.[83] The "first self" is the temporal in the self or the self as it exists in the temporal, the

---

79. Cf. Niebuhr, *Responsible Self*, 45.
80. *EUD*, 313.
81. *LR*, 108.
82. *TUD*, 36.
83. *EUD*, 313.

self as it is drawn to the momentary, the temporal and the fleeting. We might say that, for Kierkegaard, the "first self" is the self whose subjective state is malleable before the crowd. The "deeper self," with its "eternal claim" seems clearly to be the conscience.[84] The "first self" reaches out for the external, craving achievement, applause, good fortune, and in general all the dubious "somethings" valorized by the crowd's "fraudulent" criteria that deceive a person into thinking she knows herself. As the first self goes about its business the "deeper self" calls it "back from the external" so that now, Kierkegaard claims, the first self has a choice: "the first self either must proceed to kill the deeper self, to render it forgotten, whereby the whole matter is given up; or it must admit that the deeper self is right."[85] The first self can either choose to hear the deeper self's claim or willfully silence it "by letting the roar of inconstancy drown it out."[86] In either case, whether the first self will heed the deeper self's claim or become deaf to it, Kierkegaard's point is that the self must make a choice.

A person's inward turn to conscience is a choice, Kierkegaard believes, but he does not think we are left all alone to make this choice from an act of sheer will. He claims that God allows nature and, above all, hardship to aid us in this choice, to help us "strike a fatal blow" to our worldly way of thinking and awaken our conscience.[87] With or without warning nature can evoke a sense of wonder within a person that begins the process of "inward deepening."[88] Nature can do this, Kierkegaard believes, because God, invisible and unknown, is manifest in nature; nature evokes a sense of wonder in a person because she has an immediate "sense of God."[89] The sense of wonder that everything in nature means to evoke Kierkegaard calls "the beginning of all deeper understanding," because wonder "wants to see where it's going and no longer walk in the dark."[90] The self-manifestation of God in nature evokes a sense of wonder in a person because she has a sense of the presence of God and the sense of wonder that inexorably wants to know more. This *sensus divinitatis* has a magnetism that draws the wonderer further inward and the longer she remains with it the more its "persuasion" mounts, stealing "the temporal" from the person: "every moment you continue to contemplate it," he writes, "that which ought to be forgotten sinks deeper and deeper into oblivion." Such a person ultimately finds herself alone "in league with the eternal."[91]

---

84. *EUD*, 313; cf. *UDVS*, 128.
85. *EUD*, 313.
86. *EUD*, 313.
87. *EUD*, 300.
88. Kierkegaard discusses the person who heeds the imperative to regard the lilies and the birds as well as the person who happens to be struck by something in nature and pauses to consider it further (cf. *TUD*, 18).
89. *TUD*, 18; cf. *UDVS*, 193.
90. *TUD*, 18.
91. *UDVS*, 186.

Kierkegaard clearly thinks that God's self-manifestation in creation ought to be able to precipitate a person's break from the crowd and the movement of inward deepening in which a person awakens his or her conscience. But the primary means to this break and movement, Kierkegaard claims, is hardship. Recall again his axiom that conscience is installed in eternity as the "only voice" of eternity in a person, and consider his claim that every person has "eternity's hope" in the "innermost being" like "a whisper"; he then asks, "what, then, does hardship want?" It wants, he writes,

> to have this whisper brought forth in the innermost being. But then does hardship work against itself, must not its storm simply drown out this voice? No, hardship can drown out every earthly voice; it is supposed to do just that. But it cannot drown out this *voice of eternity* deep within. Or the reverse. It is *eternity's voice* within that wants to be heard and in order to gain a hearing it uses the clamor of hardship. When all the irrelevant voices are silenced with the help of hardship, then it can be heard, this voice within.[92]

Likewise, he prompts his reader,

> Imagine hidden in a very plain setting a secret chest in which the most precious treasure is placed—there is a spring that must be pressed, but the spring is concealed and the pressure must be of a certain force so that an accidental pressure cannot be sufficient. The hope of eternity is concealed within a person's innermost being in this way and hardship is the pressure. When the pressure is put on the concealed spring and forcefully enough, the content appears in all its glory.[93]

Every person has a conscience but it is hard to hear it, and so hardship enters a person's life and silences all the extraneous voices and directs a person's attention to the only constant voice in her life. Hardship has the effect, Kierkegaard assumes, of isolating a person from the crowd,[94] of making her more conscious that she cannot live entirely in the momentary,[95] and consequently of increasing the volume of her conscience. Hardship removes a person from the state of "immediacy," makes her aware of the inconstancy of the temporal, and alerts her to that within her that is heterogeneous to the temporal; hardship therein encourages a person to ponder the eternal in her being, to see her essential "abstraction" from "externality."[96] Not every person who experiences hardship will necessarily receive the help it offers; this is the earlier point that every person who breaks away from the crowd, isolates

---

92. *CD*, 109, emphasis mine; cf. *UDVS*, 128.
93. *CD*, 111.
94. Cf. *UDVS*, 100–22.
95. Cf. *CD*, 78.
96. *SUD*, 54–5.

the voice of her conscience, and listens to it has chosen to do so. But hardship nevertheless brings a person to this moment of decision and encourages her to make the right choice.[97]

Singularity and Authenticity as the Disclosure of Conscience

At this point we can summarize Kierkegaard's theory of conscience like this: every person has a conscience which is the knowledge every person has of himself or herself in relation to God; through the moral self-awareness of conscience a person becomes transparent to herself as she begins to know herself as she is known by God as God is intimately present to her. Every person has this "relation of conscience" but every person must also choose to enter into it or choose to awaken it. Kierkegaard therefore frequently refers to conscience as a voice or a whisper that a person chooses to hear or to deafen.[98] A person willfully renders conscience mute by sinking herself in the crowd or she accepts the help of nature or, especially, hardship to bring her to the stillness of silence so that she might hear the voice of her conscience.

When a person chooses to hear the voice of conscience, what does she hear? If in hearing the voice of conscience a person begins to become transparent to herself, what does she begin to see? The short answer, of course, is that she sees herself more clearly as a single individual. And since we have already defined Kierkegaard's "single individual" as the individual constituted distinctly and above all in his or her relationship to God, we have already sketched an answer to these questions. But we must unfold this answer further if we are to have the full sense of Kierkegaard's theory of conscience. Kierkegaard clearly thinks that conscience is the locus within a person in which she becomes disclosed to herself in relation to God, and he is clear that this disclosure entails both what we will call an indicative-imperative disclosure and a judicial disclosure.[99] As we will see, Kierkegaard thinks that if a person breaks away from the crowd, isolates the voice of her conscience, and draws near to God, then she will know more clearly who God is—the creator who creates every human being for a relation to God—and she will know more clearly who she is before this God—a single individual created with a "given self" and so created for a distinct and authentic relationship to God. But when a person isolates the voice of her conscience and is disclosed to herself before God, then she will also become disclosed to herself as guilty before God because she fails to respond to God's summons as she knows she ought to respond.

---

97. *CD*, 113.
98. *UDVS*, 129.
99. Walsh means the same thing when she describes Kierkegaard's theory of conscience as having "positive" and "negative" roles (*Living Christianly*, 34).

The Indicative-Imperative Disclosure of Conscience

In the indicative-imperative sense, Kierkegaard describes conscience as the awareness in each person of *being* a single individual in relation to God, and the awareness of what it means *to live* as a single individual in relation to God. Kierkegaard explains that the "more common expression for the relationship of conscience" is "to question the single individual."[100] Recall also the earlier claim that the crowd—the absence of conscience—represents the place where a person hides from God's inspection of a person as a single individual. Conscience, then, is where God questions a person about how she has acted as a single individual. Therefore, at the end of "Purity of Heart," when Kierkegaard turns to the "voice of conscience," which "is installed eternally in its eternal right to be the only voice,"[101] he imagines an examination in which a person is asked, "Are you living in such a way that you are aware as a single individual that in every relationship in which you relate yourself outwardly you are aware that you are also relating to yourself as a single individual, that even in the relationships we beautifully call the most intimate you recollect that you have an even more intimate relationship, the relationship in which you as a single individual relate yourself to yourself before God."[102] Of course, it is Kierkegaard who is posing this question to his reader, but he insists that the "upbuilding discourse" intends to awaken a person to that which she already knows; he wants such questions to arise for his reader as if they had sprung from her own inner being. And so here, in the form of a question, conscience makes a person aware that she is a single individual and that she is to live as a single individual; and further, conscience makes a person aware that to live as a single individual is to relate to God in every aspect of her life. Conscience is therefore the knowledge a person has of herself in relation to God as God, present to that person, makes both an indicative claim that to be a human being is *to be* a single individual in relation to God, and an imperative claim that a human being is *to relate* to God accordingly. Whether or not a person becomes fully conscious of this indicative-imperative claim, it is there within a person as the most basic consciousness of every human being. It is this consciousness that "conscience want[s] to emphasize."[103]

Kierkegaard does not think that a person's conscience fully wakes up all at once; he does not think, that is, that a person becomes conscious all at once of everything living as a single individual entails. He claims that God knows that this consciousness is, in fact, too much to take in all at once and that it must increase gradually.[104] When a person first begins to hear the voice of her conscience she

---

100. *WL*, 138.
101. *UDVS*, 128.
102. *UDVS*, 129.
103. *UDVS*, 133. For a nice discussion of this awareness but without reference to conscience, see Rae, *Kierkegaard and Theology*, 92.
104. Cf. *EUD*, 305.

begins to become aware that there is a providence that has made her an object of care.[105] A person becomes aware that she depends upon God for everything and that God cares for her, and in this awareness she also understands that she has a responsibility to be content to be a human being.[106] The first awakening of conscience consists, then, of a knowledge of oneself as an object of God's care and a sense of obligation to be content.

It is axiomatic for Kierkegaard that such knowledge does not stop in its movement inward. Once a person becomes conscious of being a single individual in relation to God it is very hard to turn back. And so a person mines a little deeper and becomes conscious that "implied" in the consciousness of being an object of God's providential care is the knowledge that God singles out the human being, has created the human being in God's image, and has made each human being as spirit with the duty to live in correspondence to God.[107] In particular, having become conscious of the distinct human correspondence to God as spirit, a person becomes conscious of the imperative to become "nothing" before God. Kierkegaard means here that a person becomes conscious that she is nothing without God, that she has her very being from God, and is therefore capable of nothing in and of herself. Kierkegaard thinks that Promethean fantasies tempt all of us: we all want to become something of our own accord, to be our own masters in the castles we build on our own.[108] But to succumb to these temptations is to go against the grain of our very being because God establishes the human being as a synthesis of the temporal and the eternal, as spirit, as a being fundamentally or primordially in relation to God, and so as a being with the task consciously to live in relation to God. A person's aim should be to live as "the Lord's envoy," to become nothing in oneself and to surrender oneself to God.[109] Ultimately, when a person becomes conscious of being spirit, of being a being that corresponds to God, she becomes conscious of the imperative to worship. What Kierkegaard means by this the apostle Paul captures when he offers the exhortation, "whether you eat or drink or whatever you do, do it all for the glory of God."[110] The point here complements the claim we saw earlier about worship, that in whatever a person does "he absolutely must not forget—to worship."[111] A person acts as a single individual in relation to God when she lives every moment self-consciously for God, when she surrenders everything of her life to God, when she lives in such a way that her life expresses that her relationship to God is the most intimate and basic facet of her being.[112]

---

105. *UDVS*, 188.

106. *UDVS*, 177.

107. *UDVS*, 190.

108. *SUD*, 68–9. Here is, then, another volley against the charge that Kierkegaard licenses the modern moral autonomy MacIntyre or Hauerwas identify.

109. *EUD*, 311.

110. 1 Cor. 10:31–33.

111. *UDVS*, 194.

112. Kierkegaard makes this same point in his account of the "first" and "deeper" self. He explains that once these two have become "reconciled," the first self can go about its

Finally, Kierkegaard also variously describes this summons to relate to God as a single individual by becoming nothing in worship as a summons to will the good in truth,[113] to "permeate all of life" with the God-relationship,[114] to hold fast to God in all things,[115] and to bring the eternal into every moment of life.[116]

Conscience makes a person aware that she is a single individual and it makes a person aware of what it means to live as a single individual. So far, we have been considering the way Kierkegaard describes this awareness of conscience in the form of a universal summons or in the form it takes equally for every single individual. Kierkegaard insists that because God is present to every person and because, consequently, every person equally has this relation of conscience, it must follow that every person who awakens his or her conscience becomes aware of the same summons; every person who awakens his or her conscience becomes aware that God summons him or her to become a single individual in relation to God and every person who hears this summons knows what it means. God is present to every individual in his or her conscience asking the question, "Are you living in such a way that you are conscious of being a single individual."[117] And Kierkegaard assumes that every individual who hears this question, by virtue of being human, understands what it means.[118] The summons to live as a single individual, in short, is a universal summons, equally present and accessible in every person by virtue of the relationship to God every person has in his or her conscience. Sylvia Walsh rightly explains that for Kierkegaard, "based on the spiritual equality of all persons before God, every individual possess the capacity to actualize the universally human in his or her life."[119] God makes it possible, Kierkegaard writes, "for everyone actually to grasp the highest."[120] Kierkegaard explains that God constitutes human beings with eternity in their hearts,[121] and consequently every individual has the capacity to know and to do what God requires of human beings. "The eternal," Kierkegaard writes, "speaking about the highest calmly assumes that every man can do it and merely asks, therefore, whether or not he has done it."[122] To be a human being, in short, is to be a being summoned to live as a single

business in the world so long as it does so with the "deeper self's consent," that is, so long as it does so conscientiously (*EUD*, 317).

113. *UDVS*, 48, 59, *et passim*.
114. *WL*, 129.
115. *WL*, 361.
116. *UDVS*, 11, 13, 48, *et passim*; Cf. Mackey, *Points of View*, 33; Evans, *Subjectivity and Religious Belief: A Historical, Critical Study* (Lanham, MD: University Press of America, 1982), 111.
117. *USVS*, 127. "To question the single individual," he writes, "is the more common expression for the relationship of conscience" (*WL*, 138).
118. *UDVS*, 126.
119. Sylvia Walsh, "Introduction," in Kierkegaard, *DCF*, 8.
120. *JP*, 1:36.
121. *UDVS*, 11, quoting Eccl. 3:11.
122. *WL*, 79.

individual in relation to God, and when an individual awakens her conscience and hears this summons, she hears it in exactly the same way every other person who awakens his or her conscience hears it.[123]

One of Kierkegaard's most significant presuppositions, however, is that this universal summons has a particular application for every individual. This is one of the distinguishing marks of Kierkegaard's theory of conscience and it marks a significant difference between Kierkegaard's theory of conscience and Kant's. Kierkegaard and Kant both conceive of conscience in terms of a person's singular moral self-awareness in relation to God. And like Kant, Kierkegaard thinks that everyone has the means through conscience to know himself or herself in relation to God because God's claim is universal. But, as we have seen, Kierkegaard's understanding of the universal claim God makes is quite different than Kant's understanding of that claim. Above all, while Kant thinks we should believe God makes a claim on us before the moral law for the sake of our conformity to the moral law, Kierkegaard thinks God makes a claim on us for the sake of our relationship to God. And what our conscience discloses to us about our relationship to God, according to Kierkegaard, is that God claims us for a unique relationship to God. In other words, while every person who awakens his or her conscience becomes conscious of a universal summons to become a single individual in relation to God, each single individual becomes conscious of this responsibility as a particular and unique responsibility. The summons to become a single individual in relation to God is a universal summons, "a point of unity" in the human race, but "whatever one will call it more specifically" it is contingent from person to person.[124] Every individual is capable of hearing the summons to be a single individual in relation to God but, Kierkegaard explains, each individual inevitably will have a different opinion, even a "radically different" opinion, about what this means for him or her in particular.[125] This is the case because while every person can hear the voice of conscience summoning him or her to become a single individual in relation to God, God creates every individual for a "separate and distinct" relation to God.[126] God creates each individual, he claims, from nothing for a distinct orbit or gravitation pull to God.[127] He explains in a key passage that "at every person's birth there comes into existence an eternal purpose for that person, for that person in particular. Faithfulness to oneself with regard to this is the highest thing a person can do."[128] God creates each and every person with a "given self," makes every person "a very definite something," and gives to every person at birth a distinct

---

123. On the universality of the ethical, see Evans, *Subjectivity and Religious Belief*, 99–100.
124. *UDVS*, 126.
125. *UDVS*, 126.
126. *UDVS*, 190.
127. Cf. *WL*, 103.
128. *UDVS*, 93, emphasis mine.

"divine name."[129] God commands every person, "Become something in relation to me,"[130] and gives to every person a very definite something to become.

It is on account of this close connection of singularity and authenticity that Kierkegaard thinks conscience really binds a person.[131] When a person hears the question about his awareness of being a single individual, he is to hear this question as a question about "*his* eternal destiny, about what *he* is conscious of being."[132] God creates every individual as a single individual with a particular relation to God, and every individual is created to become that single individual by freely entering into that relationship with God. God summons each individual, that is, individually to actualize this relationship. The summons to become a single individual in relation to God is not, then, an abstract principle of human conduct, nor is it an alien imposition from beyond the person. Rather, the summons to become a single individual in relation to God is, Kierkegaard argues, a summons to live with the grain of one's own given self, to be faithful to oneself as a particular self, to live into one's God-given name. God summons every individual to live in relation to God and God brings every individual into existence for a particular relation to God and so a person's task in life is to awaken her conscience, to discern who from her creation ex nihilo she really is,[133] and then to live accordingly.

Colliding with the World, Drawing Closer to God in Conscience

In sum, when a person awakens her conscience she becomes conscious of herself as a single individual in relation to God, conscious that God summons her to live her life at every moment as a single individual in relation to God, and conscious that God gives her a very particular way to respond to this summons. A person must isolate herself from the crowd if she is to hear the voice of her conscience, then, not only because the crowd sets up a "fraudulent criterion" and encourages an evasion of the relation with God in conscience, but also because a person's relation to God is unique and ultimately only each individual can discern how God in the relation of conscience summons him or her. But what this means, Kierkegaard thinks, is that listening to conscience not only requires a distance from the crowd but also that it will invite a collision with the crowd. Listening to conscience invites this collision because once a person awakens her conscience to a certain degree, a person becomes conscious that she must make a choice between God and the world. To live "for the eternal" means a person has to die to the temporal, die to herself and to the world.[134] To will to have a conscience, Kierkegaard concludes,

129. *SUD*, 36, 68, 34.
130. *CD*, 127.
131. Without reference to conscience but for a general corroboration, see Mackey, *Points of View*, 31.
132. *UDVS*, 129, emphasis mine.
133. *WL*, 115; cf. Zachman, *Reconsidering*, 145.
134. *UDVS*, 208.

ultimately brings a person into collision with the world because it means she heeds the claim God makes upon her in her conscience and even just the act of listening to the conscience, much less acting upon it, makes a claim on the world that the world is something she must resist if she is to become the distinct individual God created her to become. But the world does not like being dispensable and does not like it when a person receives her orders from somewhere beside itself.[135] Kierkegaard exhorts his reader to be encouraged by this resistance because it signals the world's tacit acknowledgment that she is acting as a single individual before God and that she is finding her satisfaction and purpose where she ought to find it, not from the world but from God.[136]

Kierkegaard's assumption is that if a person recognizes the world for what it is and rightly understands why the world resists her, then the more the world opposes her and scorns her for not finding her satisfaction and purpose in it, the more she will sense her need for God and the more she will hold fast to God.[137] And the more a person holds fast to God the greater her consciousness of herself as a single individual in relation to God. The more deeply a person holds fast to God, that is, the more deeply she partakes of God's knowledge of her as the particular single individual in relation to God that God created her to be and calls her to become. The "greater the conception of God," Anti-Climacus writes, "the more self."[138] The longer one looks to God, the more of the self a person sees reflected back. The more clearly a person sees herself reflected in God's gaze, the more clearly God's universal summons appears to her; and the more clearly God's universal summons appears to her, the more clearly her own particular God-given way to actualize this summons appears to her; and, finally, the more clearly her particular self or her particular calling to actualize God's summons appears to her, then "the more will" she has to will to respond to God's summons and to become herself in relation to God.[139]

Conscience and the Consciousness of Guilt (or Conscience in Judgment)

The more clearly a person partakes with God in this knowledge of herself as a single individual created by God for a particular relationship to God, however, the more clearly this knowledge appears to be a knowledge of herself in judgment; in her conscience, that is, she increasingly knows herself in terms of the gap between who God calls her to be and who she is in actuality.[140] The more a person holds fast to God and sees herself as God sees her, the more everything for her becomes

---

135. Cf. *CD*, 39.
136. *LR*, 91. Cf. Kirmse, *Golden Age*, 290.
137. Cf. *EUD*, 303.
138. *SUD*, 114.
139. *SUD*, 29.
140. Cf. Walsh, *Living Christianlty*, 8.

"upside down,"¹⁴¹ the more "everything appears reversed."¹⁴² With an awakened conscience a person begins to see everything rightly: what once seemed like sobriety is actually intoxication.¹⁴³ And in this vision a person sees the extent of her own failure to be what she knows in her conscience God summons her to be. This vision, he writes, "engenders regret."¹⁴⁴

Conscience represents for Kierkegaard our participation with God in God's knowledge of us, and it turns out that this participation is a participation in God's knowledge of us in judgment over who we are in actuality in light of the single individual God calls us to be. If we look to God long enough as God is looking at us then embarrassment and shame are inevitable. Anti-Climacus writes that the "relationship of conscience" consists of a person's transparency to God and that "the person sitting in the showcase is not as embarrassed as every human being in his transparency before God." He explains that "the arrangement is such that through the conscience the report promptly follows each guilt and the guilty one himself must write it. But it is written with invisible ink and therefore first becomes clearly legible only when it is held up to the light of eternity."¹⁴⁵ The point here echoes what we have seen again and again: every person has a conscience by virtue the fact that every person has a relation to God and is a single individual in the gaze of God. In this relationship a person is fully known to God, naked before God in total transparency. And now the emphasis is that when a person turns inward within herself to the relation of conscience and begins to see herself transparently in the light of eternity what she sees is her guilt, her failure to act according to the claim God makes upon her in her conscience.¹⁴⁶

141. *EUD*, 321.
142. *UDVS*, 135.
143. *JFY*, 117.
144. *UDVS*, 135.
145. *SUD*, 124.
146. Kierkegaard can be somewhat confusing on this point because sometimes he claims that to see oneself transparently with the eyes of God seems immediately to evoke the consciousness of guilt, but at other times he claims that to see oneself transparently with the eyes of God is more like a precondition for the consciousness of guilt. The sequence in "An Occasional Discourse," for instance, does appear to be that a person becomes conscious of his responsibility before God and then comes before God in judgment (*UDVS*, 150). Correlatively, in the first part of *The Sickness Unto Death* Anti-Climacus discusses the consciousness of being a self in relation to God well before the self becomes conscious of being guilty as a self in relation to God, a consciousness that he suggests requires a great deal of inward deepening to acquire and is rarely seen in the world. Where the transition comes or when this further consciousness awakens in a person's conscience is never entirely clear but it is also not the important point. The point is that the knowledge we have of ourselves is a knowledge we have in a complex and dynamic relation to God. In this relation a person becomes conscious of herself as a single individual in relation to God and conscious of her guilt in relation to God. To will to have a conscience entails for Kierkegaard that a person draws near to God and sees herself as God sees her and sees herself as God summons her

Kierkegaard is clear that once a person awakens her conscience to the degree that she becomes conscious of her guilt, she comes to a momentous crossroads: she can choose to endure the transparency in which she is guilty and be honest with herself before God about her guilt and consequently remain with God and remain with the claim God makes upon her. Like Kant, then, Kierkegaard assumes conscience plays an important role to drive a person toward repentance. And like Kant, Kierkegaard acknowledges that a person can also refuse to confess her guilt and stand in defiance against the knowledge she has of herself in God's judgment. The height of this defiance, Kierkegaard claims, appears with the person who is conscious of her failure to become the single individual God has created her to be, and who is therefore conscious of this failure as a failure in relation to God, but instead of acknowledging her guilt as her own she lays the guilt on God. "It is as if," he writes, "an error slipped into an author's writing and the error became conscious of itself as an error and now this error wants to mutiny against the author out of hatred toward him, forbidding him to correct it and in maniacal defense saying to him: No, I refuse to be erased; I will stand as a witness against you, a witness that you are a second rate author."[147] It is this possibility Anti-Climacus has in mind when he warns that despair is the most dangerous of illnesses, even if it is a necessary illness since only in the consciousness of despair can a person find the cure. But to become conscious of oneself to the degree that one becomes conscious of one's guilt is also the precondition for the possibility of self-conscious refusal to receive help, of self-conscious abdication of guilt. This state of absolute, demonic defiance is as far as a person can be from the cure.

The person who, on the other hand, is honest before God about her guilt and comes to God in confession manages, Kierkegaard claims, to "win the eternal." To "win the eternal," he explains, means that a person "is confirmed in the consciousness that he is a single individual."[148] To be confirmed in the confession of guilt that a person is a single individual is the way to win the eternal because when a person confesses her guilt she draws near to God and agrees with God about who God is and agrees with God on the goodness of what God requires, and she acknowledges her failure rightly to respond to this requirement. Kierkegaard's assumption is that God will meet the confessing person in her need, will draw near to this person and continue to be the God who summons this person to a particular relationship with God. Kierkegaard loves the Epistle of James and he loves in particular James's exhortation: "Keep near to God, then he will keep near to you. Cleanse your hands, you sinners, and purify your hearts you double minded."[149] He devotes an entire discourse to this claim and concludes the discourse with a

---

to be, and also that she draws near to God in God's judgment over how she has lived before this summons. What is clear is that the indicative-imperative and judicial aspects of the relationship of conscience are distinct but inseparable.

147. *SUD*, 74.
148. *UDVS*, 152–3.
149. Jas 4:8; *UDVS*, 24, 121.

lengthy call to confession.[150] His assumption is that a person draws near to God and God draws near to a person when she wills to be a single individual, and when, guilty and in need, she humbly confesses to God her failure to do so. The person who confesses therefore does not lose God; in her confession she finds that God will continue to be her God, and that God will continue to summon her to become the single individual in relation to God that God created her to be. To come before God in confession is "to win the eternal," then, because it is to "win God."[151]

Conscience and the Self before Christ

The consciousness of guilt and the act of confession marks a crucial and somewhat baffling transition in Kierkegaard's thought. The person who is conscious of herself in relation to God and conscious of her guilt in this relation draws near to God in such a way that, inevitably it seems, she finds herself before Jesus Christ.[152] The movement is from the single individual aware of herself as a single individual in relation to God, to the single individual "Christianly aware" of herself as a single individual before God.[153] The logic behind the transition seems to be that since the inward deepening of becoming conscious as a single individual in relation to God never stops, that since the knowledge of God and the knowledge of self continue toward deeper and deeper levels, a person will finally reach God in God's final and clearest manifestation in Jesus Christ.[154] God creates every human being to become a single individual in relation to God, summons every human being to rest transparently in God as the power that establishes them, and goes so far to help every human being to respond to this summons that God "comes to

---

150. *UDVS*, 122–54.

151. *CD*, 132. Cf. Walsh, *Living Christianly*, 40; Mackey, *Points of View*, 31.

152. The transition from Part One to Part Two of *The Sickness unto Death* is a good example of this quick, seemingly inevitable transition to Jesus Christ. See Walsh, *Living Christianly*, 12.

153. *CD*, 33.

154. Of course, as Kierkegaard describes the movement of inward deepening, of awakening conscience, that eventually leads a person to Christ, he has described the movement of a person who has broken away from the crowd and, consequently, is most likely experiencing hardship since the world inevitably resists such people. And so such a person is weary. And this person also in this struggle with the world holds to God to such an extent that she also realizes that she cannot overcome herself; she has come to see herself so clearly in her relationship to God that she becomes keenly aware of her guilt. And so she is heavy laden. A favorite passage of Kierkegaard's is Christ's invitation in Matthew 6, "come unto me," and he thinks those who are weary and heavy laden will be the ones who can really hear this invitation. But this still begs the question, why this invitation? Cf. Evans, *Subjectivity and Religious Belief*, 113–15.

the world, allows himself to be born, to suffer, to die and implores and beseeches" every human being "to accept the help that is offered."[155]

To put this more clearly in terms of Kierkegaard's theory of conscience, Kierkegaard's claim is that the God with whom we know ourselves in our conscience is the God most fully revealed in Jesus Christ. It seems almost axiomatic for Kierkegaard that once we awaken our conscience, the inexorable path of its inward movement will lead us finally to God's revealed Word. Conscience eventually therefore reaches a point at which it can no longer serve as the exclusive locus of the knowledge we have of ourselves with God. There is a threshold of what we can know by ourselves with God in our conscience, what we can know equipped only with our conscience, and that threshold is revealed in Jesus Christ. Once we reach this threshold, our participation with God in God's knowledge of us about who we ought to be and who we are can only be advanced upon by means of God's revealed Word.[156]

It is through this inexorable movement toward God's revealed Word that Kierkegaard answers the charge that his theory of conscience might sanction a "subjectivity that as such regards itself as the truth." If the single individual who awakened her conscience did not finally come to God's Word in Christ, then perhaps Kierkegaard would have no answer to this charge. If Kierkegaard's claim is that God gives to each individual a distinct moral identity in relation to God and that the conscience clearly discloses to the individual the full picture of who she is in relation to God, it is hard to imagine how Kierkegaard has not with his theory of conscience at least paved the way for the self-asserting, autonomous modern moral subject. I am not saying that Kierkegaard's theory of conscience up to this point does license this subject. His individual is an individual in relation to God, who knows herself as a moral agent in relation to God. Her assertion of her moral identity against the claims made upon her by the crowd is an assertion not of herself simply considered, but of herself as she knows herself in relation to God. But if Kierkegaard were claiming that the single individual's sense of herself in relation to God is given entirely by the conscience, it would be at least difficult to know if the individual is asserting her moral identity as it is in relation to God or if she is licensing an autonomous self-assertion in the name of her relation to God.

But Kierkegaard's point is that if a person really awakens her conscience she becomes restless. What her conscience discloses to her about who she is in relation to God is not without a good deal of substance, but it is not enough; she still does not understand fully—and she knows she still does not understand fully—what God requires of her. Or rather, she does not yet know how to be who it is God calls her to be. And so if she stops and goes no further than the testimony of her conscience then she will not, ultimately, live the life as a single individual God created her to be. She continues toward that life only if in her restless inward deepening she comes upon the one who says, "Come unto me …

---

155. *SUD*, 85.
156. Cf. Evans, *Subjectivity and Religious Belief*, 118.

I will give you rest." Through her conscience, the single individual knows herself in relation to God, but it is only before Jesus Christ that she begins to see the full picture of what it means for her to live as the single individual in relation to God she was created to be. We will see shortly that what Christ discloses to her is that she lives as a single individual in relation to God when she lives her life in love. What is important to note here is that the individual cannot stop with conscience, she must come before Christ. If she stopped with her conscience, it becomes all too easy for her to complete the picture herself of who she thinks she is supposed to be in relation to God. God's self-revelation in Christ precludes the individual from conjuring up for herself willy-nilly who it is she thinks she is supposed to be in relation to God. Consequently, Kierkegaard is clear, the individual must come before God's revelation in Christ if she is to discern fully the claim God makes upon her.

There is a clear difference between Kierkegaard's and Kant's theories of conscience that we should here make explicit. Both Kant and Kierkegaard think that conscience plays a significant role to drive a person toward repentance. But when Kant discusses this conscience-induced movement toward repentance, he does not—as we can see Kierkegaard does—turn to God's self-revelation in Christ. To give an account of the complex place of historical faith in Kant's moral theology or to compare Kant's and Kierkegaard's Christologies would take us too far afield. What is salient here is that for Kant our conscience drives us to repentance by holding us accountable to the kind of life we know by virtue of our practical reason we should live. We should, of course, believe that God calls us to live this moral life, but our conception of who God is follows from our prior knowledge of morality. And while Christianity as a historical, revealed faith can help us as we strive to be moral, it discloses to us nothing about the kind of life we should live that our practical reason does not already know.

Kierkegaard differs from Kant here because he thinks that our sin precludes us from knowing all that God wants with us. Kant, of course, has a theory of original sin and he thinks, as we saw in the previous chapter, that we are inclined to act otherwise than the way we know we should act or that we might act rightly but for the wrong reasons; moreover, Kant thinks we are quite capable to corrupt one another and to help each other justify as decent our indecent behavior. We are prone, he thinks, to deceive ourselves. But Kant does not think, ultimately, that the salve to the "dear self" and to our self-deception is divine revelation; the salve is our conscience holding us accountable to the life we know in our practical reason we should live. As we are willing to hear the testimony of conscience and begin to live in accord with our practical reason, then he grants we find encouragement from our recognition of the presentation of morality in the Christian revelation. But revelation adds nothing in essential detail about the kind of life we are to live. If it did, Kant thinks, then morality would not be truly binding because it would not be accessible to all. Kant does not think, in short, that a person comes to the threshold Kierkegaard posits, the threshold in which a person must have God's revelation in Christ if she is to have the full disclosure of what God wants with her as a single individual.

Unlike Kant, then, Kierkegaard thinks we come upon a threshold where, if we are to know what is required of us and know ourselves before what is required of us, we must turn to God's revealed Word. But it is worth emphasizing at this point that Kierkegaard clearly thinks that prior to this threshold a person can know by herself a great deal about God and about herself: A person can know that God is the Creator who creates human being to live in relation to God; she can know that God is her creator and has created her for a very particular relationship with God; she can know not only that she is an object of God's care and a creature bearing God's image, but also that she has an essential and authentic self that God has given to her for her specific relation to God. All of this conscience knows without any external communication, so that the single individual only has to find solitude and to awaken her conscience if she is to know all this about God and herself. Kierkegaard, of course, thinks that to succeed in this task is an amazing achievement because it is incredibly difficult.[157] But he is clear that everyone can do it.[158] Kierkegaard clearly thinks a person by herself with God in her conscience can know a great deal and he clearly affirms that a person is capable to act on what she knows; and yet he still thinks that a person's self-disclosure in the relationship of conscience is not enough. Revelation is necessary if a person is to know further about who God is, what God requires, and who she is before this requirement.

The awakening of conscience is therefore an essential precondition for a person's self-disclosing encounter with God's revealed Word. That is, the awakened conscience is the precondition for becoming a Christian according to Kierkegaard, because otherwise, he thinks, why else would a person come to Jesus Christ?[159] Now Kierkegaard will say the same things about the single individual in relation to Jesus Christ that he said about the single individual in relation to God: "Christianity's essential view of the human race," he writes, is "first and foremost to view all these countless ones as the single individual."[160] Likewise, he claims that "for Christ, as for God's providence, there is no number, no crowd; for him ... all are individuals."[161] God's self-revelation in Jesus Christ, Kierkegaard claims, is the revelation that "every single human being ... is infinitely important to God—incomprehensible love!"[162] To the question, then, why does God become human, Kierkegaard replies: for the single individual. Jesus Christ is the revelation of just how far God is willing to go so that each individual might become the single individual in relation to God that God creates him or her to be. And so if what Jesus Christ offers is eternity's help to become the single individual in relation to God that God creates a person to become, a person must awaken and develop her relation with God in conscience where she becomes ever more aware

---

157. *JFY*, 91; *JP*, 1:320.
158. *JP*, 1:446.
159. Cf. Evans, *Subjectivity and Religious Belief*, 101–4, 114–15.
160. *WL*, 138.
161. *WL*, 69.
162. *JFY*, 156.

of herself as that single individual.¹⁶³ A person is a single individual in relation to God by virtue of God's creation of that individual for a singular relation to God and consequently a person comes before Jesus Christ as that single individual. A person's relationship to Jesus Christ therefore is a relation between that person as the single individual God created her to be and God in Jesus Christ helping her to become the single individual God created her to be. Jesus Christ, in short, sees a person as the particular single individual she is and wants to help a person become that individual.¹⁶⁴

The Help of Christ: The Mirror of God's Word

Conscience leads the single individual to Jesus Christ but before Jesus Christ what does she learn? How does Jesus Christ help a person to become the single individual God created him or her to become? What, that is, according to Kierkegaard, is the nature of his offer of help? Jesus Christ wants to help each individual to become the single individual God created him or her to become first of all by revealing that the God who is their creator and who creates each individual for a particular relationship to God is love and creates each individual from love and for love. Kierkegaard's conclusion of what Jesus Christ reveals as the "God-man,"¹⁶⁵ as the final revelation of the divine and the human, is that "God is love, and God wants to be loved—this is the Christianity of the New Testament."¹⁶⁶ The single individual is helped by Jesus Christ, then, first of all by the revelation that what God requires of each individual is love because the God who is love creates each individual from love and for love.¹⁶⁷ God's self-revelation in Christ, in other words, discloses to the single individual the fulfillment of her

---

163. I agree with Rae that since Jesus Christ, according to Kierkegaard, is the "prototype" of the human race, Jesus Christ clearly informs what Kierkegaard thinks it means to be a human being. I do not think this means, however, that Kierkegaard's anthropology is "thoroughly Christological." See Rae, *Kierkegaard and Theology*, 98.

164. Kierkegaard's conception here of the Christian's relation to the "congregation," as he calls the Christian community, follows along the same lines as his account of the single individual and genuine community. We cannot miss his great emphasis on the individual, but we should not assume in light of that emphasis, he has nothing to say about a Christian sociality. It is just that that "fellowship is a lower category than the 'single individual.'" What Kierkegaard wants to emphasize is that, by virtue of the individual's direct relationship with God—a relationship he now conceives as a direct relationship with God in Christ—if a person is to join with other "pilgrims" on the way, she alone chooses to do so (*PC*, 223; cf. *UDVS*, 220); "No third person," he writes, "can know whether he knows you; that you must know with him and with yourself" (*DCF*, 59).

165. *JP*, 3:285.
166. *JP*, 3: 55; cf. *JP*, 3:143.
167. Cf. *CD*, 127–8.

being in love and discloses the nature of that love: love, according to Kierkegaard, is a giving of oneself wholly to God. Love is a total self-disposal before God, and insofar as to love others is to help them to be totally self-disposed before God, love is a sacrificing of oneself. If, that is, I am truly to love another person, then I help him or her grow into her relation with God; but this means I must say of myself in this relationship, like John the Baptist said of Christ, "He must become greater; I must become less."[168]

Kierkegaard insists that it is "life of Jesus Christ" that reveals that God is love and that God summons the single individual's love, and when we look at the life of Jesus we glean that the love God summons is a "matter of conscience."[169] "Christianity," he writes, "wants to permeate everything with the relationship of conscience," which is to say, it wants a person's relation to God to "permeate everything."[170] And since Jesus Christ reveals that the God with whom a person relates in conscience is love, love becomes a "matter of conscience." The God who is always present and looking at us in our conscience is love and so when we look back to God "in everything" we are looking back to and seeing ourselves in the love that created us.[171] Consequently, he writes, "to love God is to love oneself truly; to help another person to love God is to love another person; to be helped by another person to love God is to be loved."[172] Love, in short, "is the only thing worth living for, and without this love you are not really living."[173] To say that Jesus Christ reveals that the love God summons is a "matter of conscience" is to say, therefore, that God summons a person to become a single individual in relation to God by living every moment of his or her life in love to God.

Recall that the person who awakens her conscience eventually realizes that to be a single individual in relation to God requires everything of her because it requires she choose at every moment to die to the world and to herself in order to live "for the eternal."[174] Jesus Christ reveals, ultimately, that to live for the eternal in everything is to live in everything in the love of God; and so it is the love of God, in every sense, that claims the entirety of our lives. "By love," Kierkegaard writes, "God understands self-sacrificing love that sacrifices everything in order to make room for God."[175] Jesus Christ reveals, then, that God creates human beings out of love and summons human beings to relate back to God in love; furthermore, because Jesus Christ relates to each individual as the single individual God creates him or

---

168. Jn 3:30.
169. *WL*, 101, 135–54.
170. *WL*, 130, 112.
171. *WL*, 377.
172. *WL*, 107.
173. *WL*, 375: The gospel is the revelation, Kierkegaard claims, that love is "the only thing worth living for and without this love you are not really living."
174. *UDVS*, 208.
175. *WL*, 199.

her to be, Jesus Christ reveals that it is through love that a person responds to the particular summons God lays upon him or her in his or her distinct individuality. God in Christ therefore summons every person to a life of love and gives to every individual a particular way to actualize this love.[176]

Jesus Christ reveals that the love of God is what God's love requires if a person is to become the single individual God creates her to be, but Jesus Christ also reveals that the world will despise this love. What the world calls love, he explains, is really "an alliance in self-love." The "world thinks that the object of love … shall judge whether or not affection and devotion are evidenced and whether or not the evidenced devotion and affection are love."[177] Consequently, the person who really loves will be despised in the world just as Jesus Christ was despised. The world "does not really believe in God," Kierkegaard writes, which is to say that the world does not really believe in love.[178] And so when a person loves God and makes room for God in everything, the world sees a challenge to its way of being; it sees a person who does not love what it loves, and so it sees this person as a threat it cannot abide.[179] The madness of Christianity, Kierkegaard thinks, is that it asks a person to give up everything, to become nothing in the love of God and precisely in doing this to suffer for it: "When a person obeys God in this way, cares solely and exclusively about his will and has no interest, as the saying goes, in howling with the wolves he is together with, that is, when he thinks only about understanding and doing God's will and not about being understood by men—then he is *eo ipso* sacrificed."[180] Why else, Kierkegaard asks, does it go with Jesus as it does when he reveals God's love? He is the perfect manifestation of divine and human love and ultimately this revelation offends everyone—even his best friends—to the point that he is put on a cross.[181]

---

176. A person only loves another person, correlatively, when she helps the other to relate alone in love to God. The lover must presuppose that God in love is present in the beloved and that God is in the beloved summoning the beloved's love, summoning the beloved to become a self in love in relation to God. The lover must consequently make herself inconspicuous, make herself nothing, annihilate herself so that the beloved might become something in relation to God and not in relation to the lover (*WL*, 218). Furthermore, because the lover presupposes the divine claim of love present in every person, her love knows no "natural determinates"; whatever a person's condition in life, he or she has her existence most fundamentally in the relation to God, and to love that person is to love God in that relation, and not to love according to the outward conditions (*WL*, 56). The literature on love in Kierkegaard's works is enormous. Ferreira's *Love's Grateful Striving* is exemplary and surveys much of this literature.

177. *WL*, 113.
178. Cf. *WL*, 225.
179. *JP*, 2:223.
180. *JP*, 2:112.
181. Cf. *JP*, 4:240.

To See Oneself before Christ in the Mirror of God's Word

I have argued that Kierkegaard thinks a person first must awaken her conscience and know herself with God as a single individual created by God for the sake of relating to God in a particular way, and that as she feels her need for God's help in this task increasing, she comes to God's self-revelation in Jesus Christ. Conscience is the engine that drives a person toward Jesus Christ, but once a person comes to this point, she rightly knows herself with God when she looks not to her conscience but to the life of Jesus Christ. But conscience is not simply a precondition for a person's encounter with God in Christ. Conscience remains central, however, because conscience now assumes the responsibility of binding a person to God's revealed Word, of ensuring that when a person comes to God's self-revelation in Jesus Christ she sees herself reflected in it. A person is now genuinely bound in conscience by God's Word, that is, because God's Word reveals to her with ultimate clarity what it means for her to live as a single individual in relation to God, and God's Word reveals to her the help God offers to her in particular to become the single individual in relation to God that God created her to be. This is why a person must become conscious first of being a single individual in relation to God before she comes to God's Word, and this is why a person must read God's Word with her conscience. "What should be insisted upon is this," he writes,

> There is a book called the New Testament, I feel obligated by it in this way and that. But I do not theorize, I do not obligate others. I simply say—I feel obligated in this way and express it in action. Truth is not trying to get a random bunch of people obligated to me or my conception. Truth is that it became known that there is a book called the New Testament and that everyone must alone by himself before God become obligated by it.[182]

Just as Kierkegaard does not tell his reader what exactly it means for her in particular to become the single individual God created her to become since only the single individual can know this in her conscience, so also he will not say exactly what a person's life ought to express when she becomes obligated by the New Testament, because, again, Jesus Christ comes to help single individuals. The help Jesus Christ offers the single individual she must discern for herself; universally, it is the offer to become a single individual in relation to God, but particularly, this means something different from person to person.[183] Kierkegaard's "Christian prescription" is, he writes, "a very simple matter. Pick up the New Testament; read it," and then "consult" with no one but God about what you read.[184] In this way a person reads the New Testament in a "personal subjective relation to it," continually saying to herself, "it is I to whom it is speaking; it is I about whom it is

---

182. *JP*, 2:419.
183. This is contra Ziegler, "A Christian Context," 98–100.
184. *JP*, 3:268.

speaking."[185] To read scripture in this way is to read it with the conscience because he claims to read it otherwise—to read it in consultation with others,[186] to read it objectively and impersonally (the way he thinks most people read scripture)—signals "neither more nor less than a lack of conscience."[187] Therefore, a person only truly reads God's Word when she takes it into her room, and alone by herself reads it with her relation to God in conscience.[188] This does not mean, of course, that Kierkegaard is giving a person permission to read the New Testament any way she wants. The single individual encounters in the New Testament in the life of Christ a very substantive account of love that claims her. Through her conscience she knows herself with God before this claim. And as a single individual she knows with God in her conscience the very particular kind of life in love God created her to live.

By means of our conscience, Kierkegaard claims, we are to see ourselves reflected in God's Word, and he explains that when we read God's Word with our conscience and see ourselves reflected in it, our experience will be like David's before the prophet Nathan.[189] When a person sees the world crucifying love, his conscience strikes him with the claim "You are the man."[190] "Deep within every person's heart," he explains,

> There dwells his preacher of repentance. If he speaks, he does not preach to others, he does not make you into a preacher of repentance—he preaches only to you. He does not preach in any assembled crowd; he preachers in the secrete recesses of the soul—and to you, whether you want to listen to him or not. He has nothing whatever to attend to than to attend to you, and he sees to it that he is heard in that moment when everything around you is still, when the stillness makes you completely solitary.[191]

Conscience becomes the preacher of repentance when we take God's Word into our relationship with God in conscience because when we read, it asks us how we fare much as a parent who catches a child in an act of misbehavior still asks the child about the misbehavior. For example, when we read Paul's claim "all things serve us for good—'when' we love God," Kierkegaard thinks our conscience will prick us by simply asking, "When?" The conscience preaches repentance in this instance because when it asks us "when" as we read "all things serve us for good—'when' we love God," it intends immediately to wound us by catching us in our lack of love (and therefore in our unbelief).[192] When we see ourselves reflected in God's

---

185. *FSE*, 36.
186. *JP*, 3:268.
187. *FSE*, 40.
188. Again, contra Ziegler, "A Christian Context," 100.
189. Cf. Ferreira, *Kierkegaard*, 143.
190. *FSE*, 39.
191. *CD*, 192. Cf. Kirmse, *Golden Age*, 351.
192. *CD*, 192.

Word before Jesus Christ, Kierkegaard concludes, "you get a glaring guilt laid on your conscience—namely that you too are an accomplice in his innocent suffering and death."[193] When we read the New Testament with our conscience we become conscious that our conception of love is the world's conception, that our love is really an alliance in sinful self-love, and that when God in Jesus Christ reveals love to us we are among those who crucified love. Before God's self-revelation in Jesus Christ we become conscious that we are sinners, not simply sinful or guilty in this or that act, but categorically and essentially sinful before the "Holy One."[194] We become conscious, that is, not simply that we are guilty in our failure to become the single individual that God summons each of us to be, not simply that we are guilty of kicking against the goads of our own being, guilty against ourselves, but also that our crime is before God and against God and therefore that it is infinitely heinous.[195]

To summarize so far, when we bring the New Testament into the relationship with God in conscience we become conscious of who God is and what God requires of us, and we become conscious of who we are before this God. We discover that the God present to us in our conscience is love and summons us to a faith that is to become manifest in love and that rests transparently in God as the power that established us. Jesus Christ's life expresses this faith and summons us to it. But when we see ourselves by means of our conscience "contemporary" with Jesus Christ then we see ourselves among those offended by him and who crucified him, and so we see ourselves as infinitely sinful before God.[196] When we bring the New Testament into our relationship with God in conscience, then, we get a double terror laid upon our conscience. First, there is the terror of what Christianity requires. The self-revelation of God in Jesus is the revelation that God's love claims the entirety of our lives and this is terrifying. "To become a Christian," he writes, "is the most fearful operation of all."[197] Second, there is the terror that strikes us when we realize, as God reveals God's love to us, that we are participants in putting that love to death. God creates each of us to become a single individual in relation to God, but we shrink back in horror when God fully reveals in Jesus Christ how we are to become that single individual in relation to God. When we see ourselves reflected in God's Word, we are terrified in our conscience to see the categorical separation our sin creates between us and the loving power that establishes us.

Strikingly, then, for Kierkegaard, the terror of the anguished conscience belongs to a right understanding of the gospel.[198] Kierkegaard criticizes Luther for separating law and gospel and consequently for fostering a Christianity of "sheer

---

193. *CD*, 174.
194. *UDVS*, 285.
195. *SUD*, 80. Cf. Walsh, *Living Christianly*, 24–5.
196. Cf. *PC*, 39, 63, 64, *et passim*.
197. *JP*, 1:199.
198. Contra Walsh, *Living Christianly*, 33–4; Ferreira, *Kierkegaard*, 169; Rae, *Kierkegaard and Theology*, 143.

leniency."[199] The traditional division of law and gospel as the division between terrifying requirement and reassuring grace is, Kierkegaard claims, a "shameful abuse." "No," he explains, "the gospel itself is and must be terrifying at first."[200] Consequently, he explains that "all of Christianity"

> must be traced back to the struggle of the anguished conscience. Remove the anguished conscience, and you may as well close the churches and turn them into dance halls. The anguished conscience understands Christianity ... an atonement is necessary only in the understanding of the anguished conscience."[201]

It is because the gospel itself is terrifying that Kierkegaard thinks the reassuring, comforting gospel preaching of his day that is an attempt to "eliminate conscience."[202] It is, he writes, "the greatest possible relapse" when the gospel is preached, as he thinks it is preached in Christendom, "in the following manner: You have a God who has atoned—now you may really enjoy life."[203] The gospel is not, Kierkegaard suggests, God's provision for us in Christ for our failure to live according to an abstract principle of human conduct in the form of the law.[204] Rather, the gospel is the revelation that what God requires of us is that we come to Jesus in faith and we do this when we decide to follow him by responding to God's love in every moment of our lives with love to God, like Christ and with Christ's help; the gospel is the revelation that God summons our love because the God who created us is love, created us from love and for love and becomes a human being in order to help us live in that love.[205] And if we really understand the gospel, if we really see Jesus

---

199. *JP*, 3:103. Given the importance of law and gospel in Luther's theology, this is clearly no small criticism. Cf. Zachman, "Conscience in the Theology of Martin Luther and Søren Kierkegaard." For readings that interpret Kierkegaard in closer step with Luther; cf. Walsh, *Living Christianly*, 38, 40, 155. Ferreira, *Kierkegaard*, 19.

200. *JP*, 4:240.

201. *JP*, 1:521.

202. *JP*, 1:217.

203. *JP*, 1:217.

204. This is Gerald McKenny's helpful way of summarizing the relation of law and gospel in Luther's theology. See McKenny, *The Analogy of Grace: Karl Barth's Moral Theology* (New York: Oxford University Press, 2010), 167.

205. I don't want to get too far afield from Kierkegaard's theory of conscience, but obviously the relation in Kierkegaard's theology of grace and works, gospel and law plays an important role in what Kierkegaard says about conscience, the anguished conscience in particular. Kierkegaard thinks that a proper understanding of the atonement, that is, consists in the revelation of Jesus Christ "as prototype and the Redeemer, and in turn the Redeemer and the prototype" (*JFY*, 147). The order here is crucial. Kierkegaard clearly claims that the gospel first asks us in faith to strive to come after Jesus Christ, to walk in his footsteps as our prototype, as the exemplar of the truly human life God summons us to live (cf. *JP*, 3:44; *SUD*, 82). As we come after Christ, we find that he is our redeemer who comes to our aid in our striving so that we might continue to strive to come after

Christ as the New Testament portrays him, and if we really understand that Jesus Christ's invitation "Come to me" addresses us personally and that it summons us in everything to give our lives in love to God, then we will experience the terror of an anguished conscience. Why else, Kierkegaard asks, "did it go with Christ as it did when he said: Come to me—and they all went away, they fled from him."[206] When we see ourselves by means of our conscience reflected in God's Word, we see ourselves among those who are terrified by the summons of God's love in Christ and who, consequently, fled.

But when we see ourselves by means of our conscience reflected in God's Word we see ourselves fleeing from our only way to remain with God and to remain with God's command in love, "Become something in relation to me." Kierkegaard's conclusion is that if "you are not conscious of being a sinner to the degree that in the anxiety of the anguished conscience you do not dare anything other than to commit yourself to Christ—then you will never become a Christian. Only the agony of the consciousness of sin can explain the fact that person will submit to this radical cure."[207] Through the awakened conscience and the Word of God a person finds herself in anguish before Jesus Christ because before Jesus Christ she comes to know herself as God knows her in Jesus Christ as one who rejects God and God's claim on her life. Jesus Christ, in short, is the final and clearest revelation of who God calls a person to be and who she is in actuality in light of this call. Before Jesus Christ she comes to know herself in the "enormous weight of God,"[208] as loved by God with such infinite love that God becomes a human being to show her the way and to die in order to be her way to become the single individual in relation to God that God created her to become. When a person knows herself before Jesus Christ she is terrified because before Jesus Christ she knows herself in her sin before the perfect manifestation of the requirement that God's love lays upon her. But in this terrified self-knowledge a person also finds Jesus Christ as the one who implores and beseeches her with his offer to help.[209] Before Jesus Christ, the help looks like madness—everyone else runs away from it—but in the anguish of her conscience she knows herself as God knows her, as one who has rejected the divine love that established her, and so as one so profoundly sick that only this radical cure of coming unto Jesus Christ can save her.

---

him as our prototype. Kierkegaard insists that the life of the God-man, the prototype-redeemer-prototype, expresses grace from first to last but that grace lays a requirement on us (*JFY*, 153).

206. *JP*, 4:240.

207. *JP*, 1:199. Cf. *PC*, 67-8. For a more Lutheran interpretation of this passage, cf. Walsh, *Living Christianly*, 47; Amy Laura Hall, *Kierkegaard and the Treachery of Love* (New York: Cambridge University Press, 2002), 16-17; Rae, *Kierkegaard and Theology*, 174.

208. *SUD*, 120.

209. *SUD*, 85.

Summary and Conclusion

We can summarize Kierkegaard's theory of conscience, in conclusion, in terms of the individual and her relationship to God the Creator. Every individual has a conscience but there is a sense in which conscience only begins to exist for a person when he or she moves away from the crowd where the masses deceive themselves by living their lives according to false criteria about what it means to be a human being. A person must break away from this deceitful public life and move to the location where conscience becomes audible. The location is the place of stillness and solitude where everything is quiet so that the individual can acquire through inward deepening a transparency to herself about who she really is. In this still, removed, and quite place she discovers who she really is because she discovers her relationship to her creator. In stillness and solitude she discovers that God is, that God is present to her and looking at her. As she looks back to God in this relationship of conscience she knows herself with God as a creature in God's image created to live in worship before God; and as she looks back to God in this relationship of conscience she knows further that God has created her to live before God in worship in a unique way; with God she begins to know her divinely given name and she begins to know what it means for her in particular to live into this name. She is bound in her conscience not by a standard alien to her but by her own very being, because God summons her in her conscience to become the single individual in relation to God that God created her in particular to become. But as she continues to move more deeply inward, partaking more deeply with God in God's knowledge of her as this particular individual who is summoned to live in this particular way, she also begins to know herself with God in her guilt because she begins to know how far her life in actuality is from what God summons her to be. And for this reason she feels that much more her need for God, and so she confesses her guilt and in so doing she holds fast to God and discovers that God will hold fast to her.

Kierkegaard more or less takes for granted that the individual who delves deeply enough in her conscience to know herself with God as God knows her in her guilt will inexorably come upon God's self-revelation in Jesus Christ. The God with whom she knows herself as an individual languishing in guilt is the God before whom she hears the plea, "Come unto me all you who are weary and heavy laden." Having come to this offer of help, a person now no longer knows herself solely through her relationship with God in her conscience. Now she is to bring God's revealed Word into her relationship with God in her conscience and by means of her conscience she is to see herself reflected in and obligated by God's Word. She is bound by God's Word because it is the final revelation of what God requires of her if she is to become the single individual God created her to become. God's Word reveals especially that God is love and that God creates every individual from love and summons every individual to relate to God in love. In the presence of Jesus Christ, then, a person sees the way God has given her to become herself as God has created her to be. If by means of her conscience, however, she sees herself reflected in God's Word then she knows herself among those terrified by what God in Christ reveals about what it means to become a single individual in relation to God; and if she knows herself, further, among those terrified by the requirement of God's love, then she knows herself as complicit with those who put love on the cross. When she reads God's Word with her conscience and sees herself reflected in it she is terrified by what Jesus Christ reveals and she is terrified to see herself among those rejecting God, who she knows as source and goal of her life. But when she sees herself by means of her conscience reflected in God's Word she also sees herself before God as he implores her with his help to come after him and to find rest in him. In the anguish of her conscience she sees no other way to be the individual God summons her to be than to rush headlong into this madness where she finds her cure.

Clearly, the Son of God is a central figure in Kierkegaard's theology, and obviously, he plays a central role in the individual's relationship to God in her conscience. But Kierkegaard's theory of conscience is best summarized in terms of the single individual and her relationship to God the Creator, because it is this relationship that Jesus Christ serves to repair. Consequently, at the center of Kierkegaard's theory of conscience is the single individual who God the Creator creates for a singular and authentic reciprocal relationship with God. To be a human being, Kierkegaard assumes, is to be a being made for a singular relationship to God and the *sine qua non* of every human life as such is God's summons to live at every moment for God. Conscience, for Kierkegaard, is the knowledge every person has of himself or herself in this relation; it is the knowledge of who she is in this relationship and who she ought to be. Jesus Christ is *the help* she needs to live as God summons her to live.

We can say in conclusion that Kierkegaard's theory of conscience falls within the heritage of thinking about conscience that we found in Kant's practical philosophy and moral theology, namely that conscience is (or in Kant's case, is the means to) the knowledge a person has of herself in relation to God. But Kierkegaard is distinct from Kant in his insistence that a person knows herself in relation to God for the sake of that relation. His theory of conscience is about the individual who is created to be "God's bondservant," created to find her highest satisfaction in the summons God lays upon her in order finally to rest transparently in God. Kierkegaard thinks that every individual is singularly bound by the summons to be God's bondservant, because he believes that God creates every individual with an essential self, with a unique existential DNA uniquely binding him or her to God. Every individual is an "original edition" from God's hand created for a very specific relationship to God. And so when a person knows herself rightly in her conscience under God's summons to be God's bondservant, she knows herself under the summons to be faithful to herself, because for her to be God's bondservant means she lives as the single individual God created her to become. Conscience is the knowledge every person has of himself or herself in this relationship established by God at the creation of every individual; through the conscience every individual is able to know himself or herself with God as an individual created by God and redeemed by God for a unique relationship with God, for a unique way, that is, to realize the summons in love, God the loving Creator lays on every human being.

Chapter 4

CONSCIENCE AS SINGULAR MORAL SELF-AWARENESS: AN OUTLINE

Introduction: Conscience as Singular Moral Self-Awareness before God

The aim of this book is to recommend, especially for contemporary Christian ethics, a theory of conscience as an individual's moral self-awareness before God. This recommendation takes shape in the previous two chapters through close studies and defenses of the distinct ways this theory of conscience appears in the works of Immanuel Kant and Søren Kierkegaard. What these chapters establish is that Kant and Kierkegaard present conscience as a sharing with God in God's knowledge of us as God sees and judges the moral quality of our actions and our character. And Kant and Kierkegaard both claim that an individual's moral self-awareness in relation to God is distinct from an individual's moral self-awareness in relation to others, as it might be conditioned, that is, by other individuals and communities. Conscience is, for Kant and Kierkegaard, about an individual's awareness of moral accountability before God that they insist is distinct from an awareness of moral accountability before human communities, though it is a moral self-awareness significantly about life in community with others. Kant and Kierkegaard present conscience, in short, as an individual's singular moral self-awareness in relation to God, singular in the sense that the individual exists in a distinct moral relation to God and that God knows and judges that individual distinctly. In other words, while Kant and Kierkegaard differ in important ways about what it means to have knowledge with God and what it means to be an individual in relation to God, they share a theory of conscience broadly conceived as individual's singular moral self-awareness in relation to God.

The aim of this chapter is to outline and defend a theory of conscience along these lines, drawing on central themes and basic contours from the chapters on Kant and Kierkegaard and situating those themes and contours within a broader biblical and theological tradition about conscience as an individual's moral self-awareness before God. The previous chapters therefore provide important context for this chapter, which I intend to be a culmination of the book's argument. But I appreciate also that different readers will have different degrees of interest in the content of those chapters, as each focuses on distinct aspects and figures in the history of modern Christian thought about conscience. And so as this chapter draws on the previous ones, especially the ones on Kant and Kierkegaard, there will be some repetition of the most salient earlier points so that this chapter can to a certain extent stand on its own, or at least make sense to a reader who has needed to pass quickly through those earlier chapters. An important caveat, however, is that a major burden of this book is historical because, as I have argued, there is a close connection between a certain misreading of Kant and, to a lesser extent, Kierkegaard, and the decline of interest in conscience as moral self-awareness in twentieth-century and contemporary theological ethics. The heart of this book, in other words, are the historical studies of Kant's and Kierkegaard's theories of conscience. The burden of this chapter is to make a more sustained case that passing through Kant and Kierkegaard as we have can help us conceive of conscience in a way that makes good theological sense and that retrieves an important theme from the Bible and the history of Christian thought about the nature of individual moral accountability before God. There are surely different ways to draw on these figures than I will draw on them here, and the case for conscience this chapter outlines is not necessarily one that either Kant or Kierkegaard would fully endorse. My hope is to persuade readers that conscience as an individual's moral self-awareness has an important place in the Christian tradition and, to that end, that Kant and Kierkegaard can help illuminate what conscience is and how it works.

There should be no hiding the fact that this theory of conscience promotes an individualism that might make many readers suspicious. But my hope, at the very least, is to persuade readers that a certain kind of individualism simply belongs to a broadly Christian understanding about God's relation to human beings. When Kierkegaard writes about the moral and spiritual implications of God's intimate presence to each person, a presence that "changes everything,"[1] he is not necessarily striking a modern, existentialist tone or advancing a novel individualism; rather, he is at least echoing the language of the Bible, of Jesus himself, who is straightforward about the individual's very personal and private relation to God.[2] Kant does not endorse what Kierkegaard means here since Kant believes that a person who claims to have a familiar relation to God is delusional,[3] guilty of an irrational, enthusiastic zeal, a zeal that in its familiarity with God simply cannot be universal.[4] A special, personal relationship to God is clearly not something Kant wants to affirm. This does not mean, however, that, according to Kant, we are not each singularly accountable to God. He insists we should believe in a God who sees our hearts, and he clearly means by this a God who sees each of our hearts in particular. In a qualified sense, then, it is correct to say that Kant's theory of conscience is about a private matter between the individual and God—even if Kant objects to the idea of a special, familiar relationship to God. Kant affirms that God

---

1. *UDVS*, 125.

2. For an excellent account of the way Jesus singles out individuals and the way individual identity is thereby established in this singular relation (as clearly differentiated from an individual's relation to a community), see Richard Bauckham, *Gospel of Glory: Major Themes in Johannine Theology* (Grand Rapids, MI: Baker Academic, 2015), 1–20.

3. *Religion*, 6:201.

4. *Religion*, 6:68.

sees my heart and judges me. I am accountable before God for the quality of my life's conformity to a moral law I can justifiably think of as promulgated by God. We might say, then, that Kant and Kierkegaard present a range of perspectives for how to understand the individual's singular relation to God, from a more strictly moral perspective to one that is more familiar and personal.

The Unwelcome Individual in Contemporary Theology and Ethics

Neither perspective appears very welcome in much contemporary discourse in theology, ethics, and biblical studies. And so here I will briefly revisit both the critique of the type of individualism that Kant's and Kierkegaard's theory of conscience allegedly supports, and the communitarian turn that has quietly dismissed conscience as an important feature of Christian ethics. The revolution in Pauline studies Krister Stendhal helped inaugurate with his essay, "The Apostle Paul and the Introspective Conscience of the West,"[5] has generally moved in an anti-individualistic interpretation of the Pauline epistles. Stendhal argues that since Augustine, and most significantly with Luther, theologians have imposed a psychological interpretation on Paul and find in Paul a struggle in conscience oriented around the individualistic question, "How can *I* find a gracious God."[6] Paul's problem, Stendhal writes, is not this individualistic one. Paul himself, he argues, clearly does not have the anxious conscience Western theologians since Augustine attribute to him.[7] Rather, Paul grapples with how the inclusion of the Gentiles into the church makes sense of God's promises to Israel.[8] N. T. Wright and Richard Hays are among the many, and certainly two of the most influential, who follow Stendhal in his dismissal of the tradition that reads Paul as an anxious proto-existentialist concerned about his individual standing before God. Wright and Hays argue that Paul's moral vision is about God's faithfulness to his promise that Abraham would be the father of a worldwide family under God's kingly rule.[9] Wright makes concessions to the presence of the "old style" concern for the individual in Paul's theology so long as this concern falls within the broader corporate vision of salvation;[10] but the overall tenor of

---

5. Stendhal, Krister, *Paul among Jews and Gentiles and Other Essays* (Philadelphia, PA: Fortress, 1976).

6. Stendhal, *Paul*, 83, emphasis mine.

7. Stendhal, *Paul*, 84.

8. Stendhal, *Paul*, 84–5.

9. Hays and Wright are prolific authors, but see, for instance, Richard Hays, *The Echoes of Scripture in the Letters of Paul* (New York: Yale University Press, 1993) and *The Moral Vision of the New Testament: Community, Cross, and New Creation* (New York: HarperCollins, 1996), 16–59; N. T. Wright, *Paul: In Fresh Perspective* (Minneapolis, MN: Fortress Press, 2005), 21–40, 108–25, and *What Saint Paul Really Said* (Grand Rapids, MI: Eerdmans, 1997), 19–36.

10. Wright, *What Saint Paul Really Said*, 16.

his and Hays's interpretation of Pauline theology dismisses the significance of the individual in conscience before God. This is nowhere more evident than in their total inattention to the place conscience does in fact have in Paul's theology. Whether or not Paul's conscience was an anxious one, and whether or not Paul's primary question was about the individual's standing before God, Paul appeals to conscience quite a few times throughout his letters. As we will see, Paul clearly affirms that in conscience each individual stands in distinct moral accountability before God. I do not mean to gainsay the general advances figures like Wright and Hays have offered to our understanding of the New Testament; but because major Pauline scholars like them since Stendhal have been so concerned not to return to the "old," anxious-in-conscience, individualistic Paul, they disregard the positive valence of conscience and the reality of the individual before God in Paul's theology and therefore encourage theologians and ethicists to do the same.[11]

Popular Reformed Christian philosopher James K. A. Smith, for example, laments that the core concern of "modern Christianity" has become "the individual," rendering the church "simply a collection of individuals." The Christian faith is, in turn, impoverished, Smith argues, since it is conceived as "a private affair between the individual and God;" consequently, much of modern American Christianity "finds it hard to articulate just how or why the church has any role to play other than providing a place to have fellowship with other individuals who have a private fellowship with God."[12] In short, "modern Christianity tends to think of the church either as a place where individuals come to find answers to their questions or as one more stop where individuals can try to satisfy their consumerist desires."[13] Against "modern Christianity," then, Smith wants to "resist talking about Christians as individuals" and instead simply to "speak of the church" as "an organic model of community" that "counters the modernist emphasis on the individual."[14] It is not difficult to discern the influence of Hauerwas in these anti-individualistic claims. Hauerwas is clear that any affirmation of an individual's direct relation to God

---

11. Bauckham suggests that this is an unfortunate succumbing to certain academic "theological" or "sociological" pressures to overemphasize corporate life at the expense of the individual and the individual's singular relation to God (*Gospel of Glory*, 19).

12. James K. A. Smith, *Who's Afraid of Postmodernism: Taking Derrida, Lyotard, and Foucault to Church* (Grand Rapids, MI: Baker Academic, 2006), 29.

13. Smith, *Who's Afraid*, 29.

14. Smith, *Who's Afraid*, 30. According to Bauckham, a claim like this represents precisely the kind of flattening "of the contours of the [biblical] canon to the detriment" the genuine singularity of the individual before God we find in the fourth Gospel (*Gospel of Glory*, 19). As we have seen earlier, Abraham Kuyper, a fountainhead of Smith's particular Reformed tradition, claims, that the individual submits his conscience "as to a direct *sensus divinitatis* through which God Himself stirs up the inner man, and subjects him to His judgment" (*Lectures on Calvinism*). That Smith can make such a contrary assertion with so little criticism is evidence of how influential the communitarian turn has become.

is theologically irresponsible. He suggests that we simply should not allow any possibility for directness or "immediacy" in the individual's relation to God.[15]

It is a short step, Alisdair MacIntyre argues, articulating a major worry tacit in claims like Smith's and Hauerwas's, from the individual directly before God to the individual who acts as a law unto herself, in whose life moral formation and the careful cultivation of practical reason are not matters of great concern. MacIntyre finds in Reformation figures like Luther and Calvin a novel creation of an individual "alone before God ... [therefore] stripped of all social attributes, abstracted ... from all his social relations" and "continually before God."[16] For such an individual, MacIntyre continues, his moral identity

> now is only that of the bearer of a given name who answers as a matter of contingent fact to certain descriptions ... and he has to make his own choice among the competing possibilities. From the facts of his situation as he is able to describe them in his new social vocabulary, nothing at all follows about what he ought to do. Everything comes to depend upon his own individual choice. Moreover, the sovereignty of individual choice is not only a consequence of his social vocabulary, but of the theorizing derived from theology.[17]

Because the self is alone before God and at the whim of God's commands, "about ends" his reason "must be silent,"[18] and so his arbitrary power of choice must acquire its own sovereignty. In sum, according to MacIntyre, it is a short step from the Reformation's alleged invention of a self alone before God to a modern reduction of morality to personal preferences. Whether or not this is a charitable or persuasive interpretation of Luther or Calvin,[19] it nevertheless captures something important in the worries about what might result from theological affirmations of the individual before God.

As we have seen, though, it is Kant who provokes some of the strongest criticisms for licensing modern individualism. For at least the past few decades a standard view in Christian ethics (prevalent also in moral philosophy), especially under the influence of MacIntyre and Hauerwas, has been to treat Kant as the principal architect of the morally relativistic, banal individualism of contemporary Western life. Our contemporary culture is Kantian, Hauerwas claims, insofar as the common assumption is that morality is a subjective, creative endeavor from

---

15. Hauerwas, *Peaceable Kingdom*, 27.

16. MacIntyre, Alisdair, *A Short History of Ethics: A History of Moral Philosophy from the Homeric Age to the Twentieth Century*, second edition (Notre Dame, IN: University of Notre Dame Press, 1998), 81.

17. MacIntyre, *Short History*, 81.

18. MacIntyre, *After Virtue*, 54.

19. For a clear and persuasive critique of MacIntyre's account of Luther and Calvin, see Richard J. Mouw, "Alisdair MacIntyre on Reformation Ethics," *Journal of Religious Ethics*, vol. 13, no. 2 (1985), 254, 255.

one individual to the next.[20] In other words, if you were looking for the intellectual framework that ultimately gives rise to the self-asserting, atomistic, autonomous individual of contemporary Western life—the individual who determines for herself what her morality will be—the standard view has been to look to Kant. Kierkegaard receives less attention than Kant in this regard, but MacIntyre situates Kierkegaard within this Kantian trajectory, and influential theologians like Karl Barth have worried about the subjective caprice Kierkegaard might license.[21] The charge about conscience, in this alleged Kantian paradigm, is that it becomes the means by which the morally sovereign individual holds herself accountable to the moral laws she has prescribed for herself. Conscientious self-consistency—being true to oneself—is the moral ideal.

And while this book challenges oversimple declension narratives that unfairly confine major figures like Kant to the role of villainous foil with little insight to offer, it is nonetheless true that the present situation appears to be as such narratives describe (even if the interpretation of figures like Kant is often suspect). We do live in a time in which there is widespread confidence that it is right and good to regard one's own subjectivity as the first and last word on what is right and good. And in this view, conscientious self-examination would indeed serve the purpose of helping a person to be consistent with his self-posited moral identity. Semester after semester, in my own experience in the classroom with young college students in ethics and theology courses, I hear now familiar aphorisms like "You do You!" and "Live your truth!," aphorisms that convey a clear affirmation of a "a subjectivity that regards itself as truth" (this is the subjective caprice noted above that Barth thinks Kierkegaard might license). Along these lines, sociologist of religion Christian Smith conducted a wide-ranging study of American teenagers about their views on religion and morality and found strong corroboration for the morally relativistic, sovereign individual of MacIntyre's account.[22] Smith concludes that the most accurate way to describe American youth—across a wide range of religious traditions—is that they are "moralistic therapeutic deists."[23] In other words, what Smith found most common among his sample group of American teenagers is that while they believe a God exists who wants them to be "nice" to others, what makes a religious tradition or moral system valid is that it makes a

---

20. Hauerwas, *Resident Aliens*, 98.

21. Karl Barth, "A Thank-You and a Bow—Kierkegaard's Reveille," 99.

22. Christian Smith, "On 'Moralistic Therapeutic Deism' as U.S. Teenagers' Actual, Tacit, De Facto Religious Faith," in *The 2005 Princeton Lectures on Youth, Church, and Culture: With Imagination and Love: Leadership in Youth Ministry* (Princeton, NJ: Princeton Theological Seminary, 2005), 57 n. 2. Available at http://youthlectures.ptsem.edu/?action=tei&id=youth-2005-05, accessed June 2018.

23. The major study is Christian Smith and Melina Lundquist Denton, *Soul Searching: The Religious and Spiritual Lives of American Teenagers* (New York: Oxford University Press, 2005), see especially 118–71.

person feel good about himself.²⁴ What really matters when it comes to religious and moral conviction is that each person figure out what makes him happy and what helps him to "get along with others," so that everyone "can then together hold hands and declare in unison, 'Each person decides for himself!'"²⁵

The Consequent Communitarian Turn and the Implications for Moral Self-Awareness

The very understandable response to the reality of this prevalent, relativistic moral individualism has been the strong communitarian turn in Christian ethics. I defined this communitarianism earlier as the belief that our moral identity is not something a person creates but that comes into being as she is embedded in a public world, as she is given a role in the life of a particular, historical, moral culture that lives according to particular sociolinguistic conventions. Her task, then, is to acclimate herself to those conventions, discover her role within them, and learn what it means to live into that given role. Theological renderings of this commitment find God at work in and through the historical community. And so she can trust that God is present in her life as her identity is conformed to or sublimated in the life of the community.

An important question at stake here is to what extent the contingencies of our lives determine our moral identity. Is there anything about who we are as moral agents that is noncontingent, anything, that is not determined by social-historical contingencies? MacIntyre and Hauerwas argue that modern, Kantian-influenced individualism is about abstracting ourselves from our concrete social contexts, and that what is, in that scheme, essential about our moral identity is ahistorical, noncontingent, and consequently, up to each of us individually.²⁶ MacIntyre thinks this is a mistake because we are "in key part" what we inherit from our history, from our past relations with others from a particular time and place.²⁷ It is a little unclear if MacIntyre is arguing that our moral identity is entirely contingent, entirely a social construct or a historical artifact since "in key part" is an ambiguous phrase. That seems to be his argument, though, as he goes on to say that all we can do as moral agents is to take ownership of the moral identity given to us through our lives with others. We possess "only the resources of psychological continuity," he writes, which is to say we do not create our moral identity, but we can give an account for it.²⁸ Hauerwas is less ambiguous, echoing MacIntyre's claim that

---

24. Smith, "On 'Moralistic Therapeutic Deism,'" 47. Smith is clear that these teens are most likely simply reflecting the beliefs of their parents and the culture more broadly (54).

25. Smith, "On 'Moralistic Therapeutic Deism,'" 55.

26. MacIntyre, "The Virtues," 105; with Kant in view, 106. Hauerwas, *Peaceable Kingdom*, 35.

27. MacIntyre, "The Virtues," 105.

28. MacIntyre, "The Virtues," 103, emphasis mine.

we can take ownership or responsibility for the identity given to us, but claiming without qualification that that identity is fully "historically determined," fully socially constructed.[29] There is no transcendent dimension, no relation to God alongside or independent of our socially constructed, historically determined moral identities; rather, for Hauerwas, if there is a transcendent relation to God, it shapes us only as a historical community mediates it to us.[30]

There is therefore no moral self-awareness, in this account, that exceeds the bounds of a person's social context, no moral self-awareness that is not fully determined by the community's own self-understanding. Since a person's moral identity comes into being through the life of a community, it is before the community's norms that she knows herself as accountable. These norms, furthermore, are not static ideals the community safeguards; rather, they emerge in and through the community's life, through its examination of its own habits and practices, its self-reflection on its "ongoing experience," as Hauerwas writes.[31] And so, for Hauerwas, the moral constraints a person encounters in her moral self-awareness indicate "the markers of the outer limits of the communal self-understandings."[32] In other words, when a person finds within herself some sense of moral accountability before a particular prohibition, that prohibition is telling her that to continue in this or that course of action is to act out of step with the community that shapes her.[33] This sounds very much like H. Richard Niebuhr's conception of conscience as a person's internalization of external social mores, as an encounter within a person of an Other who represents the general ethos of a particular formative community. And I suggested earlier that Hauerwas could perhaps develop a theory of conscience along these lines, with a distinct focus on how the life of a particular Christian community might shape the nature and function of a person's conscience. This would be as useful as a way to describe the "resources of psychological continuity" by which a person conforms her life to the life of the community and what is going on when a person encounters a community's prohibitions.[34]

But useful as it might be, Hauerwas seems wary to move in this direction. Conscience takes place within a person; it is where a person discerns how well her life conforms to the community's moral norms. Such discernment vaguely indicates a buffer between a person and the community, something about a person's moral identity that is distinct from the community, which suggests, for Hauerwas, an unwelcome "ahistorical view of the self, a transcendental self somewhere always behind my character."[35] The turn inward, then, is to be discouraged. The proper

---

29. Hauerwas, *Peaceable Kingdom*, 35.
30. Hauerwas, *Peaceable Kingdom*, 27.
31. Hauerwas, *Peaceable Kingdom*, 119.
32. Hauerwas, *Peaceable Kingdom*, 119.
33. Hauerwas, *Peaceable Kingdom*, 119.
34. Hauerwas cites this passage from MacIntyre in *Peaceable Kingdom*, 40.
35. Hauerwas, *Peaceable Kingdom*, 39.

locus of moral self-awareness is the community. And so the individual looks not within but without, to the community as it examines the relation between its habits and practices and its particular history.[36] There does appear to be a real tension here, one that Hauerwas tacitly acknowledges,[37] between a notion of moral agency that allows for some degree of noncontingency, some degree of abstraction from the contingencies of social context and history, and a moral agency entirely shaped by the contingent, historical community. But Hauerwas clearly wants to discount anything that suggests something noncontingent in a person's moral identity.[38]

I should note here that while Hauerwas's own particular brand of communitarianism may be less prominent in the field of Christian ethics than it used to be, the general communitarian commitments about the nature of moral agency have not been seriously challenged. The response to Hauerwas, that is, largely has not been to reassert the role of the individual in the Christian life or to consider further how moral identity might not be a social construct shaped entirely by a community. Indeed, perhaps bearing Hauerwas's influence, I think it is a fair generalization that community identity, as signified through social practices and as the proper locus of ethical reflection, is a dominant theme in contemporary Christian ethics. In other words, with respect to any affirmation or interest in individual identity or moral self-awareness that is distinct from community identity and awareness, it is fair to assume that Hauerwas's position is broadly representative of the scholarly consensus.

Beyond the Dichotomy: An Individual Not Sovereign but before God

Hauerwas makes evident a dichotomy present throughout the worries about modern individualism we have been considering. On the one hand there is the individual whose moral self-awareness comes into being as he finds himself embedded in a community with a particular history signified through certain habits, practices, and sociolinguistic customs; on the other hand there is the modern individual, bearing an allegedly Kantian genealogy, who asserts his own moral identity, unencumbered by history and social convention, and who therefore lives by laws of his own making, and is, as such, accountable ultimately to himself. The options appear to be the individual whose identity is realized only as it is sublimated in the life of a community and the individual who asserts his identity against history and community, who exists morally as an atom in empty space. H. Richard Niebuhr, for instance, contrasts the existence of a moral agent defined in relation to an abstract moral law and the moral agent who is "essentially a social structure."[39] MacIntyre contrasts the noncontingent, ahistorical autonomous

36. Hauerwas, *Peaceable Kingdom*, 46.
37. Hauerwas, *Peaceable Kingdom*, 39.
38. For Hauerwas, we are fully determined by our history, our history gives us our character, and "we are our character" (*Peaceable Kingdom*, 39).
39. Niebuhr, *Responsible Self*, 72.

individual and the individual who finds himself as one shaped by a tradition-bearing, historical community.[40] James K. A. Smith tells us that to talk about individuals at all is to jeopardize a much more fruitful attention to the community. And Hauerwas, again, presents us with a fully, historically determined, socially constructed individual as the necessary corrective to the modern, autonomous, ahistorical Kantian self.[41] To this end Hauerwas finds an ally in Augustine when Augustine declares to God, "you were more inward than my most inward parts and higher than the highest element within me."[42] Hauerwas notes that here Augustine does not lay the groundwork for the detached interiority of the modern Kantian self because "when Augustine looks 'internally' he finds God, not self."[43] And this discovery, Hauerwas claims, supports his own argument about the construction of individual moral identity through the habits and practices of the historically embodied community.[44]

But does it? Does Augustine's discovery of God's presence to him not indicate another possibility beyond the dichotomy of a socially constructed, historically determined self and an ahistorical, atomistic, autonomous self? Augustine's address to God as the one "more inward than my most inwards parts" sounds more like an expression of a singular relation to a personal God than an expression of a self whose moral identity in relation to God has been socially constructed and entirely mediated through the habits and practices of a particular historical community. Along these lines, Augustine appeals to God as one who cares "for each one of us *as though the only one in your care*, and yet for all as for *each individual*."[45] And it certainly sounds like Augustine assumes a singularity before God when he says to God, "Before you I lay my heart and my memory," and as

---

40. MacIntyre, "The Virtues," 105–6.
41. Hauerwas, *Peaceable Kingdom*, 39.
42. Augustine, *Confessions*, trans. Henry Chadwick (New York: Oxford University Press, 1991), 3.6.11, p. 43. Hauerwas clearly alludes to this passage when he defends Augustine against the claim that Augustine lays the groundwork with his focus on the interior life for the modern notion of the self. Hauerwas objects: "when Augustine looks 'internally' he finds God, not self" (Hauerwas, "Agency Going Forward by Looking Back," 194). Hauerwas offers this parenthetical note on Augustine in the course of making a strong claim about the social construction of moral identity through the narrative and practices of communities. His concern with Augustine is that Augustine does not license the modern self. The dichotomy he sets up is, on the one hand, a socially constructed personal identity through story, etc. and, on the other hand, the modern emotive self. And this dichotomy seems to have caused Hauerwas to miss that it is Augustine, the singular human being, who turns inward and finds within himself, the presence of God. Augustine, indeed, does not license the modern self. It is the presence of God to Augustine that makes all the difference for Augustine about who Augustine the individual is.
43. Hauerwas, "Agency Going Forward by Looking Back," 194.
44. Hauerwas, "Agency Going Forward by Looking Back," 189, 194.
45. Augustine, *Confessions*, 3.9.19, p. 50.

he recalls a time when God was "putting my shameful errors before my face (Ps. 49: 21) so that I would see and hate them."[46] We are entering the territory of an individual's moral self-awareness in relation to God with this passage (and warrant from the Psalms) but the point for the moment is that Augustine's language seems to indicate a directness in relation to God as God, intimately present to Augustine, addresses him.

Karl Barth, to take another major theologian Hauerwas claims for his particular communitarian agenda,[47] likewise resists the dichotomy between the detached interiority of the modern individual and the communitarian self whose being is embedded in the ecclesial community. As John Webster notes, Barth vigorously denies the detached interiority of the modern moral subject. Like Hauerwas and others, Barth "refuses to allow" that an autonomous, self-subsistent "moral consciousness is basic."[48] But what often goes unnoticed is that "Barth does not undermine the primacy of interiority by exploring the embeddedness of moral self-hood in a public world—in the ethical self-descriptions which the Christian agent absorbs from participation in the linguistic and social conventions of the church considered as a form of moral culture."[49] In other words, Barth shares the worries of MacIntyre or Hauerwas about a certain kind of modern individualism, but he does not share their solution, because Barth considers human moral agency to be constituted by the "self-bestowing, communicative personal presence" of a God who claims us each individually.[50] Barth's theory of conscience is relevant here as it pertains to the individual's direct encounter with God in which the individual shares with God in God's knowledge of her as God claims her in a distinct relation to God.[51] For Barth this direct encounter with God is eschatological, following Paul's claim that only eschatologically will we see "face to face" and know ourselves with God as we are "fully known,"[52] but, according to Barth, God allows this direct encounter to break into our present,[53] however weakly we might experience

---

46. Augustine, *Confessions*, 5.7.11, p. 79.

47. Hauerwas is very clear about his lifelong debt to Barth in his recent memoir, *Hannah's Child: A Theologian's Memoir* (Grand Rapids, MI: Eerdmans, 2010). See, for example, 37, 59, 108, *et passim*. See also, "How 'Christian Ethics' Came to Be," in *The Hauerwas Reader*, especially 45–9. Hauerwas here makes a strong assertion (without qualification) for the essential Barthian inspiration and orientation of his own work as an ethicist.

48. John Webster, *Karl Barth's Moral Theology: Human Action in Barth's Thought* (Grand Rapids, MI: Eerdmans, 1998), 42.

49. Webster, *Barth's Moral Theology*, 42.

50. John Webster, *Barth's Moral Theology*, 42. Through the conscience, Barth writes in his Ethics lectures, God addresses the individual and "makes each individual responsible as such," as one singularly claimed (Karl Barth, *Ethics*, trans. Geoffrey Bromily (New York: Seabury Press, 1981), 494, cf. 491, 508. See also Barth, *The Holy Spirit and the Christian Life* (Louisville, KY: Westminster John Knox Press, 1993), 65–6).

51. Cf. Barth, *Ethics*, 477, 481, 497, 499.

52. 1 Cor. 13:12.

53. Barth, *Ethics*, 465, 480; *Holy Spirit and the Christian Life*, 60–2.

it,[54] and it is instructive, in any event, that Barth affirms this direct relation to God as at the end of God's ways with us.

It is instructive because Barth and Augustine both draw our attention to a way of talking about the individual as neither a solitary sovereign nor a social construct. They do indeed affirm that the individual is constituted in relation, but in relation to God. That is, they suggest that a singular relation to God is an important aspect of human moral identity and, in particular, with respect to what it means for a human being to be morally accountable and morally self-aware. And they are not without good biblical warrants. Augustine's discovery of God as more inward than his most "inward parts" recalls Psalm 139, where David declares to God, "For you formed my inward parts; you knitted me together in my mother's womb."[55] A major emphasis of the Psalm is David's experience of the inescapable, interrogating presence of God to him in particular. And when David declares to God, "O Lord, you have searched me and known me!" he is too specific as to how God searches and knows him for one to object that the Psalm should be taken as a reference to the life and moral self-awareness of a community:

> You know when I sit down and when I rise up;
> you discern my thoughts from afar.
> You search out my path and my lying down
> and are acquainted with all my ways.
> Even before a word is on my tongue,
> Behold, O Lord, you know it altogether.[56]

The singularity of the individual before God is here unmistakable. And a central point of the Psalm is not simply that God's omniscience and omnipresence entail a direct relation to each person, that everything a person does God knows because God is present to each person. David's concern is ultimately the quality of his life before God, and he calls on God to share with him what God knows about the quality of his life. David tells us that God has searched and known him, continues to search and know him, and will always search and know him. Having declared to God all the many and various ways God knows everything about David, David then asks God: "Search me, O God, and know my heart; test me and know my thoughts. See if there is any wicked way in me and lead me in the way everlasting."[57] After everything David has said about God in the Psalm, this final request seems redundant. It seems odd that he would ask God, who he clearly describes as the searcher and knower of his heart, to search and know his heart. But what David

---

54. Barth, *Ethics*, 484, 463, 495.
55. Ps. 139:13.
56. Ps. 139:2-4.
57. Ps. 139: 23-24. Given that here alone we can count six first person possessive pronouns in a direct address to God, surely we can question the responsibility of saying we should give up all talk of Christians as individuals.

is doing here is examining himself with God prayerfully in God's presence. He is telling us that we know ourselves rightly when we draw near to the one before whom we are fully transparent. David's prayer could be paraphrased like this: you have searched me and known me God, now disclose me to myself, allow me to know myself with you so that I might live well in your sight.[58] And all this implies, again, a singular relation to God—a moral accountability directly before God that cannot be reduced to or sublimated in a moral accountability before a community. In a related context, this certainly appears to be the implication of God's words to Samuel, as Samuel searches for Israel's next king, telling Samuel quite clearly that for God to see the heart is to know a person in a way other people cannot.[59] And so, applied to Psalm 139, for a person to know her heart with God is to know herself in a way that is distinct from how she knows herself in relation to other people and how other people might condition her to know herself. As a Psalm there is, of course, something corporate going on here; there must be some axis between the individual drawing before God in self-examination and the life of the community that recites or sings the Psalm together. We will consider this corporate-individual axis later in the chapter. For the moment, we should not miss the clear singularity of the individual before God the Psalm presents.

In the Sermon on the Mount Jesus likewise draws attention to the singularity of the individual before God, who sees the individual in a relation of distinct moral accountability.[60] A refrain as Jesus discusses such things as a person's charity, wealth, and piety is that God sees the person's "secret" intention,[61] or as it is clear from the context, God sees the heart.[62] And the emphasis on God seeing what is "secret" certainly would seem to suggest a relation in which a person is singled out before God—God sees this person in particular at a remove from the group. Jesus's counsel, as with the pattern of Psalm 139, is that a person should therefore withdraw to a solitary place to be before God who sees the heart. The Lord's Prayer makes for an interesting example of this exhortation to prayerful self-examination before God, since the prayer is framed in the collective, "Our Father in heaven ... Give us this day our daily bread ... Forgive us our sins," and

---

58. Likewise, Augustine writes, "May I know you, who know me. May I 'know as I also am known' (1 Cor. 13:12)." This sharing of self-knowledge appears to be what Augustine claims is "the benefit I derive from making confession to you." He does not allow himself, when he comes before God in this way, to hide from himself by hiding from God (*Confessions*, 10.2.2., p. 178).

59. 1 Samuel 16:7

60. In concert with the argument of this paragraph is Richard Bauckham's assessment of the Gospel of John as not excluding the importance of corporate life but as also pointing clearly and consistently to the "individual experience that is not reducible to the corporate" (Bauckham, *Gospel of Glory*, 19).

61. Matthew 6:4, 6, 18.

62. Matthew 5:8, 6:21, 15:18-20; See also Luke 16:15, "You are those who justify yourselves before men. But God knows your heart."

so on.[63] But while framed in the collective, Jesus prefaces his instruction with the exhortation, "whenever you pray, go into your room and shut the door and pray to your Father who is in secret; and your Father who sees in secret will reward you."[64] The directness of this private, transactional (to be somewhat crude) interaction is striking. But what is also noteworthy is that the only commentary Jesus offers immediately following this prayer has the inevitable effect of directing the one who prays to solitary, inward self-reflection: "For if you forgive others their trespasses, your heavenly Father will also forgive you."[65] What Jesus means here about the nature of God's forgiveness is up for debate; but there is a clear dynamic Jesus presents in this instruction about how to pray: if you go into your room, draw near the one who sees you in secret, and pray in the way Jesus suggests, then you, alone in your room with the door shut,[66] will be confronted with this "if." In other words, as with Psalm 139, Jesus directs the individual to draw near the one who sees in secret in a way that must result in the individual acquiring some transparency about herself, since she cannot pray in secret for God's forgiveness without also being confronted before God about her own willingness to forgive others. To pray as Jesus instructs, that is, involves the individual coming before God in a manner that leads to self-disclosure; it involves, we can plausibly say, a submission before God to have one's heart searched and known.[67]

Psalm 139 and the Sermon on the Mount are not explicitly about conscience but about the heart. Similar references to the heart throughout the Hebrew Bible, though, nicely foreshadow and ground early Christian views about conscience as an individual's singular moral self-awareness before God. Martin van Creveld finds a litany of passages in which the heart acts as a site of self-disclosure before God, such as "The Lord examines hearts and kidneys," and "O Lord of hosts, that judges righteously, that triest the reins and the heart."[68] Van Creveld concludes that the heart exists as a locus of a person's direct accountability before God, as that place within the person that "Lord can look right into ... and will know what sinners have done regardless of how hard they work at concealing their thoughts."[69] In other words, there is a close conceptual proximity between the heart and the conscience as we have been considering it. This close conceptual proximity is further evident in the way the Septuagint renders the Hebrew of Job's claim, "My heart does not reproach me for any of my days,"[70] as "I do not know with myself

---

63. Mt. 6:9-13.

64. Mt. 6:6, emphasis mine.

65. Mt. 6:14.

66. Mt. 6:6.

67. One might say that this is obviously a very Kierkegaardian gloss on the Sermon on the Mount and the Lord's Prayer, but equally we might reply that Kierkegaard's theology bears a strong imprint of this Synoptic Gospels' theme of the individual in secret before God.

68. Psalm 26:2; Jeremiah 11:20. Quoted in Martin Van Creveld, *Conscience: A Biography* (London: Reaktion Books, 2015), 15.

69. Van Creveld, *Conscience*, 15.

70. Job 27:6.

that I have done anything amiss."[71] Paul Lehmann argues that what we see in Job is indicative of the Hebrew Bible more broadly, that the heart acts as a semantic equivalent of conscience as "the nexus of human responsibility;" consequently, the moral self-awareness ascribed in the Hebrew Bible to the heart lays a foundation for the direct, intimate, and personal knowledge later associated with conscience.[72] And we see this impulse to make conscience and the heart more or less equivalent when Origin, for example, translates the *kardia* of 1 Jn 3:21, "if our hearts [*kardia*] do not condemn us, we have confidence before God," as "conscience."[73] Indeed, Origin's translation is in concert with general patristic idea about conscience, which, according to Oliver O'Donovan, was "that of an inner created space within the seat of human agency, the heart."[74] Having surveyed a broad range of patristic theologians, O'Donovan finds the essence of their understanding of conscience as the individual's "self-opening to the probing interrogation and challenge of an encounter with God."[75]

This patristic consensus was no innovation; rather it is a faithful reflection of the New Testament's presentation of the individual in judgment before God. My aim here is still the prefatory one to defend the claim that the notion of an individual distinctly before God is not a modern innovation but is rather quite fundamental in early Christian literature.[76] And now we can see how that idea comes to inform a conception of conscience as an individual's moral self-awareness. Resonant with Augustine's claim above that God cares for each person as though the only one in God's care, 1 Peter describes God as one who "judges each one's work impartially."[77] Likewise Paul, defending his apostolic credentials, tells the Corinthian church, "I care very little if I am judged by you or by any human court ... It is the Lord who judges me."[78] The passage is a bit difficult for our purposes, in all fairness, as Paul also says, "I do not even judge myself. My conscience is clear, but that does not make me innocent. It is the Lord who judges me." Paul's point is perhaps that the judgment of conscience is provisional before the judgment of God, which is absolute. And so in a literal sense, only God truly judges and what goes on in conscience is an indirect and approximate judgment. This would make for a helpful corroboration to the interpretation of Kant's theory of conscience as an approximation of divine judgment, but it's also not entirely clear that is Paul's meaning. But what is very clear from the passage is that the

---

71. Lehmann, *Ethics*, 352.
72. Lehmann, *Ethics*, 352–3.
73. Cited in van Creveld, *Conscience*, 50.
74. O'Donovan, *Ways*, 305.
75. O'Donovan, *Ways*, 305.
76. Indeed, as Bauckham argues, "in the perspective of Christian history, there is nothing strange about a focus on the individual's intimacy" with God (Bauckham, *Gospel of Glory*, 19).
77. 1 Pet. 1:17.
78. 1 Cor. 4:3-4.

judgment of the particular ecclesial community—or any human community—is distinct from the judgment of God. Paul insists that the two judgments are distinct and that his standing—his singular standing, I might add—before God is the one that matters most of all.

The singularity of the individual's moral self-awareness before God in conscience is also manifest in Paul's reflection on the freedom of conscience in his discussion about eating meat sacrificed to idols. Paul writes,

> But if someone says to you, "This has been offered in sacrifice," then do not eat it, both for the sake of the one who told you and for the sake of conscience. I am referring to the other person's conscience, not yours. For why is my freedom being judged by another's conscience? If I take part in the meal with thankfulness, why am I denounced because of something I thank God for?[79]

Relatedly, in Romans Paul explains,

> One person considers one day more sacred than another; another considers every day alike. Each of them should be fully convinced in their own mind. ... You, then, why do you judge your brother or sister? Or why do you treat them with contempt? For we will all stand before God's judgment seat. ... So then, each of us will give an account of ourselves to God.[80]

It is at the very least plausible to conclude from both passages that God's judgment of the individual is distinct from the judgment of any other person—and I think we can add, any community of persons—and that this entails the singularity of the individual's standing before God, before whom, Paul insists, we must each give an account of ourselves. Communal mediation of God's judgment and the individual's moral accountability and self-awareness feel quite alien to these texts. Paul is talking here about liturgical rites, and in particular about a certain social practice (eating meat) as it pertains to liturgy and the sacred. But about such a practice, he is clear, it is not the community's consensus, if there were one, that is authoritative, but what each person is convinced of "in their own mind." The context of this passage is Paul's association of conscience and the individual's assurance before God. As Herman Ridderbos explains in his helpful commentary, "freedom in Christ is mirrored in the conscience as the believer knows himself to have been cleansed from sin and in what he does receives the assurance of being blameless before God."[81] And by "before God," Ridderbos means that this Pauline individual is distinctly before God and not any human community. Freedom of conscience, that is, makes the individual "independent of the judgment of men (1 Cor.

---

79. 1 Cor. 10:28-30.
80. Rom. 14:5, 10-12.
81. Ridderbos, *Paul: An Outline of His Theology* (Grand Rapids, MI: Eerdmans, 1975), 292.

10:29) and consists positively in inner certainty (Rom. 14:5), in not condemning oneself."[82] In short, freedom of conscience entails a person's consciousness of being "bound to God" in a way that sets him apart from the human community, giving him the ability to discern for himself before God the moral quality of his actions in variable, morally unclear circumstances.[83]

Conscience as Tribunal and Self-Testimony

It is hopefully clear at this point that there is a strong and persistent biblical and early theological testimony to the singularity of the individual before God, that God knows and judges each individual distinctly and that conscience in some way draws a person before God and engenders moral self-awareness. But now we can turn more specifically to how conscience works. What does it mean that conscience opens a person to "to the probing interrogation and challenge of an encounter with God." Paul's famous account of the Gentiles in Romans 2 gives some indication. He writes,

> For it is not those who hear the law who are righteous in God's sight, but it is those who obey the law who will be declared righteous. (Indeed, when Gentiles, who do not have the law, do by nature things required by the law, they are a law for themselves, even though they do not have the law. They show that the requirements of the law are written on their hearts, their consciences also bearing witness, their thoughts sometimes accusing them and at other times even defending them.) This will take place on the day when God judges people's secrets through Jesus Christ, as my gospel declares.[84]

Paul begins the chapter introducing the idea of God's wrath, which will be visited upon "each person according to what they have done."[85] Those with an "unrepentant heart" are in an especially precarious position (and there is a clear parallel between the heart and conscience in the chapter).[86] God will judge lawlessness with wrath (whatever that might mean), Paul writes. The judgment comes from God, from outside the person in response to the life that person lives before God. But, Paul continues, there is also something internal, something within a person that responds to the moral quality of a person's actions. And Paul calls this internal, self-reflexive judgment "conscience." C. A. Pierce's paraphrase of Paul is helpful: "'And even more than [God's wrath],' Paul goes on to say, 'have I not met, universal among the Gentiles, this plainly valid experience of conscience, the internal counterpart

---

82. Ridderbos, *Paul*, 292.
83. Ridderbos, *Paul*, 292.
84. Rom. 2:13-16
85. Rom. 2:6.
86. Rom. 2:5

and compliment of [God's judgment], which adds its vital testimony to my present contention?'"[87] Pierce is clear that conscience here for Paul—and in the New Testament generally—represents a self-disclosing "moral reflex" within a person that reacts to a person's actions as that person lives before God.[88] The image, then, is of a reality external to the human being and a corresponding internal reaction. God sees the person's heart, singles the person out, sees the person in secret, and passes judgment; and within the person there is this experience of conscience that somehow corresponds to this experience with God. Conscience directs a person to this judgment, reminds her of it, making her aware, as Ridderbos writes, that she is "bound to a divine standard of judgment standing above [her], by which [she] is to measure [herself]."[89] There is the relation to God, then, on the one hand, the singularity of a person's moral standing before God; and, on the other hand, there is the conscience within the person making a person aware of that relation, making her aware of the moral quality of her actions as she lives before God. There is a parallel in the passage, that is, between conscience as it accuses and defends a person and God as God "judges people's secrets."

It is on this Pauline basis that we can understand conscience as a kind of internal, judicial, reflexive self-awareness, or as a kind of tribunal within a person in which she is disclosed to herself. In this respect Calvin finds it necessary to describe conscience as a "forum" in which a person finds herself as a defendant before "a sense of the divine justice ... as a witness which ... does not allow them to hide their sins ... but hales [them] before God's judgment."[90] Like a "guardian," Calvin writes, conscience does not allow a person to hide from wrongdoings, to let them "remain buried in darkness. Hence the ancient proverb, 'Conscience is a thousand witnesses.'"[91] Likewise, we find anticipations of Calvin's "forum" and "sentinel" language in John Chrysostom who asks, "Why has God set in the mind of every one of us such a continuously watchful and sober judge? I mean the conscience. For there is no judge, no judge at all among men as sleepless as our conscience."[92] Even when social sources of accountability fail, Chrysostom writes, this judge within will not let us off the hook: "Even if a long time passes, the conscience never forgets what has happened" and maintains its prosecutorial role.[93] We may not always feel its presence very keenly, he explains, especially when we are in the midst of some immoral action, but its testimony will come nonetheless.[94] Augustine also casts

---

87. C. A. Pierce, *Conscience in the New Testament* (London: SCM Press, 1955), 85.

88. Pierce, *Conscience in the New Testament*, 113, on conscience as "moral reflex," see 111-13 on the correspondence of conscience to God's judgment and as focused on specific acts.

89. Ridderbos, *Paul*, 288.

90. Calvin, *Institutes*, III.19.15, p. 848.

91. Calvin, *Institutes*, III.19.15, p. 848.

92. Chrysostom, *Wealth and Poverty*, 88.

93. Chrysostom, *Wealth and Poverty*, 88.

94. Chrysostom, *Wealth and Poverty*, 88.

conscience in this role of internal, self-disclosing witness, remembering when "the day had come when I should be naked to myself and my conscience complained within me;" he describes conscience as gnawing at him, witnessing against him so that he became filled with a guilty self-awareness.[95]

It is clear that this forum has to do with how an individual finds himself accountable before God, but what is also implied is that this forum involves a kind of self-dialogue or self-testimony. Chrysostom, for instance, describes conscience in terms of "self-accusation and self-condemnation," and says that the person "who commits sin condemns himself."[96] Calvin describes conscience as existing "between God and man, not suffering man to suppress within himself what he knows."[97] William Ames, following Calvin, makes the self-dialogue aspect of conscience even more explicit, claiming that conscience entails a person's "judgment of himself, according to the judgment of God."[98] It is also in this vein that Kierkegaard describes conscience as the place where "you as a single individual relate yourself to yourself before God."[99] And, again, Paul is in the background, associating conscience with our own thoughts that accuse or defend us as we stand before God in judgment. Conscience is about a person's moral self-awareness in relation to God, that is, and this entails a person's relation to himself, his own testimony about himself to himself before God.

What I want to affirm is that conscience is both a person's singular self-disclosing encounter before God and a self-disclosing testimony or witness to herself. Or, rather, part of what it means for conscience to be a singular self-disclosure before God, to be a sharing with God in God's knowledge of us, is that it entails this aspect of self-dialogue or testimony. Kant's theory of conscience can be helpful here because of his systematic treatment of conscience in both of these senses. He is careful to distinguish, that is, how conscience functions practically as a person's encounter with or testimony to herself and how this testimony also qualifies as a person's moral self-awareness before God. To make this point clear, I will retrace some of the most salient aspects of the earlier treatment of Kant's theory of conscience. Recall Kant's definition of conscience as an "internal judge" that observes and threatens and keeps a person in "awe," respectful of the moral law.[100] Sounding much like Chrysostom, Kant explains that conscience watches over a person from within but also, so it seems, without that person's consent—conscience is there whether she likes it or not. She might try to ignore conscience but it will not stop its prosecution, and however hard she tries to block it, the testimony of conscience will, even if only occasional, break through.[101] Conscience

---

95. Augustine, *Confessions*, 8.7.18, p. 145.
96. Chrysostom, *Wealth and Poverty*, 90, 88.
97. Calvin, *Institutes*, III.19.15, p. 848.
98. Ames *Conscience*, 1.
99. *UDVS*, 129.
100. *Metaphysics of Morals*, 6:438.
101. *Metaphysics of Morals*, 6:438.

is part of our being, a constituent aspect of human nature, Kant claims, but we experience it as if it were someone else, as if it were a kind of internal judge who has called a court to hear the arguments of the prosecutor and the advocate.[102] It feels like an encounter with an "actual or a merely ideal person" within us but it is, in fact, a person our own reason "creates for itself."[103] Conscience is a "business," he writes, we have with ourselves, even if it is an involuntary business we are "constrained" to "carry out ... as at the bidding of another person."[104] We do not have any control over conscience—it comes to us willy-nilly—but it is nonetheless our own testimony to ourselves accusing or defending us in our actions.

It is our own testimony to ourselves, Kant insists, but curiously, we should not think of the other we encounter in conscience either as ourselves or as an abstract generic other, but as a being like God, as a judge with authority and with the power to search the heart and to see the quality of a person's conformity to the moral law. And so it is best to view conscience as "the subjective principle of being accountable to God for all one's deeds."[105] Kant concludes that God "in fact ... is always contained in the moral self-awareness of conscience."[106] Kant does not mean, though, that conscience is God's voice, or that the experience of conscience warrants belief in God, or that belief in God is necessary to be conscientious.[107] To understand our experience of conscience in terms of accountability before God is a helpful way to understand our accountability to an absolute, universal moral standard.[108] So conscience is our testimony to ourselves, but, precisely because Kant wants to avoid licensing the kind of banal, individualistic moral relativism figures like MacIntyre and Hauerwas attribute to him, he insists that we should think of the judgment of conscience as if it were God's judgment. We should think of the judgment of conscience as if it were the judgment of a being whose will is in perfect conformity with the moral law, which, as rational beings, we know as the "fact of reason,"[109] but which, as creatures of sensible inclinations, we do not necessarily follow.[110] And so imagining our testimony to ourselves as the judgment of God is, for Kant, a psychologically useful analogy to help us understand what is going on in our conscience, to understand the nature of our accountability before a moral standard that holds for all.

And yet Kant believes in God and argues that we have good grounds to believe God exists as the searcher and knower of our hearts, as the "authorized judge of conscience." I will not retrace Kant's moral argument for the existence of God.

---

102. *Lectures*, 132.
103. *Metaphysics of Morals*, 6:438.
104. *Metaphysics of Morals*, 6:438.
105. *Metaphysics of Morals*, 6:438; cf. *Religion*, 6:99.
106. *Metaphysics of Morals*, 6:438; cf. *Religion*, 6:99.
107. *Metaphysics of Morals*, 6:439.
108. *Metaphysics of Morals*, 6:439.
109. *Practical Reason*, 5:31.
110. *Groundwork*, 4:414.

What is important now is that Kant insists that we are "driven to believe" in God as the "moral ruler" of the world;[111] and while what we can know about God is limited by human morality, we nonetheless can know something about God and should believe in God as the giver of the moral law, as the "holy guardian" of the human race, and as the judge of our actions.[112] "Reason, heart and conscience all teach this" about God, Kant concludes, "and drive us to it."[113] Kant's theory of conscience, then, provides a way to understand how conscience brings us before "the bar of God," to use Calvin's phrase, and how it consists of our own testimony to ourselves. Kant's theory of conscience asks us to hold together our own judgment of ourselves, our own "self-accusation," as Chrysostom holds, and God's judgment of us. In conscience our own practical reason "creates for itself" the judge of our actions, but, at the same time, Kant insists conscience represents "the divine judgment seat; it weighs our dispositions and actions in the scale of a law which is holy and pure; we cannot deceive it, and lastly we cannot escape it, because, like the divine omnipresence it is always with us."[114] In our conscience we are disclosed to ourselves by our own accusation and defense as if we were being disclosed before God as the "scrutinizer of hearts," and we should believe that God indeed exists as the one who scrutinizes our hearts. Kant's theory of conscience accounts for something like William Ames's claim that conscience is a person's self-judgment that accords with God's judgment. In other words, for Kant conscience is the principle of our accountability before God for all our actions because it is through our conscience that we strive to judge ourselves according to God's actual judgment of us.[115] We each exist before an omnipresent God who holds us each singularly accountable, who sees our hearts in secret, and in our conscience we endorse what we take this judgment to be. It is by means of our conscience that we search ourselves in an effort to know ourselves as we are known by the "one who knows the heart" and who judges "the worth of [our] actions."[116] Kant's theory of conscience, in sum, provides a way to construe the juxtaposition Paul presents: "we all stand before God's judgment seat," and therefore we must each "give an account of ourselves to God."[117]

The Passive Experience of Conscience and the Activity of Conscientiousness

Giving an account of ourselves indicates an activity or voluntariness about conscience. But I also noted earlier Kant's claim that conscience is an involuntary

111. *Religion*, 6:139.
112. *Religion*, 6:139.
113. *Religion*, 6:144–145.
114. *Lectures*, 133.
115. *Metaphysics of Morals*, 6:438.
116. *Religion*, 6:99.
117. Rom. 14:10, 12.

business that we are "constrained" to carry out. The image of conscience as something that "will not desist," as Chrysostom describes it, that follows us like our shadows is also an image of us in flight from our conscience as it testifies to us, whether we like it or not (and the idea is that we often do not like it). In this vein, H. Richard Niebuhr explains that the others we encounter in our conscience are "unbidden" and that "the self does not have the power over them to fashion them in its own image."[118] And this makes sense of Paul's account of conscience as our own thoughts accusing and defending us, not letting us off the hook in our actions before God. Of course, as a testimony or witness, conscience is something we are meant to hear. We can ignore it and try to numb ourselves to its verdicts, which is how we can understand 1 Timothy's description of conscience as "seared with a hot iron."[119] Kant claims we can try to stun ourselves or put ourselves to sleep.[120] But we can also stop and listen to conscience. Listening to conscience is an action we can decide to do. It is in this regard that Kierkegaard claims that while conscience is something everyone has, it is also something everyone must "will to have."[121] Conscientiousness, in other words, is a strenuous achievement.[122] Conscience bears witness to us whether we like it or not, but conscientiousness is also an activity we can freely undertake.

Considering the relation between conscience and moral feeling can help illustrate the passive experience of conscience and the activity of conscientiousness. Kant holds that conscience is distinct from moral feeling but that it provokes moral feeling within us.[123] In this vein, Pierce explains that across the New Testament, in the Pauline epistles especially, conscience is consistently depicted as causing the pain of guilt when a person acts badly.[124] Conscience is not itself the guilt but is its source. Guilt is the moral feeling most frequently associated with conscience in the New Testament, though conscience is also qualified in terms of more positive moral feelings, as "clear," "clean," "purified," "perfected," or "good" when a person has feelings assurance before God.[125] We cannot help having these moral feelings—we cannot help it when we feel guilty. But we can help whether or not we will pay attention to those feelings. And, as Kant argues, when we do actively consider

---

118. Niebuhr, "The Ego Alter Dialectic and the Conscience," 355.

119. 1 Tim. 4:2.

120. *Metaphysics of Morals*, 6:438.

121. *JFY*, 91.

122. *JP*, 1:320. Likewise, he explains, every person has a conscience but everyone nonetheless must become "equipped ... with a conscience" (*JP*, 1:321).

123. *Metaphysics of Morals*, 6:401. Pierce explains that across the New Testament conscience is consistently depicted as causing the pain of guilt when a person acts badly (54, 112). It is not itself the guilt but is its source. Guilt is not the only moral feeling conscience evokes in the New Testament—conscience is also described in terms of assurance, as "good" (1 Tim. 1:19), "clean" (Heb. 10:22), and "clear" (1 Cor. 4:4).

124. Pierce, *Conscience in the New Testament*, 54, 112.

125. Rom. 9:1, 1 Tim. 1:5, 3:9; 2 Tim. 1:3; Heb. 9:14, 13:18; 1 Pet. 3:16.

them and follow them down to their source what we find is the testimony of our conscience about the moral quality of our particular actions.[126]

Kierkegaard describes this dynamic in terms of "becoming guilty." Kierkegaard is less systematic than Kant and seems to associate conscience and the experience of guilt (or, what is the same for him, regret and shame) more closely; it's not entirely clear, that is, when he describes regret and guilt as a "voice," if this voice is a guise conscience puts on or if regret and guilt are more like heralds of conscience.[127] For the sake of clarity I will assume Kierkegaard means guilt and its cognates are heralds that direct a person to conscience. His point is generally the same as Kant's, that a person has an involuntary experience of guilt and then should voluntarily follow that feeling down to the testimony of her conscience. Kierkegaard's claim is that each of us is a pilgrim traveling either on the road of the good or on the road of perdition.[128] To go astray from the good is always a danger, but as an aid against this danger, Kierkegaard argues, regret is given as a guide; in fact, he claims, "if the voice of this guide is never heard, then it is precisely because the way of perdition is being followed."[129] Regret is so significant in this regard, Kierkegaard writes, "that there is nothing more terrible than to have escaped it entirely."[130]

The experience of guilt is an involuntary encounter, but Kierkegaard does not construe guilt only in these passive terms. He insists of regret, for example, that it "must be an *action* with a collected mind."[131] Actively to regret is to heed regret's call and to make the step back to the good.[132] The person who actively regrets, in this regard, makes use of the experience of guilt as a "safeguard" for "the journey." The "casual traveler" is someone who goes about his life in a hasty and unreflective way and so he "does not get to know" the road he is on in the same way as the person who regrets, "the traveler with his burden."[133] This person who actively regrets does so by "laboriously" gathering "up the experience."[134] The person who regrets, that is, collects himself, gathers up his experience of guilt,[135] considers

---

126. *Lectures*, 133. We can see how conscience itself is not, according to Kant, moral feeling since moral feeling is something we can deaden. Conscience pronounces a verdict that wants me to feel guilty, but I may ignore the feeling and, consequently, ignore the verdict. But if I keep ignoring the feeling, the feeling eventually will weaken and perhaps vanish altogether. But conscience itself, Kant insists, will continue to pass its verdict whether I feel badly about my action or not.

127. *UDVS*, 13.

128. The language of being on the road toward or away from the good appears throughout "An Occasional Discourse," but see, especially, 16–19.

129. *UDVS*, 13.

130. *UDVS*, 13.

131. *UDVS*, 16.

132. *UDVS*, 14.

133. *UDVS*, 14.

134. *UDVS*, 14.

135. *UDVS*, 14. It is not entirely clear what the referent is for "experience" or "burden" in this passage, but the most plausible interpretation is that it is regret.

his life,[136] and in this way actively fosters the "deep inwardness of concern" that "vividly" sets his guilt before him.[137] A person's conscience pricks him with "the sanctity of shame" when he avoids his responsibility before God,[138] and the great temptation that person feels is to hide from conscience.[139] If regret serves a person as a "rescuing attendant,"[140] then for a person to heed regret's call and not avoid it would indicate a person's admission that he indeed has something to regret, that his guilty feelings are on the mark because he has acted badly. In other words, regret and shame as subjective feelings of guilt mean to bring a person before the objective reality of his guilt, before the testimony of his conscience. And like a person who does not want to admit that certain symptoms might indicate a serious illness, the guilty person does not want to listen to the gnawing voices that direct him to his guilt.

But like a person whose only recourse to wellness is to acknowledge the symptoms of illness, the irresponsible person can only begin to move toward responsibility by first actively listening to her guilt and coming to grips with it. The task is actively to endure the disclosure of guilt, to "appropriate" the guilt,[141] or self-consciously to "increase the acknowledgment of guilt."[142] The passive experience of guilt should prompt a person to find stillness before God, where Kierkegaard claims she has her conscience,[143] so that she can then endorse her guilt. This is what Kierkegaard means in the repetition of his exhortation that a person must "become guilty" or "become a sinner."[144] In "An Occasional Discourse," Kierkegaard guides the reader through an array of questions to help her evaluate the quality of her life, but if the reader is taking the questions seriously, he insists these questions can only "sound like indictments."[145] What, then, is the reader to do? If she wants to act rightly as one with "responsibility before God," then she must first actively "endure this rigorous judgment of singularity."[146] When guilt arises in a person, then, the task it presents is not to run from it but actively to face it, to seek it, to follow it

---

136. *UDVS*, 127.

137. *UDVS*, 17.

138. *UDVS*, 45.

139. Kierkegaard, *Three Discourses on Imagined Occasions*, Kierkegaard's Writings, vol. 10 (Princeton, NJ: Princeton University Press, 1993), 11.

140. *UDVS*, 52.

141. Kierkegaard, *Three Discourses*, 37. On the significance of appropriation and the appropriation of guilt; see also *Three Discourses*, 21 and *UDVS*, 17.

142. Kierkegaard, *Three Discourses*, 29.

143. *TUD*, 11–12.

144. This exhortation suffuses *Three Discourses*. On "becoming a sinner," see *Three Discourses*, 28, 29, 31, and 36; on "becoming guilty," see 12, 14, and 40.

145. *UDVS*, 150.

146. *UDVS*, 150.

down from the pain it inflicts to conscience, the "sacred source" of that person's singularity before God.[147]

The point of this brief focus on moral feeling and the experience of guilt has been to draw attention to the way conscience entails both a passive experience and an activity. Conscience testifies to us about ourselves whether we like it or not; it prompts us with feelings of guilt or assurance that we cannot control. But we have a choice about whether or not we will listen to the testimony of our conscience and heed it; we have a choice about whether we will regard or ignore the moral feeling conscience prompts within us. With precedents like Romans 2 in view, the perspective that I have taken has been that to have a conscience is part and parcel of what it means to be a human being; to claim that someone does not have a conscience, that is, should be taken to mean that a person pays no heed to it, ignores it, or hides from it.[148] To refer again to Psalm 139 as an analogy and model for conscientiousness, a person is transparent before God, is searched and known by God, but then also actively should draw before God to be searched and known, to be self-disclosed.

There is another sense in which conscience is both a passive experience and an activity. Or, to be more precise, there is more to say about the activity of listening to conscience. To listen to conscience is to hear testimony about the moral quality of particular actions, but this particular disclosure then enables a person to discern the moral quality of her character. There is a movement, that is, from the knowledge of self in particular actions and a knowledge of self as a moral agent. The central idea at work in this conception of conscience and its role in self-knowledge is the tree that is known by its fruits.[149] The quality of fruit helps to disclose something fundamental about the tree. There is knowledge about the action, on the one hand, and there is more fundamental knowledge about ourselves, as moral agents, on the other hand. As we have seen, Kant and Kierkegaard present different versions of this act-person dynamic: Kant distinguishes conscience as the knowledge of the moral quality of a person's action from conscience as the means to a person's knowledge of her heart ("heart" understood here as a person's fundamental disposition, or character, as distinct from the earlier reflections on the language of the "heart" in earlier biblical literature as anticipating the language of "conscience" as it appears in later New Testament epistles). Kierkegaard likewise distinguishes the knowledge of the moral quality of particular actions and knowledge of a person's moral identity before God, but he locates both forms of knowledge within conscience itself. For both Kant and Kierkegaard, we might simply say that the movement from the particular knowledge about action to the broader knowledge about the person belongs to a more widely understood concept of conscientiousness.

---

147. Kierkegaard, *Three Discourses*, 35. The singular encounter with God is the source of the "sacred pain," the source of the guilt that is the root of a person's break from the self-deceived stance a person takes hiding in the crowd.

148. Cf. Timmerman, "Kant on Conscience," 297, 304. Cf. *Lectures*, 130.

149. Mt. 7:15-20; Lk. 6:43-45.

We find good precedent in the biblical testimony of this back-and-forth dynamic between conscience as knowledge about particular actions and conscience as somehow associated with a broader view of the person as a moral agent. On the one hand, it is as the individual confronts the prospect of a certain decision about eating meat sacrificed to idols, for instance, that conscience preemptively passes judgment.[150] And Paul certainly seems to construe conscience in a rather punctiliar, act-oriented way when he says conscience "sometimes" accuses and "other times" defends.[151] It is with respect to a particular misdeed that Paul writes, "if you do wrong, be afraid ... not only because of possible punishment but also as a matter of conscience."[152] But, on the other hand, there are instances where Paul's invocation of conscience appears more oriented to a broader understanding of himself before God, such as his declaration that his "conscience is clear" with respect to his apostolic authority.[153] Likewise, Paul later writes, "What we are is plain to God, and I hope it is also plain to your conscience."[154] The appeal to the other's conscience is a bit confusing, but there does seem to be a clear connection between personal identity ("what we are") and the conscience. In other words, taken with the related "clear conscience" of the earlier correspondence, it is quite plausible to read Paul's "I hope it is *also* plain to your conscience," as implying "as it is with ours." In short, the judgment of conscience pertains to particular actions, but it is also the case that conscience at the least has an association with a person's knowledge of something broader about his moral identity before God. Pierce proposes that the New Testament construal of conscience broadly is in reference first "to specific acts" and then "to character" as disclosed or "expressed in certain acts."[155] And it is in this vein that Kant claims that we can trust the verdicts of our conscience to provide us with a reliable means to "extract [the] disposition from the deed,"[156] "not directly" but approximately.[157] From the particular verdicts of our conscience, that is, "it must be possible to assume" the more fundamental disposition behind them.[158] What is common to both Kant and Kierkegaard, consistent with the biblical testimony, is that through our conscience we acquire knowledge about the moral quality of our actions in relation to God, and we can move from this knowledge toward a kind of knowledge of ourselves more broadly as moral agents in relation to God.

Kierkegaard's account of this movement from the particular to the general is also evident in his account of a person's need to "become guilty." A person

---

150. 1 Cor. 10:28.
151. Rom. 2:15.
152. Rom. 13:5.
153. 1 Cor. 4:4.
154. 2 Cor. 5:11.
155. Pierce, *Conscience in the New Testament*, 42.
156. *Religion*, 6:77.
157. *Religion*, 6:76.
158. *Religion*, 6:21, emphasis mine.

"becomes guilty," that is, not only by acknowledging the particular guilt but also by moving to a broader self-assessment. And, somewhat as an aside, I want to note that while this exhortation to such a negative global self-assessment appears morose, it is not exceptional. After all, the writer of 1 John exhorts his Christian audience always to remember, "if we say we have no sin, we are deceiving ourselves and the truth is not in us."[159] And it is in a late Pauline epistle that the Apostle Paul (or the Pauline persona) describes himself as the "greatest of sinners."[160] The fact of the lateness of this claim by an apostolic voice underscores the Christian witness, at least, to the ineradicable quality of a person's experience of guilt in this life. This is not to say this witness should have the last word, though as Jennifer Herdt argues, so long as it is set "within a broader context of global affirmation and acceptance,"[161] a range of Christian traditions still affirm the reality "that humans have failed globally to meet the moral standard and thus" that the experience of guilt and even shame—as a global self-assessment—"is appropriate."[162] It is appropriate, but as Kierkegaard writes, "you are not to withdraw and sit brooding over your eternal accounting."[163] Kierkegaard's point, like Kant's, is that a person can understand something fundamental about herself from the particular guilt, the particular testimony of conscience. But a person should not despair, ruminate, or brood. A good example here is the sober alcoholic who introduces herself at Alcoholics Anonymous, saying, "Hi I am so and so and I am alcoholic." She is not berating herself or confessing a regrettable bad action; rather, she is making a wise and admirable self-aware admission about herself in a global sense, a self-admission that helps steel her resolve to remain sober.

To summarize the theory of conscience I have outlined up to this point, it is a theory of conscience predicated on the idea that God knows and sees each individual distinctly and holds each individual accountable as such. Again, while Kant (like Hauerwas) rejects the idea of a personal, familiar relationship to God, his analogy that conscience is "like the divine omnipresence … always with us," is, as I have argued, complex but sincere. What we do in our conscience corresponds to what we should believe is the case in our direct moral relation to God. And as we saw for Kierkegaard, it is the "presence of God," that "changes everything."[164] For Kierkegaard (as for Paul and Augustine, and many others), God is always present to everyone, but the more you know that God is present to you, the more you become aware of the task, he claims, "before God of paying attention to yourself."[165] I have argued that this is indeed individualistic, but no more so

---

159. 1 Jn 1:8.

160. 1 Tim. 1:15.

161. Jennifer Herdt, "Guilt and Shame in the Development of Virtue," in *Developing the Virtues: Integrating Perspectives*, ed. Julia Annas, Darcia Navarez, and Nancy E. Snow (New York: Oxford University Press, 2016), 250.

162. Herdt, "Guilt and Shame," 250.

163. *UDVS*, 137.

164. *UDVS*, 125.

165. *UDVS*, 125.

than the individualism apparent as Jesus tells his audience to remove themselves from the crowd to be before God who sees them in secret, or Paul's assertion that God's direct judgment of him is distinct from and trumps the judgment of any human community, or his claim that each must give an account before God, or Peter's corresponding claim that God judges each of us impartially, or Augustine's claim that God cares for each person as if the only one in God's care. I could keep going with this litany, but I think I have made the point. One might object that these texts are more complicated or could accommodate a more communitarian interpretation, but that does seem to bear a heavy burden of proof. The plain sense of these texts, the sense that passes through Kant's and Kierkegaard's theory of conscience, is that God knows each individual and holds each individual singularly accountable for the life she lives before God, and that as such each individual has the capacity to share with God in God's knowledge of her. Finally, it should be clear, at this point, that the theory of conscience I am outlining here, drawing from Kant and Kierkegaard and a broader biblical and theological tradition, is not about self-assertion but submission. Kant and Kierkegaard both present theories of conscience, in line with the biblical and patristic and later theological sources we have considered, that have to do with the individual in conscience approximating, appropriating, or endorsing God's judgment. They assume that the individual is not accountable to herself but singularly accountable to God and in conscience she holds herself accountable as a way to share in God's judgment.

Conscience against Self-Deception

An important implication of an individual having the capacity to share with God in God's knowledge of her has to do with the how an individual can make a drastic change of course in life, how, that is, an individual repents from one way of life and converts to another. To repent from one way of life or course of actions and convert to another is an intrinsically self-reflective activity. There must be some realization that what I am doing, how I am living, and, consequently, who I am fundamentally is, to a certain extent, a lie—that I have been deceiving myself. There is, therefore, an individualistic aspect of repentance and conversion that commends the theory of conscience I am outlining. I realize that what I thought was good and right to do, or what I took for granted as fine to do, turns out actually not to be good and right or fine to do. And so I find myself at a point where I want to distance myself from what I did and who I was, and, perhaps, also from the people with whom I lived as that kind of person. This is why Kant and Kierkegaard—and the way of thinking about conscience they represent—associate conscience with repentance and conversion. I will come back to repentance and conversion shortly. What precedes them—or what is a person's first act in this movement—is the person's fight against self-deception, and conscience here plays a crucial role. There are different forms and degrees of self-deception, but two very basic forms of self-deception we will consider concern how a person either does not realize an immoral action is in fact immoral or does not realize a moral action was committed for immoral reasons.

It is possible for a person's own right actions to be sources of self-deception, to mask a discord between ostensibly good actions and a corrupt center of agency.[166] Jesus has plenty to say, for instance, about those whose outward appearance of righteousness conceals an inner self-serving immorality.[167] An act's intention matters, in other words. In this vein, recall Kant's conviction that we are especially prone to self-deception about the moral quality of our hearts when our actions make us appear good in the eyes of others. We can be easily self-deceived about the moral quality of our hearts by our good deeds.[168] We can act morally, Kant explains, but if we really consider what is behind our actions, we constantly find selfish motives.[169] A person can act rightly and have good morals but not necessarily be a morally good person.[170] For one reason or another a person might rarely find himself in a position where he is tempted to lie, cheat, or steal and might think of himself for those reasons as an exemplary person. And it is quite possible, Kant claims, that such a person, most likely unwittingly, uses his formally good life conduct to hide an immoral heart from others and from himself.

But Kant is clear that this is precisely where conscience is so important because its verdicts extend to the intention behind the action and so the selfish person of good morals will not go without internal testimony to his selfishness; he will not go without some awareness that there is a gap between his outward moral self-presentation and his inner self-serving intention and disposition. I gave the example in an earlier chapter of a father who wants to do what is right for his children and, after much deliberation, decides to send his children to a good private school. But inwardly he also relishes a host of selfish reasons for this decision, reasons pertaining to the status and respect he gains indirectly by sending his children to the good school. Kant insists that such a person will hear the voice of his conscience, even if he has become fairly deaf or aloof to it. He will wake up "from time to time" and hear its testimony against him in these outwardly good actions (trying to give your children a good education) that carry selfish intentions.[171] This is in the same spirit as Paul's suggestion that the witness of conscience renders all without excuse or Chrysostom's claim that however often conscience bears witness, "whether it

---

166. We are not considering the person who says or ostensibly believes some conduct is immoral but nonetheless frequently acts in just that way (e.g., the religious conservative who is outspoken about the immorality of extramarital sex who is also cheating on his spouse). We are assuming, as Kant does, that the person who both professes some behavior to be moral and whose action is consistent with that belief has a greater likelihood of self-deception, since the behavior can more easily mask a selfish intention. We are taking for granted that the more willful hypocrite who says one thing and does another is, or at least at some point has been, quite morally self-aware of the hypocrisy.
167. e.g., Mt. 6:1-4, 6:16-18, 7:21-23, 15:7-9 23:27-28.
168. *Religion*, 6:68.
169. *Groundwork*, 4:407.
170. *Religion*, 6:31.
171. *Metaphysics of Morals*, 6:438.

speaks once or twice or three times or innumerable times, and you do not pay attention, it will speak again, and will not desist until your last breath."[172] Likewise, for Kant, the possibility of conscientious self-disclosure is always possible, making the hypocrisy of the person of good morals at least a semi-conscious activity for which he is responsible.[173]

To be fair, it is not entirely clear that this way of understanding conscience as exposing a person's covert incentives requires a commitment to conscience as a person's singular moral self-awareness; it is not clear, that is, that it requires a commitment to thinking about the self-disclosure of conscience as doing something other than making a person aware of the gap between how he is acting and the social role that has been given to him. If a person's moral identity comes into being through the life of a particular community and if his conscience is understood as his internalization of that community's ethos or norms, there's no reason to think his conscience could not expose his covert incentives and in that way disclose him to himself. Take, again, the example of the father who wants to ensure his children get a good education but who covertly relishes the personal advantages that might accrue to him by sending his children to private school. It might be, however, that he comes from a family and a community that consistently manifest a love of learning for its own sake and a vibrant commitment to the intellectual life as intrinsically valuable for the common good and for a happy life. Consequently, as he finds within himself these selfish reasons for sending his kids to a good private school for a good education, he will also encounter in his conscience the figure of some other, a family member or former teacher or mentor, who will represent this ethos that calls such selfishness into question. The other in his conscience will make him aware that his incentives for acting in this particular way are out of sync with the community that shaped him.

The problem for such a social theory of conscience, though, is that it has a difficult time accounting for the way communities themselves can be sources of self-deception. It strikes me as self-evident that life within certain groups can make us quite comfortable doing things we would be much warier doing if we were alone. This is Kierkegaard's point when he imagines a gathering of people who say to each other, " 'Lets be part of a group,' for if we are part of a group it means good-night to conscience. We cannot be two or three, a Miller Brothers and Company around a conscience."[174] In this vein, recall, Kant insists that we have a propensity to "corrupt each other's moral dispositions and make one another evil."[175] Kant might sound like he is describing us as much more self-consciously malicious than he intends. What he means is that we are quite capable of slowly and tacitly training each other, through our life together, to see our shared vices as virtues, or at least as non-vicious. So long as my vice is "common to a class,"

---

172. Chrysostom, *Wealth and Poverty*, 89–99.
173. Despland, "Can Conscience Be Hypocritical," 366.
174. *JP*, 2:417.
175. *Religion*, 6:93.

I can eventually come to regard it as not really a vice.[176] This is the danger of what Kant calls "self-incurred minority," when a person allows others to determine for her what counts as virtuous behavior, when contingent customs are confused for moral norms.[177] Kierkegaard, likewise, worries about this confusion of social custom and a person's moral responsibility. There is a very common form of social life, "the crowd," that encourages a person to see the "demand of the times" as the good to be done.[178] Kierkegaard therefore depicts "the crowd" as a place where a person hides from her genuine moral responsibility, especially by conflating it with contingent cultural mores.[179]

A good corroborating example of the kind of social malformation and social source of self-deception that Kant and Kierkegaard worry about, along with the hope that the individual's moral self-awareness can be a source of resistance to such self-deception comes, perhaps surprisingly, in Pope Francis's account of the "technocratic paradigm" in his encyclical *Laudato Si'*. Francis devotes a considerable amount of time in *Laudato Si'* to diagnosing how we have come to act, especially in communities across the Global North, with a "cheerful recklessness" with regard to the environment.[180] By "cheerful," Francis means that we go about our daily lives fairly ignorant or insufficiently concerned or just plain aloof about the disastrous ecological consequences of many of our mundane habits and practices.[181] Francis talks in *Laudato Si'* about a widespread "numbing of conscience" about the environment, which he describes in terms of a shortsighted way of living in which a person does not fully recognize or rightly care about ecologically irresponsible actions as irresponsible and does not recognize or care about environmental issues as issues before which he is accountable.[182]

How this scenario has come about is complicated but it has a great deal to do with how we act together and what we tacitly sanction as producers and consumers of goods. Francis defines this way of life together as the "technocratic paradigm" because we have ceded the rapid increase of technological power to business interests.[183] Because the growth of technological power has been so rapid it has outpaced, he says, the "development in human responsibility, values, and conscience."[184] New things are constantly on display before us so quickly and accessibly that we are discouraged to reflect on whether they should have been produced at all, how they were produced, or where they came from.[185] "The alliance

176. *Religion*, 6:33.
177. "Enlightenment," 8:35–36.
178. *UDVS*, 42.
179. *UDVS*, 57.
180. Pope Francis, *Laudato Si': On the Care of Our Common Home* (Vatican City: Libreria Editrice Vaticana, 2015), §59.
181. Pope Francis, *Laudato Si'*, §49.
182. Pope Francis, *Laudato Si'*, §49.
183. Pope Francis, *Laudato Si'*, §109.
184. Pope Francis, *Laudato Si'*, §105.
185. Pope Francis, *Laudato Si'*, §113–14.

between the economy and technology," Francis explains, "ends up sidelining anything unrelated to its immediate interests."[186] The technocratic paradigm represents a shortsighted concern for immediate consumption and maximizing profits, which overlooks "the rhythms of nature" and the long-term threats to biodiversity and general ecological health.[187] This sounds a bit like Francis is saying that powerful corporate interests have a self-conscious, deliberate anti-ecological agenda (which is partly true), but the point is more that as a society of producers and consumers of goods, we continuously, tacitly sanction a way of life that cares more for ease and convenience than for an ecological responsibility that might require more austere measures.

When we think of this dynamic at work in a local community—in something like Hauerwas's church of "parking lots and potluck dinners"—then we can see more concretely how such a community might be a source of subtle malformation and self-deception, a "crowd"-like hiding place, or a locus of "self-incurred minority." Since, for Hauerwas and Smith and the like, it is through a community's practices like its potluck dinners that individuals participate in a kind of morally formative liturgy, let's take the potluck dinner itself as an example. One of the ways the technocratic paradigm subtly insinuates itself in our everyday life is through our food, since most of the food produced in the United States comes through a technologically advanced, industrial agricultural system that gives us very cheap access seemingly to anything we want to eat. And because it does this on such a large scale and relatively out of view, we are generally unaware of the disastrous ecological and social harms it creates and that we perpetuate. A person can learn, though, through a general ecological education such as he might get from *Laudato Si'* or a documentary film about modern industrial agriculture, that buying meat and produce from a "big box" store, for instance, has myriad adverse implications for animal welfare, biodiversity, general public health, and for poor and marginalized people. And so he starts trying to make informed choices, starts going to more farmers markets, even though this is less convenient and more expensive. But what happens when he shows up at the church potluck dinner and sees that it has been almost entirely sourced with cheap industrial food? He had started to feel uneasy with this food but now he sees Pastor Bill blessing it and he watches the pillars of his church community buying and eating it without qualm. He does not have to simply accept this behavior. He might try to implement a "Food and Faith" educational series at the church and initiate conversations with Pastor Bill, church leadership, and his friends. And this might have an impact. But it might also very well be that by the next potluck dinner very little change has occurred; there is Pastor Bill blessing the industrial food again and there are his fellow parishioners eating without qualm. They might have more awareness about what they're doing but they also don't think a significant change is really possible. They came away from his "Food and Faith" series understanding the

---

186. Pope Francis, *Laudato Si'*, §54.
187. Pope Francis, *Laudato Si'*, §190.

message but also doubting that much can be done about a system so powerful and seemingly omnipresent. And the food is just too cheap and convenient and, frankly, delicious. This might end up being the source of tension for this person and his church community, but it might also be that their nonchalance becomes his own. He begins to see his former culinary conscientiousness as overwrought; yes, the consumption of this food perpetuates all kinds of bad ecological and social outcomes that he does not want to perpetuate, but, shaped by his church and their potluck dinners, he comes to realize there is just not much that can be done about it; he has been convinced that he was perhaps being naive and unrealistic. And while something needs to be done about those bad outcomes, perhaps some more "realistic" solution can be found, because for now, having shared a table again and again with these people who eat this food without qualm, he eventually gets past his inhibitions and digs in.

Perhaps this anecdote is too contrived. But I find it nonetheless a plausible description of the role a community's habits and practices can play to help routinize or normalize an unjust paradigm in a person's practical reason and moral self-awareness. To be plain, the point is that in everyday life people find themselves at odds and alienated from their formative communities. And sometimes a person's real virtue can devolve as she sublimates her life into the life of the community. This is a concession to the fact that we are of course malleable beings who bear the imprint of our social contexts. This is not something either Kant or Kierkegaard deny, as I argued in previous chapters (and as we will consider again shortly). It is also not something Pope Francis would deny, for that matter, since his account of the technocratic paradigm is an account of a societal malformation, of the ways our lives together tacitly shape us into ecologically irresponsible moral agents. The key question is not whether a community influences or shapes a person's moral agency, but how extensively and what is it that enables a person to find herself at odds with one of her primary communities of influence. If a person's moral identity comes into being only as she finds herself embedded in the public world of a particular community with particular sociolinguistic conventions, what makes it possible for a person eventually to break from that community (which I assume must be possible)?

Repentance, Conversion, and the Universality of Conscience

We considered earlier the conundrum this question poses for accounts like Niebuhr's and Hauerwas's and will not relitigate that here, but instead offer a positive response based on Kant's and Kierkegaard's assumption that when communities make irresponsible or unjust demands upon us, explicitly or implicitly through their habits and practices, we have a capacity for discernment and resistance. Moral repentance and conversion, in other words, are concepts well suited to conscience as an individual's singular moral self-awareness. Kant's and Kierkegaard's assumption is that communities, including (and sometimes especially) ecclesial communities, can be exceedingly malicious and unjust and that the individual must have some kind of access to something beyond the power or influence of the community that allows her to call that community (and herself as a participant of that community) to account, or to enter into the life of another community that challenges the first community's malice and injustice. For the sake of the common good, that is, Kant and Kierkegaard assume there must be a source of moral agency and a locus of personal accountability that cannot be reduced to the moral norms expressed in a particular community's life, a locus of moral self-awareness that must be distinct from the corporate self-understanding of a particular community.

Through conscience, according to Kant and Kierkegaard, a person finds herself accountable to a standard that is not contingent and so when an empirical, contingent community makes an irresponsible or unjust claim upon her, she has the capacity for a moral self-awareness that will give her pause, that will enable her to distance herself from those claims and, if necessary, from that community. This is Kant's point that however accustomed to our vices a person might become—and he is clear that social life can play a significant role in the acculturation[188]—conscience will continue to flicker within, so that a person must wake up "from time to time" and hear "its fearful voice."[189] Kierkegaard's account of a person's "first self" and "deeper self" makes a similar point. He describes the "first self" in negative terms, as person's susceptibility to the crowd's bad influence to follow its life and accept its customs as morally authoritative; whether the "first self" has to be described in these negative terms is something we will consider shortly, but the key point here is that the "first self" represents that which is malleable in the self, that which is open to social influence.[190] And as the crowd's "fraudulent" criteria begins to take hold within a person's "first self," as her moral identity becomes sublimated in the crowd's life, the "deeper self," by which Kierkegaard means conscience,[191] calls a person back to her distinct responsibility before God; it does not allow her to totally embed herself in the crowd's life or render her responsibility as simply accounting for the role that community has given her.[192] A person may try, nonetheless, to conceal herself "in finitude … in the same way as Adam" did who hid "among the trees," but to no avail because God, "the unconditioned," in conscience "unconditionally" will catch sight of her and she will find herself in her singular accountability.[193]

We are not malleable all the down, in other words, and we find within ourselves a locus of accountability that is distinct from the contingent customs all around us. To return to *Laudato Si'*, this is precisely Pope Francis's claim as to why we are not defeated by the technocratic paradigm. "Yet all is not lost," he writes toward

---

188. *Lectures*, 134.
189. *Metaphysics of Morals*, 6:438.
190. *EUD*, 313.
191. *EUD*, 313.
192. *EUD*, 313.
193. *JFY*, 113.

the end of the encyclical, striking a resoundingly hopeful chord after many pages of a fairly grim diagnosis of the social forces that have corrupted our moral agency.[194] While we might be deeply compromised by the technocratic paradigm, which embroils us and our communities in ecological and social harms, Francis finds hope nonetheless. The depth and breadth of the technocratic paradigm's reach is profound but, as Francis writes, no "system can completely suppress our openness to what is good, true, or beautiful."[195] Significantly, even as the "mental and social conditioning" of the moment directs us away from ecological responsibility, making us, as he says, "capable of the worst," Francis insists that this conditioning is not the last word; human beings, he writes, "are also capable of rising above themselves, choosing again what is good, and making a new start."[196] And here we can see a profound resonance with Kant's and Kierkegaard's theory of conscience because Francis thinks that our ability to rise above ourselves, choose the good, and make a new start is predicated upon our ability, as individuals, to undertake a conscientious self-examination. We can, he writes, "take an honest look at ourselves ... acknowledge our deep dissatisfaction, and ... embark on new paths."[197] And the reason we can do this, Francis claims, is due to the "transcendent dimension" of each person, due to the fact that each person is fundamentally open to the "Thou of God."[198] Francis is not systematic in these points, but he is clear that there is something about the fact that because we each exist in a transcendent openness before God—suggesting a transparency before God—we are also able to know ourselves in a deep and profound way. We cannot be reduced to our social contexts. We are more than that and can know ourselves as more than that. Perhaps a person does not know this is exactly what is going on when he takes an honest look at himself, but, Francis suggests, the fact of a person's openness to God means he is open to a moral claim and a corresponding self-disclosure that transcends the contingent demands and conditioning of any particular time and place. In short, in spite of a profound social conditioning that moves a person in one direction, he has the capacity to move in the other direction, to go against the grain and respond to "a summons to profound interior conversion ... which entails the recognition of errors, sins, faults, and failure, and leads to heartfelt repentance and the desire to change." All this despite the overwhelming social pressures to the contrary.[199]

A key point I want to underscore here, in concert with Francis, is that conscience is something unconditioned and universal. This is the sense, again, of the Pauline claim that, at least in part on account of conscience, all are without excuse—that no one is off the hook. Paul accepts conscience, Pierce explains,

---

194. Pope Francis, *Laudato Si'*, §205.
195. Pope Francis, *Laudato Si'*, §205.
196. Pope Francis, *Laudato Si'*, §205.
197. Pope Francis, *Laudato Si'*, §205.
198. Pope Francis, *Laudato Si'*, §119. Recall, this is exactly what Hauerwas claims we do not have.
199. Pope Francis, *Laudato Si'*, §217, 218.

"as a universal experience."[200] And in this vein Bernard of Clairvaux rhetorically asks, "to whom does conscience not speak?"[201] And so Francis has good reason to present an imperative to honest self-examination, repentance and change in an encyclical addressed to every human being on the planet. Like Kant and Kierkegaard, he is assuming something basic about the human being as a being constituted with moral accountability before God. His wager, that is, is that his universal plea for honest self-examination can hit its mark, that it does not ring out as a meaningless abstraction but that it resonates with something fundamental within a person. Pope Benedict is perhaps in the background here, as Benedict writes that conscience "should represent the transparency of the subject for the divine, and thus constitute the very greatness and dignity" of the human person.[202] Conscience, Benedict writes, pertains to a person's "openness to the ground of his being, the power of perception of what is highest and most essential."[203] Benedict explains that in conscience every human being encounters "the perceptible and demanding presence of the voice of truth ... from God."[204] Consequently, Benedict concludes, resonating with Francis, "conscience cannot be reduced to social advantage, to group consensus, or to the demands of political and social power."[205] And in this same spirit, addressing the universality of the individual's accountability before God in conscience, we find in *Gaudium et Spes* the striking claim that in conscience a person is "alone with God, Whose voice echoes in his depths." What this means, more precisely is that in conscience a person finds himself accountable before God to a universal law "which is fulfilled by love of God and neighbor," a law that unites all people "in the search for truth."[206] Because each person is open and accountable before God in conscience—which entails that each is open and accountable before that which is true, good and beautiful, as Francis suggests—conscience provides the grounds for hope that anyone, anywhere can change their course of life for the good.

This theme of conscience as unconditioned and universal is one that Kant and Kierkegaard share, but we should recall that it is one they understand in distinct

---

200. Pierce, *Conscience in the New Testament*, 113.

201. Cited in Evans, G. R., *Bernard of Clairvaux*, 35.

202. Benedict, *On Conscience* (San Francisco, CA: Ignatius Press, 2007), 22. And in a similar vein as Francis's claim about a person's ability to rise above herself, Benedict writes that "Paul can say that the gentiles are a law unto themselves ... in the much deeper sense that nothing belongs less to me than myself. My own 'I' is the site of the profoundest surpassing of self and contact with [God] from whom I came and toward whom I am going" (33).

203. Benedict, *On Conscience*, 16.

204. Benedict, *On Conscience*, 25.

205. Benedict, *On Conscience*, 26.

206. *Pastoral Constitution on the Church in the Modern World—Gaudium et Spes* Promulgated by Pope Paul VI (Vatican City: December 7, 1965), §16. Available at http://www.vatican.va/archive/hist_councils/ii_vatican_council/documents/vat-ii_const_19651207_gaudium-et-spes_en.html, accessed June 2018.

ways. Both claim that every person is equally, singularly accountable before God in conscience; and so conscience as a person's moral self-awareness before God is therefore, in a sense, the same for every person. For Kant, this has to do with the universality of the moral law that each person should believe God promulgates to her and according to which her conscience holds her accountable as if before God. And I have tried to show, here in this chapter and in the chapter on Kant, that there are very sound biblical and theological resonances for thinking about conscience in this way. The dominant one is the Pauline emphasis that every person has a conscience wherein she finds herself accused or defended in her direct accountability before God. Wherever and whenever a person finds herself—in whatever community she lives—she is accountable before God in conscience. How else, Paul would ask, can we say that no one is without excuse?

Kierkegaard also assumes that in conscience each individual is accountable before God for quality of his life before a moral law or standard that God universally gives to all. But for Kierkegaard, as I noted at the start of the chapter, this accountability before God entails a more personal telos. While God lays the same summons on every person to live responsibly before God, so that there is a "point of unity" in the human race, God also makes a specific claim on each person, giving each person a distinct way to realize his responsibility before God.[207] This is his point that God endows every person with a particular purpose so that faithfulness to God becomes manifest in a faithfulness to a person's given purpose.[208] God creates each and every person with a "given self," makes every person "a very definite something," and gives to every person at birth a distinct "divine name."[209] What distinguishes Kierkegaard's theory of conscience here is that he incorporates into it a concept of vocation, somewhat like the concept of "haecceity" John Hare finds in Dons Scotus and Gerard Manly Hopkins. This is the idea, Hare explains, that each person has a specific, individual nature constituted by God. In clear resonance with Kierkegaard, Hare writes that this "*haecceitas* ... can be associated with the name of each one of us, written on a white stone, which we are told in the book of Revelation God knows but we do not yet know."[210] We do not yet know fully, is Hare's point, because our responsibility before God, he explains, is "to grow into this individual character" or name or calling.[211] I might add to Hare's warrant from the book of Revelation the sentiment that it is God who knits each person together,[212] or the many times God directly encounters very specific people and gives them very specific missions for which they are

---

207. *UDVS*, 126.
208. *UDVS*, 93, emphasis mine.
209. *SUD*, 36, 68, 34.
210. Hare, *God's Call*, 77.
211. Hare, *God's Call*, 77.
212. Psalm 139 is perhaps the most well-known of such passages. But see also Jer. 1:1-4, Job 31:14, and Lk. 12:7.

accountable.[213] Kierkegaard's point is that to be singled out by God in this way is itself a universal feature of human life, and that to be conscientious entails a person's striving to know himself as one to whom God has given a distinct way to fulfill that which is the highest good for everyone, to live as a single individual in relation to God.

There are of course tensions here between Kierkegaard's and Kant's thought, but rather than adjudicate between them I have tried to show that they both draw our attention to themes we have found good reasons to affirm. We have good reason to affirm, that is, both that conscience constitutes an individual's moral self-awareness of her accountability before God for the quality of her life as a moral agent bound by a universal moral law, and as an individual uniquely constituted by God for a particular relation to God. Kant does not think moral accountability can be personal in this way because it cannot be universal. But I think Kant is wrong about this and that Kierkegaard offers good reasons to think that it can be.[214] And what is common in both of these aspects of conscience as moral self-awareness is that every person is capable of it, that every person is accountable before God in conscience in these ways and so every person is capable of being conscientious. And so when the life of a community begins to move in a direction out of sync with what is right or a person's vocational responsibility, she has the capacity to resist that community.

Singularity, Sociality, and Authority

In sum, the theory of conscience I have been outlining and defending takes conscience to be a singular moral self-awareness that is universal, in the sense that to be a human being is to have a conscience and the capacity to be conscientious, and unconditioned, in the sense that the presence of conscience within a person does not emerge through contingent sociolinguistic, historical circumstances, but through the transcendent dimension of a person's standing before God. And this way of understanding conscience provides a helpful way to think about the

---

213. There are too many examples to list, but, the Patriarchs; Samuel; Isaiah; Jeremiah; Jonah; Mary, mother of Jesus; the Apostle Paul; etc. are present examples of individuals singled out by God for a particular responsibility. One might object that these are all exceptional examples, but do they not, even still, pose a problem for claims about the communitarian mediation of God's presence and demands? And furthermore, if we take something like Paul's account of the "measure of faith" given to each, in the sense that each is given a particular vocation and responsibility, it is quite plausible to see the prominent examples of divine vocation listed as models of that which applies to every person (Romans 12). Paul's discussion of individual vocation in Romans 12, of course, belongs within his "many parts, one body" account of the church, so there is some axis of individual responsibility and corporate life. I will take up this theme below.

214. Cf. Hare, *God's Call*, 118.

actions of repentance and conversion, particularly as these actions might entail an individual's break with a particular community that has been influential and formative in a person's life. This is the case because conscience as an individual's singular moral self-awareness pertains to an accountability that cannot be reduced to the life of any particular community. No human community, that is, can fully confine a person's moral identity and moral self-awareness because the transcendent dimension of a person's accountability to God enables a self-knowledge that exceeds the bounds of any community's self-understanding. A key implication, then, is that conscience does indeed entail a buffer between the individual and the community.

But to say there is a buffer between the individual and the community is not to say that there is nothing malleable about us as human beings or that other people and communities have nothing to do with how we understand ourselves in our conscience. To affirm that conscience is an individual's singular moral self-awareness before God is to affirm that an individual's moral agency and self-awareness cannot be reduced to the self-understanding of any human community. The transcendent relation to God buffers against that reduction. But this is not to say we are not social beings constituted for life together. Kant, Kierkegaard, and the tradition of conscience they represent do not deny this. And there are indications in Kant's and Kierkegaard's thought that there is something socially formed about us with respect to our conscience, that we do, consequently, need other people to help us hear our conscience, and that seeking the common good is a central aim of being conscientious. Given the critique that Kant and Kierkegaard and their theories of conscience significantly contribute to the rise of an asocial, ahistorical, atomistic individualism, a consideration of the affirmations of community in their conceptions of conscience should by itself help strengthen the case I am making.

Conscience itself, Kant and Kierkegaard are clear, is not something that needs formation. It is a constituent feature of being human and it asserts itself, in its verdicts or presence, whether we like it or not. It is our ability to hear and heed conscience that is in question.[215] What is malleable about us with respect to conscience, that is, is not conscience itself but our receptivity to it. Kant is clear that conscience per se cannot be formed; it is not a "work of art and education." But "art and education" can bring conscience to "fruition," in the sense that these morally formative, social activities can help a person more clearly discern conscience's workings.[216] Our ability to hear and heed conscience is something we can "hurt or injure" or something we can foster.[217] Kierkegaard also talks about hearing conscience as

---

215. Along these lines Karl Barth warns us that we have to be careful when it comes to conscience because "we err in our hearing of it." Describing conscience as we did above as, in part, a self-dialogue, Barth claims that it is also a constant "self-misunderstanding." Barth's point, which he shares with Kant and Kierkegaard, is not that conscience is inaccurate in its ability to disclose us to ourselves but that our perception of its disclosure can be dim, not "absolutely ... but relatively very highly so" (Barth, *Ethics*, 484).

216. *Lectures*, 133.

217. *Lectures*, 133.

something that requires an education: every person has a conscience, he writes, but there is also "no accomplishment that requires such an extensive and rigorous schooling as is required before one can genuinely be said to have a conscience."[218] Again, for Kierkegaard, as for Kant, conscience is not a work; it is not something that needs formation. But hearing conscience is a rigorous accomplishment that requires formation of some kind. We can return here briefly to Kierkegaard's account of the "first self" and the "deeper self" because it addresses this dynamic between that which is malleable about us, that which needs a "rigorous schooling," and the conscience. As we have seen, Kierkegaard describes the "first self" in fairly negative terms, as that aspect of us as moral agents that wants to conform to the crowd's life. But there is also a neutrality about the "first self." It denotes our ability to be more or less open to our conscience. It might be, fallen creatures that we are, that we are more inclined to injure our ability to hear our conscience by filtering ourselves into the crowd; we are inclined to "stun" ourselves or put ourselves to sleep, as Kant claims.[219] But Kierkegaard is clear that we can also turn the other way. The "first self" can also "admit that the deeper self is right."[220] In other words, if it is fair to assume that "the first self" represents that which is malleable in our subjectivity, Kierkegaard depicts it as something that can be shaped to be more or less attuned to conscience. In this regard, Pierce explains that the New Testament's image of a "seared conscience" is an image not of a conscience that has ceased to work but whose voice is smothered by the scars of a habitual turning away from it.[221] And so we might say that Kant's and Kierkegaard's point is that moral formation pertains to the degree to which conscience has been seared, the degree of our sensitivity to conscience.

And here Kant and Kierkegaard both affirm that other individuals and communities can play an important role in shaping a person to be more awake or sensitive to conscience. Kant claims that those who love the good, and who are therefore conscientious, will rally together so that they might "gain the upper hand over evil and its untiring attacks."[222] This might seem a bit circular: the conscientious gravitate toward the conscientious so that they might be more conscientious. But that is the point. A person does not need other people to shape the conscience within him; but as he listens to his conscience he will be inclined to congregate with others who are likewise sensitive to their conscience. And this gathering of the conscientious has the effect of keeping individuals mindful of their conscience; individuals in this society are less likely to stun themselves or put themselves to sleep. We are not the kind of creatures, Kant insists, who can go about our striving after the good alone. It is good to have a moral community to spur us on and hold

---

218. *JP*, 1:320. Likewise, he explains, every person has a conscience but everyone nonetheless must become "equipped ... with a conscience" (*JP*, 1:321).
219. *Metaphysics of Morals*, 6:438.
220. *EUD*, 313.
221. Pierce, *Conscience in the New Testament*, 93.
222. *Religion*, 6:94.

us accountable. We need, that is, a moral community to hold us accountable by keeping us always mindful of our ultimate source of accountability as individuals who live before God.[223] And so when Kant says that "art and education" are needed for a person's conscience to come to "fruition," he is sincere that these social goods of a particular moral community have an essential function in a person's striving to live a good life.

It might seem implausible to argue that Kierkegaard also affirms the positive role of other people or a community to direct a person to conscience. His worries about the ways other people and communities become occasions to ignore conscience are quite prominent. And a significant part of his counsel to a person to listen to conscience has to do with getting away from people and finding solitude. The lilies and the birds and the dead are the companions he tells us to trust.[224] But it would be a mistake to conclude that there is no place for the help of others in a person's striving for conscientiousness. His account of "little Ludvig" in *Judge for Yourself!* provides a helpful indication of how he thinks others can help. Kierkegaard asks us to think about a toddler, "little Ludvig," and his relationship to his parents:

> Every day little Ludvig is taken for a ride in his stroller. A delight that usually lasts an hour. ... Yet the mother has hit upon something new that will definitely delight little Ludvig even more: would he like to try to push the stroller himself? And he can! What! He can? Yes, look, Auntie, little Ludvig can push the stroller himself! Now, let us be down to earth but not upset the child, since we know very well that little Ludvig cannot do it, that it is his mother who is actually pushing the stroller, and that it is really only to delight him that she plays the game that little Ludvig can do it himself.[225]

Kierkegaard uses this anecdote to make a point about God's grace and human action, but it is instructive about how Kierkegaard understands healthy relationships between children and parents and humans in general. The mother's aim is to help Ludvig walk by himself; the delight he takes is his own walking, his striving to stand on his own two feet. The aim is for him to walk without her help and so she helps in a way that does not draw attention to herself. It is the love of one person for another that allows that person to flourish as the person that he is. Or, as Kierkegaard writes in *Works of Love*, the mother's love of Ludvig is the love that responds to the other's claim to let "me be something in myself, something distinctive."[226] This claim is predicated on the belief that each person has, as his or her highest good, a distinct, singular relation to God, and that God cares for each

---

223. Cf. *Religion*, 6:105.

224. Although, as I argued earlier, Kierkegaard's exhortation to a person to consider herself before one who is dead ultimately has to do with taking living persons seriously, respecting the equal dignity of each person as an individual before God.

225. *JFY*, 185.

226. *WL*, 270.

individual as if the only one in God's care (to paraphrase the passage I quoted from Augustine earlier). And so to love another person is to help a person stand in his singularity. The implication for conscience and conscientiousness is that other people can direct a person to their conscience, can help them hear it and heed it. Others do not shape a person's conscience but they can be formative in a person's willingness to be conscientious.

It is hard to know what else Kierkegaard thinks he is doing as an author, with respect to conscience, if he is not trying to do exactly that. For instance, when the conscientious person finds stillness and considers the quality of her life as a single individual before God, she does so with the aid of Kierkegaard's probing questions. She is not completely without human company in her removed location. Kierkegaard is there with her. She examines herself with a copy of *Upbuilding Discourses in Various Spirits* at her desk. His ideal reader, reading slowly and aloud to herself is prompted by Kierkegaard's carefully crafted words.[227] Kierkegaard's aim, though, is to be like little Ludvig's mother. He is guiding the reader but in such a way, he hopes, that it would be as if this question of conscience had arisen in her own heart.[228] Kierkegaard does think, then, we need other people's help to be conscientious—even if it might seem like he has appointed himself as our principal helper.

But I think Kierkegaard implies a larger community than just himself and his reader. Recall that for Kierkegaard the conscientious person must ultimately come before the Bible and find himself disclosed by it. It is before the mirror of God's Word, Kierkegaard claims, that a person is most fully disclosed to himself, but it is conscience that holds a person before this mirror. A person reads the Bible rightly, that is, when he reads it with his conscience. His advice about how to do this sounds anti-communal. A person is to read the Bible with a "subjective personal relation to it," in the sense that he reads it rightly when he is aware that it is "I to whom it is speaking; it is I about whom it is speaking."[229] Consequently, he is to "consult" with no one but God about what he has read,[230] and so he does not put any obligations on others or let others put any obligation on him.[231] It is important to be careful about what Kierkegaard is and is not saying here. He is not launching an attack on theological education simply considered. He is not telling a person not to study theology, consult commentaries, study the biblical languages, or partake of any intrinsically communal, scholarly apparatus. Gifted student of all those things that he was, that would be rather hypocritical of him. He is saying that, ultimately, when a person reads the Bible he has to remember that it is "living and active,"[232] it is not merely an object for study and reflection

---

227. *UDVS*, 124.
228. *UDVS*, 5; see also *FSE*, 3; *Three Discourses*, 5.
229. *FSE*, 36.
230. *JP*, 3:268.
231. *JP*, 2:419.
232. Heb. 4:12.

but above all a divine communication that makes a person responsible; a person rightly understands what he reads when he reads it as God's address to him.

But the Bible can be difficult and confusing. Even Peter says, after all, that some parts of Paul's letters "are hard to understand."[233] And the matrix of theological studies surrounding a person's reading of the Bible helps get to the point of what the text is actually saying. A translation of the Bible into Danish, for instance, is itself a work of theological interpretation by a community of scholars, who have, themselves, consulted traditions of interpretation. It is worth noting that Kierkegaard writes in a much more theologically and biblically literate time than our own and he perhaps takes for granted that his reader has a certain amount of theological education at hand. Even so, Kierkegaard himself does a fair bit of hermeneutical intervention in a person's reading of the text, an intervention that, again, implies a broader theological discourse. Kierkegaard insists that the conscientious person must see herself reflected in the "mirror of God's Word," but surely he is aware that he has given his reader a very particular kind of mirror, with a particular understanding of the person and work of Jesus Christ and a particular notion of the nature of self-sacrificing love. And emphasizing the centrality of Christ-like love as a central theme before which a person should see herself reflected, also represents a particular theological tradition, which also implies communities of interpretation. And his apparent privileging of the Synoptic gospels indicates interpretive preferences that have theological histories and communities behind them. I do not think Kierkegaard means to downplay these facts, and, giving him benefit of the doubt, I do not think he is being grossly naïve about what a person is capable of understanding about a text as she reads it alone in her room. His point, again, is the same as with little Ludvig and his mother. The community should act to help a person stand on her own before God's Word has it, with her conscience, discloses her to herself and makes her responsible. His exhortation to "consult with no one" has to do with the text's power as divinely inspired to obligate a person. It does not mean that the communal element of theological interpretation is not or should not be present as a person reads. The individual who takes the Bible into her room and reads a "subjective relation to it" does so with a community at her side, in a sense. How much of this communal aspect of reading the Bible Kierkegaard means to imply is not entirely clear. It nonetheless strikes me as clearly and plausibly inferred in his exhortation. To have this cloud of witnesses, of sorts, accompany a person in her reading of the text does not mean the community mediates the text's meaning or that the community is therefore, in a sense, the source of a person's accountability and self-disclosure. Rather, the community, independent of the text, can help a person understand the text's meaning. The resources of biblical scholarship, church tradition, preaching, community Bible studies, and so on can help a person get a sense of what is going on in the biblical text. But, ultimately, a person has to read it conscientiously and understand herself as reflected in it and obligated by it, and not consult anyone

---

233. 2 Pet. 3:16.

about it so as not to shuffle off her responsibility. And if a person does not read the text in this way, then she does not truly read the text.

Kant and Kierkegaard mutually affirm, then, the general idea that community has a place in helping a person to be conscientious. Conscience is not socially formed, but social forces have a role to play. And this provides a helpful way to think about the authority of a community—ecclesial communities included—with respect to a person's conscience. What I want to argue here is that when it comes to a person's conscience the community's authority is secondary or indirect. The authority is indirect or secondary because God is the ultimate "authorized judge of conscience," as Kant writes; a person is directly accountable in conscience before God. Likewise, Paul does not claim that ultimately each person must give an account of himself before a community—ecclesial communities included—but before God as distinct from any human community.[234] But the community can remind a person of that ultimate authority, can direct a person to it. The view I am taking here is not far from John Henry Newman's famous toast first to conscience, and then to the Pope, a toast Pope Benedict appreciates in his own view of conscience.[235] As Benedict explains, because conscience brings a person into contact with the ground of his being, because in conscience, a person encounters the truth from God, and because the church is entrusted with the truth from God, there should ideally be no conflict between conscience and the church. They should be corroborative.[236] But the point I have stressed is that at the concrete level, an ecclesial community can be a source of malformation and self-deception and quite out of sync with a person's conscience. But ideally—and I think this is in a similar spirit as Benedict—the ecclesial community can direct a person to his conscience, remind him that therein he is accountable to God, and can remind him even further that the God before whom he is accountable in conscience is *this God* revealed to us in a particular way in Jesus Christ. But then it still falls to the individual to discern in conscience, in a way the ecclesial community simply cannot, how precisely he finds himself accountable to God in conscience. This is, again, essentially Kierkegaard's point when he tells his reader he must find himself disclosed and accountable in conscience before the mirror of God's Word.

The distinction I am making here is like the medieval theological distinction between the Church's ability to counsel and command. The ecclesial community, O'Donovan explains, is limited in its authority by the fact that each individual is confronted by God's command "without the reinforcement of social constraint."[237] Because God addresses each individual and holds each individual responsible, the community must recognize that there is an "area of human fulfillment in which well-doing and wrongdoing are not susceptible to public observation: the inner

---

234. This seems like the clear implication of reading 1 Cor. 4:3 with Rom. 14:5.

235. John Henry Newman, *A Letter Addressed to the Duke of Norfolk: On Occasion of Mr. Gladstone's Recent Expostulation* (New York: Aeterna Press, 2015), 50.

236. Benedict, *On Conscience*, 23.

237. O'Donovan, *Resurrection*, 171.

life of thought, attitude and motive, and the response to individual vocation."[238] In other words, because the community respects the individual as one whom God "addresses directly and whose particular decisions are partly hidden from public gaze" it takes its role to counsel as its own "most characteristic form of address to the individual."[239] The ecclesial community does really counsel, though, because it is not as though it knows nothing about Christian morality. It can direct the individual to "the authority of God's revelation in Christ and to the moral teaching of Jesus, the prophets and the apostles; for it knows that right attitudes and decisions, however hidden and inscrutable in their details, are those which come from a thoughtful obedience to that revelation."[240] And so, in a similar sense in which I said that the community has a secondary or indirect authority, O'Donovan explains that the ecclesial community has an authority for the individual in its role to counsel. This is an authority secondary to the authority of God, before whom each individual stands. It is clearly evident in Paul's address to the Corinthians, "we are not lords over your faith but collaborators. ... For it is by your faith that you stand."[241] O'Donovan concludes that this authority is a "didactic" one that appeals "to the authority of a truth which stands above it."[242] The straightforward implication for conscience is simply the idea, again, that the community has the role of directing a person to their conscience. In other words, if its role to counsel is to direct a person to God's authority over him, then that would also have to include directing him to God's authority over him in conscience. And it is not implausible to claim that this idea about the church's role to counsel coheres with Kant's and Kierkegaard's thought about conscience. In their own distinct and qualified ways of understanding the ideal community it is something they can affirm. The point, in short, is that we need other people in our efforts to be conscientious. That this theory of conscience does not entail that conscience is socially constructed and that it does entail a buffer between the individual and the community does not mean it is a misanthropic, anti-communal theory of conscience.

Furthermore, and finally, Kant and Kierkegaard are both clear that the singularity of a person's moral self-awareness is for the sake of greater solidarity with others. Kant's worries about "self-incurred minority" are worries about the common good.[243] When a person fails to be conscientious, she risks, to quote Paul but capturing Kant's sentiment, being "blown here and there by every wind of teaching and by the cunning and craftiness of people in their deceitful scheming."[244] For Pope Francis, the fact of an individual's transcendent relation to God means she has the ability to resist the "mental and social conditioning" of her communities

---

238. O'Donovan, *Resurrection*, 171.
239. O'Donovan, *Resurrection*, 171.
240. O'Donovan, *Resurrection*, 171.
241. 2 Cor. 1:24, quoted in *Resurrection*, 172.
242. O'Donovan, *Resurrection*, 172.
243. "Enlightenment," 8:36.
244. Eph. 4:14.

and conscientiously to examine herself and make significant life changes. But the aim is not, of course, for the individual to enjoy some private good between herself and God. The aim is to create "a more dignified environment."[245] Francis insists that all "is not lost" for the common good of our common home precisely because individuals are capable of "rising above" their social contexts.[246] And a significant aspect of this "rising above" is the individual's turn within toward an interior self-examination. This is essentially Kant's claim as well. Conscientiousness has to do with a person's respect for the equal dignity of every person as companions within the kingdom of ends. If Kant's theory of conscience is not communitarian with respect to its nature, it does have this communitarian telos.

For Kierkegaard, as we saw earlier, to will to have a conscience before God is an essential precondition for healthy social life. Recall his claim that the single individual must first "establish an ethical stance despite the whole world"—must first will to be a single individual—and "not until then can there be any question of genuinely uniting."[247] A thriving sociality emerges, Kierkegaard insists, only on the condition that "eternity" first "takes hold of each one separately with the strong arms of conscience."[248] It is clearly a mistake, then, to miss the fact that Kierkegaard's strong emphasis on the singularity of each person before God entails a genuine concern for what unites people. And he is clear that there can be no real unity if people do not respect each person's equal dignity as a single individual before God.[249] But when people do live with this respect Kierkegaard explains that it will permeate all their relationships, it will "support and transfigure and illuminate" how people live together.[250] Somewhat in this vein, reflecting on Paul's discussion of the church as "one body with many members," each with a distinct gift or "measure of faith,"[251] O'Donovan explains,

> The more I conceive myself as an agent before God, the more I discern the path of my agency as intersecting with other paths, as occupying a particular position in the world that does not belong to everybody else, with particular obligations that do not weigh on other people. Deliberation about my responsibilities makes me one of a multitude again … because I conceive myself within the multitude as the site of a personally unique experience.[252]

O'Donovan's claim, like Kierkegaard's, is that singularity before God, far from precluding or diminishing or jeopardizing community, can generate it and

---

245. Pope Francis, *Laudato Si'*, §105.
246. Pope Francis, *Laudato Si'*, §205.
247. *LR*, 106.
248. *UDVS*, 133.
249. *UDVS*, 81.
250. *UDVS*, 137.
251. Rom. 12:4-6.
252. O'Donovan, *Ways*, 317.

support it. For Kierkegaard, above all, each person has as his or her highest good the relation to God as a single individual. But this is not a good, ultimately, to be enjoyed alone. God constitutes each person for a distinct relation to God, and yet Kierkegaard also claims that in everything a person does she must "not forget—to worship."[253] But worship is not an isolated activity; it is something one does in concert with others. It is in this vein that Kierkegaard claims that "the unanimity of the singled out is the band playing well orchestrated music."[254] And so as a person strives to be conscientious, to know herself in her singular relation to God, she will surely "find fellow pilgrims."[255]

Summary and Conclusion

I have outlined a theory of conscience in this chapter as a person's moral self-awareness before God. It is the knowledge a person shares with God about the moral quality of his life as he lives before God. There is an involuntary and voluntary aspect of this knowledge. It is involuntary in the sense that a person has a conscience, has this self-knowledge whether he likes it or not. Conscience is there within a person testifying to him about who he is in his accountability to God. But a person can heed this testimony or try to ignore it and so I defined the activity of conscientiousness as a person's efforts to listen to conscience, to strive to hear its verdicts. These verdicts, I have argued, pertain to the moral quality of a person's actions but also to the particular, vocational responsibility God lays on each individual. I want to affirm, that is, that a person is disclosed by the verdicts of his conscience in a moral and vocational sense. And a key aspect of this disclosure is the way it pertains not just to the quality of a person's actions but also to the person in a global sense, in the sense of who he is fundamentally as a moral agent. Part of the activity of conscientiousness, that is, is to move from the testimony of conscience with respect to particular actions to a broader knowledge of oneself as a moral agent, to "extract the disposition from the deed," as Kant writes. And this movement is so important because otherwise a person is easily caught in self-deception and therefore less capable of repenting a bad course of life and converting to a new and better one. To come back to the analogy of the alcoholic, the alcoholic who denies his alcoholism, for example, is unlikely to break from its destructive cycles. But the alcoholic who, after many particular bad encounters with alcohol, admits to himself that he is, in a global sense, an alcoholic is much more likely to change his course of life.

This is a good example also because the recovering alcoholic who, striving to keep this cure of self-knowledge daily in view, needs a community to help him on his way. The community does not tell him he is an alcoholic; he knows this

---

253. *UDVS*, 194.
254. *LR*, 55.
255. *UDVS*, 220.

about himself. *He* tells them what he knows about himself. But they hold him accountable, that is, to remain conscientious. The community acts to keep him mindful of what he knows about himself so that he can continue the fight to live a good and sober life. I have argued, in this spirit, that community has an important role for a person striving to be conscientious. The community does not shape a person's conscience but a good community can direct a person to conscience and can help influence or shape a person's ability to hear it. Moreover, the activity of being conscientious should also redound to the common good. Pope Francis's conscientious individual, again, is one who breaks out of the bad social conditioning of the moment in order to live a more ecologically responsible life for the sake of the common good of everyone.

Finally, I have had two principal objectives in this concluding chapter's outline of conscience. First, I have organized the outline according to key themes from Kant's and Kierkegaard's thought and surrounded those themes with precedents and warrants from the Bible and a range of theologians from the patristic era to the present. The point is not to say that Kant and Kierkegaard derived their theories of conscience from those sources, though that at times may be true. But those sources indicate a broader biblical and theological tradition that Kant and Kierkegaard seem clearly to extend in their own way. Rich and interesting and novel as their theories of conscience may be, much of what they have to say, as I have tried to show here, finds echoes across the centuries. And if drawing attention to those echoes has the effect of making Kant's and Kierkegaard's theories of conscience seem less exceptional, that's not necessarily a bad outcome here. I think they are exceptional thinkers and wrestling with their theories of conscience has been enormously gratifying, but they are also representatives of a way of thinking about conscience with deep and broad roots, a way of thinking that has been dismissed and forgotten significantly on account of misinterpretations of these two figures. Far from offering us a novel theory of conscience that helps set the stage for the subjective caprice of modern individualism, Kant and Kierkegaard can remind us of this deeper tradition and can stimulate us to think through it anew. In this regard, as I have said, I have not offered an adjudication between Kant and Kierkegaard, nor have I tried to show how divergences in their thought can be reconciled. I have, rather, tried to outline a theory of conscience that takes its cues from the various strengths of each and that sets those strengths in a broader historical theological context. Much of this chapter has been about strengths they share, but sometimes the strengths they offer are unique to just one of them. They each offer important ways to think about conscience that find strong theological resonances and make good theological and philosophical sense.

The second objective of this chapter pertains to this book's broader aim to correct a prominent misreading about the kind of individualism and social life Kant and Kierkegaard allegedly promote in their thought generally and in their theories of conscience specifically. And because the lack of interest in this theory of conscience stems significantly from those misreadings, a major burden of this book has been the historical one to set the record straight. I have argued that the general disappearance of conscience from much contemporary theological discourse stems from worries about the way appeals to conscience can bolster the relativistic, subjective caprice of modern Western life. A common assumption is that Kant and, to a lesser extent, Kierkegaard bear a great deal of responsibility for this. And the response, eager to correct this banal individualism, has been a dominant discourse in theological ethics that sublimates the individual's personal identity, moral formation, and self-understanding into the life of the community. The individual's moral agency and corresponding self-awareness, that is, are realized as the individual is embedded in the community's life and self-awareness. What this response seems to assume is that any affirmation of the individual's moral identity apart from the life of the community must, to some degree, affirm modern subjective caprice. But this is wrong and a closer inspection of Kant's and Kierkegaard's theories of conscience point us in a different direction, one in which the individual is not autonomous in the sense of being a law unto herself but in the sense of being able to endorse or recognize or appropriate her distinct, singular accountability before God. Their theories of conscience offer a vision of the individual, God, and community in a triangulated relationship: the individual exists in a distinct relation of accountability before God; a good community can help a person be mindful of this relation; and the person who is mindful of it, who is conscientious, is one who, as such, lives for the good of the community. In other words, this is a vision in which a person's singular moral self-awareness before God aims at a flourishing social life, in which singularity and solidarity go hand in hand. Kant and Kierkegaard can help us retrieve this vision and remind us of a classical Christian commitment to the moral self-awareness each individual can acquire because each individual lives singularly accountable before the One who sees the heart.

BIBLIOGRAPHY

Adams, Robert, "Introduction," in Immanuel Kant, *Religion within the Bounds of Reason Alone and Other Writings*, edited by Allen Wood and George di Giovanni. New York: Cambridge University Press, 1998.
Ameriks, Karl, *Kant and the Fate of Autonomy: Problems in the Appropriation of the Critical Philosophy*. Cambridge: Cambridge University Press, 2000.
Ameriks, Karl, *Kant's Elliptical Path*. New York: Oxford University Press, 2012.
Ameriks, Karl, "Vindicating Autonomy: Kant, Sartre, and O'Neill," in *Kant on Moral Autonomy*, edited by Oliver Sensen. Cambridge: Cambridge University Press, 2012.
Ames, William, *Conscience with the Power and Cases Thereof*. Leyden: Imprinted W. Christiaens, E. Griffin, J. Dawson, 1639.
Aquinas, Thomas, *Summa Theologica*. Notre Dame, IN: Christian Classics. English Dominican Province Translation, 1981.
Aquinas, Thomas, *Summa Theologica*, volumes 4–12 in *Opera Omnia iussa edita Leonis XIII P.M.* Rome: Ex Typographia Polyglotta S.C. de Propaganda Fide, 1918–30.
Augustine, *Confessions*. New York: Penguin, 1961.
Barth, Karl, *Ethics*, translated by Geoffrey Bromily. New York: Seabury, 1981.
Barth, Karl, *Fragments Grave and Gay*. San Francisco, CA: HarperCollins, 1971.
Barth, Karl, *The Holy Spirit and the Christian Life*, translated by R. Birch Hoyle. Louisville, KY: Westminster John Knox, 1993.
Baylor, Michael, *Action and Person: Conscience in Late Scholasticism and the Young Luther*. Leiden: E. J. Brill, 1977.
Benedict XVI, *On Conscience*. San Francisco, CA: Ignatius Press, 2007.
Biggar, Nigel, *The Hastening the Waits: Karl Barth's Ethics*. Oxford: Oxford University Press, 1993.
Bonhoeffer, Dietrich, *Creation and Fall*. New York: Touchstone, 1994.
Bonhoeffer, Dietrich, *Ethics*. New York: Touchstone, 1995.
Book of Common Prayer. New York: Church Hymnal Corporation, 1979.
Calvin, John, *Institutes of the Christian Religion*, edited by John T. McNeil, translated by Ford Lewis Battles. Louisville, KY: Westminster John Knox, 1960.
Chignell, Andrew, "Rational Hope, Moral Order, and the Revolution of the Will," in *Divine Order, Human Order, and the Order of Nature*, edited by Eric Watkins. New York: Oxford University Press, 2013.
Chrysostom, John, *On Wealth and Poverty*. Yonkers, NY: St. Vladimir's Seminary Press, 1999.
Colette, Jacques, O. P., *Kierkegaard: The Difficulty of Being a Christian*. Notre Dame, IN: University of Notre Dame Press, 1969.
Come, Arnold, *Kierkegaard as Humanist: Discovering My Self*. Montreal: McGill-Queen's University Press, 1995.
Come, Arnold, *Kierkegaard as Theologian: Recovering My Self*. Montreal: McGill-Queen's University Press, 1997.

Connell, George, *To Be One Thing: Personal Unity in Kierkegaard's Thought*. Macon, GA: Mercer University Press, 1985.
Connell, George, and C. Stephen Evans, eds. *Foundations of Kierkegaard's Vision of Community: Religion Ethics, and Politics in Kierkegaard*. Atlantic Highlands, NJ: Humanities Press, 1992.
Crites, Stephen, *In the Twilight of Christendom*. Chambersburg, PA: American Academy of Religion, 1971.
Despland, Michael, "Can Conscience Be Hypocritical? The Contrasting Analyses of Kant and Hegel," *Harvard Theological Review*, vol. 68, nos. 3–4 (July–October 1975), 357–70.
Dewey, Bradley, *The New Obedience: Kierkegaard on Imitating Christ*. Washington, DC: Corpus Books, 1968.
Dupre, Louis, *Kierkegaard as Theologian: The Dialectic of Christian Existence*. New York: Sheed and Ward, 1963.
Ebeling, Gerhard, *Word and Faith*. Minneapolis, MN: Fortress Press, 1963.
Eller, Vernard, *Kierkegaard and Radical Discipleship: A New Perspective*. Princeton, NJ: Princeton University Press, 1968.
Elrod, John, *Kierkegaard and Christendom*. Princeton, NJ: Princeton University Press, 1981.
Emmanuel, Steven M., *Kierkegaard and the Concept of Revelation*. Albany: State University of New York Press, 1996.
Evans, C. Stephen, *Faith beyond Reason: A Kierkegaard Approach*. Grand Rapids, MI: Eerdmans, 1986.
Evans, C. Stephen, *Kierkegaard's Ethic of Love: Divine Commands and Moral Obligations*. New York: Oxford University Press, 2004.
Evans, C. Stephen, *Kierkegaard on Faith and Self: Collected Essays*. Waco, TX: Baylor University Press, 2006.
Evans, C. Stephen, *Soren Kierkegaard's Christian Psychology: Insight for Counseling and Pastoral Care*. Grand Rapids, MI: Zondervan, 1990.
Evans, C. Stephen, *Subjectivity and Religious Belief: A Historical, Critical Study*. Lanham, MD: University Press of America, 1982.
Evans, G. R., *Bernard of Clairvaux*. New York: Oxford University Press, 2000.
Ferreira, M. Jamie, *Kierkegaard*. Malden, MA: Wiley Blackwell, 2008.
Ferreira, M. Jamie, *Love's Grateful Striving: A Commentary on Kierkegaard's Works of Love*. New York: Oxford University Press, 2001.
Ferreira, M. Jamie, *Transforming Vision: Imagination and Will in Kierkegaardian Faith*. Oxford: Clarendon Press, 1991.
Freud, Sigmund, *Civilization and Its Discontents*. New York: W.W. Norton, 2010.
Freud, Sigmund, *Introductory Lectures on Psycho-Analysis*. New York: W.W. Norton, 1990.
Freud, Sigmund, *An Outline of Psycho-Analysis*. New York: W.W. Norton, 1989.
Foucault, Michel, *Ethics*, edited by Paul Rabinow. New York: New Press, 1992.
Gaudium et Spes ("Pastoral Constitution on the Church in the Modern World"), in *The Documents of Vatican II*, edited by Walter M. Abbott, S. J. London: Chapman, 1966.
Geismar, Eduard, *Lectures on the Religious Thought of Soren Kierkegaard*. Minneapolis, MN: Augsburg Press, 1937.
Gowens, David J., *Kierkegaard as Religious Thinker*. Cambridge: Cambridge University Press, 1996.
Gowens, David J., *Kierkegaard's Dialectic of the Imagination*. New York: Peter Lang, 1989.
Green, Ronald, *Kant and Kierkegaard: The Hidden Debt*. Albany: State University of New York Press, 1992.

Hall, Amy Laura, *Kierkegaard and the Treachery of Love*. New York: Cambridge University Press, 2002.
Hare, John, *God's Call: Moral Realism, God's Commands, and Human Autonomy*. Grand Rapids, MI: Eerdmans, 2001.
Hare, John, *God and Morality: A Philosophical History*. Malden, MA: Wiley-Blackwell, 2009.
Hare, John, *The Moral Gap: Kantian Ethics, Human Limits, and God's Assistance*. New York: Oxford University Press, 1996.
Hare, John, *Why Bother Being Good? The Place of God in the Moral Life*. Eugene, OR: Wipf and Stock, 2002.
Hauerwas, Stanley, "Agency Going Forward by Looking Back," in *Christian Ethics: Problems and Prospects*, edited by Lisa Cahill and James Childress. Cleveland, OH: Pilgrim Press, 1996.
Hauerwas, Stanley, *A Better Hope: Resources for a Church Confronting Capitalism, Democracy, and Postmodernity*. Grand Rapids, MI: Brazos Press, 2000.
Hauerwas, Stanley, *Hannah's Child: A Theologian's Memoir*. Grand Rapids, MI: Eerdmans, 2010.
Hauerwas, Stanley, *The Hauerwas Reader*, edited by John Berman and Micahel Cartwright. Durham, NC: Duke University Press, 2001.
Hauerwas, Stanley, *The Peaceable Kingdom: A Primer in Christian Ethics*. Notre Dame, IN: University of Notre Dame Press, 1983.
Hauerwas, Stanley, *Resident Aliens: Life in the Christian Colony*. Nashville, TN: Abingdon Press, 2004.
Hauerwas, Stanley, *With the Grain of the Universe: The Church's Witness and Natural Theology*. Grand Rapids, MI: Baker Academic, 2001.
Hauerwas, Stanley, and L. Gregord Jones, *Why Narrative? Readings in Narrative Theology*. Eugene, OR: Wipf and Stock, 1997.
Hays, Richard, *The Echoes of Scripture in the Letters of Paul*. New York: Yale University Press, 1993.
Hays, Richard, *The Moral Vision of the New Testament: A Contemporary Introduction to New Testament Ethics*. New York: HarperCollins, 1996.
Hegel, G. F. W., *Elements of the Philosophy of Right*, edited by Alan Wood, translated by H. B. Nisbet. Cambridge: Cambridge University Press, 1998.
Hegel, G. F. W., *Lectures on the Philosophy of Religion*. New York: Oxford University Press, 2009.
Herdt, Jennifer, *Putting on Virtue: The Legacy of the Splendid Vices*. Chicago, IL: University of Chicago Press, 2009.
Herdt, Jennifer, "Guilt and Shame in the Development of Virtue," in *Developing the Virtues: Integrating Perspectives*, edited by Julia Annas, Darcia Navarez, and Nancy E. Snow. New York: Oxford University Press, 2016.
Hill, Thomas, "Punishment, Conscience, and Moral Worth," in *Kant's Metaphysics of Morals: Interpretive Essays*. New York: Oxford University Press, 2002.
Kant, Immanuel, *Critique of Practical Reason*, translated and edited by Mary Gregor. New York: Cambridge University Press, 1997.
Kant, Immanuel, *Groundwork of the Metaphysics of Morals*, translated and edited by Mary Gregor. New York: Cambridge University Press, 1997.
Kant, Immanuel, *Lectures on Ethics*. Indianapolis, IN: Hackett, 1980.
Kant, Immanuel, *Metaphysics of Morals*. New York: Cambridge University Press, 1996.

Kant, Immanuel, "Moral Mrongovius II, in *Lectures on Ethics*, translated by Peter Heath and edited by J. B. Schneewind. New York: Cambridge University Press, 1997.
Kant, Immanuel, "On the Miscarriage of all Philosophical Trials in Theodicy," in *Religion Within the Bounds of Reason Alone and Other Writings*, edited by Allen Wood and George di Giovanni. New York: Cambridge University Press, 1998.
Kant, Immanuel, *Religion Within the Bounds of Reason Alone and Other Writings*, edited by Allen Wood and George di Giovanni. New York: Cambridge University Press, 1998.
Kant, Immanuel, "What Is Enlightenment," in *Kant's Practical Philosophy*, translated and edited by Mary Gregory. New York: Cambridge University Press, 1999.
Kierkegaard, Søren, *Attack upon Christendom*, translated and edited by Walter Lowrie. Princeton, NJ: Princeton University Press, 1968.
Kierkegaard, Søren, *Christian Discourses*, translated and edited by Howard Hong and Edna Hong. Princeton, NJ: Princeton University Press, 2009.
Kierkegaard, Søren, *Concluding Unscientific Postscript to Philosophical Fragments*, translated and edited by Howard Hong and Edna Hong. Princeton, NJ: Princeton University Press, 1992.
Kierkegaard, Søren, *Discourses at the Communion on Friday*. Bloomington: Indiana University Press, 2011.
Kierkegaard, Søren, *Fear and Trembling/Repetition*, translated and edited by Howard Hong and Edna Hong. Princeton, NJ: Princeton University Press, 1983.
Kierkegaard, Søren, *For Self-Examination/Judge for Yourself!*, translated and edited by Howard Hong and Edna Hong. Princeton, NJ: Princeton University Press, 1991.
Kierkegaard, Søren, *Journals and Papers*, 7 volumes, translated and edited by Howard Hong and Edna Hong. Bloomington: Indiana University Press, 1967–78.
Kierkegaard, Søren, *Philosophical Fragments*, translated and edited by Howard Hong and Edna Hong. Princeton, NJ: Princeton University Press, 1985.
Kierkegaard, Søren, *Practice in Christianity*, translated and edited by Howard Hong and Edna Hong. New Jersey: Princeton University Press, 1991.
Kierkegaard, Søren, *The Book on Adler*, translated and edited by Howard Hong and Edna Hong. Princeton, NJ: Princeton University Press, 2009.
Kierkegaard, Søren, *The Point of View for My Work as an Author*, translated and edited by Howard Hong and Edna Hong. Princeton, NJ: Princeton University Press, 1998.
Kierkegaard, Søren, *The Sickness unto Death*, translated and edited by Howard Hong and Edna Hong. Princeton, NJ: Princeton University Press, 1983.
Kierkegaard, Søren, *Two Ages: A Literary Review*, translated and edited by Howard Hong and Edna Hong. Princeton, NJ: Princeton University Press, 1978.
Kierkegaard, Søren, *Upbuilding Discourses in Various Spirits*, translated and edited by Howard Hong and Edna Hong. Princeton, NJ: Princeton University Press, 2009.
Kierkegaard, Søren, *Works of Love*, translated and edited by Howard Hong and Edna Hong. Princeton, NJ: Princeton University Press, 1999.
King Jr., Martin Luther, *A Testament of Hope: The Essential Writings of Martin Luther King*. San Francisco, CA: Harper One, 2003.
Kirk, Kenneth, *Conscience and Its Problems*. New York: Longman Green, 1921.
Kirk, Kenneth, *Some Principles of Moral Theology and Their Application*. New York: Longman Green 1921.
Kirmse, Bruce, *Kierkegaard and Golden Age of Denmark*. Bloomington: Indiana University Press, 1990.
Krishek, Sharon, *Kierkegaard on Faith and Love*. New York: Cambridge University Press, 2009.

Kuyper, Abraham, *Lectures on Calvinism*. Peabody, MA: Hendrickson, 2008.
Langston, Douglas, *Conscience and Other Virtues: From Bonaventure to MacIntyre*. Penn State University Press, 1996.
Lane, Keith H., *Kierkegaard and the Concept of Religious Authorship*. Tuebingen: Mohr Siebeck, 2010.
Law, David R., *Kierkegaard as Negative Theologian*. New York: Clarendon Press, 1993.
Lehmann, Paul, *Ethics in a Christian Context*. New York: Harper and Row, 1963.
Lehmann, Paul, "Ethics," in *Karl Barth in Re-View*, edited by H. M. Rumscheidt. Pittsburgh, PA: Pickwisk Press, 1981.
Levinas, Emmanuel, *Totality and Infinity: An Essay on Exteriority*, translated by Alphonso Lingis. Pittsburgh, PA: Duquesne University Press, 1969.
Long, Edward Leroy, "Analyses of Conscience," in *A Recent Survey of Christian Ethics*. New York: Oxford University Press, 1982.
Lovin, Robin, *Christian Faith and Political Choices: The Social Ethics of Barth, Brunner, and Bonhoeffer* Philadelphia, PA: Fortress Press, 1984.
Luther, Martin, *Commentary on Galatians*, volume 26 of Luther's Works. St. Louis, MO: Concordia Publishing House, 1962.
McKenny, Gerald, *The Analogy of Grace: Karl Barth's Moral Theology*. New York: Oxford University Press, 2010.
Mackey, Louis, *Points of View: Readings of Kierkegaard*. Gainesville, FL: University of Florida Press, 1986.
MacIntyre, *After Virtue: A Study in Moral Theory*. Third edition. Notre Dame, IN: University of Notre Dame Press, 2007.
MacIntyre, *A Short History of Ethics: A History of Moral Philosophy from the Homeric Age to the Twentieth Century*. Second edition. Notre Dame, IN: University of Notre Dame Press, 1998.
Mattison, William, *Introducing Moral Theology: True Happiness and the Virtues*. Grand Rapids, MI: Brazos Press, 2008.
Mead, G. H., *Mind, Self, and Society: From the Standpoint of a Social Behaviorist*. Chicago, IL: University of Chicago Press, 1967.
Michalson, Gordon, *Fallen Freedom: Kant on Radical Evil and Moral Regeneration*. New York: Cambridge University Press, 1990.
Mount, Eric, *Conscience and Responsibility*. Richmond, VA: John Knox Press, 1969.
Mouw, Richard, "Alisdair MacIntyre on Reformation Ethics," *Journal of Religious Ethics*, vol. 13, no. 2 (1985), 243–57.
Mueller, Paul, *Kierkegaard's Works of Love: Christian Ethics and the Maieutic Ideal*, translated and edited by C. Stephen Evans and Jan Evans. Copenhagen: C.A. Reitzel, 1993.
Newman, John Henry, *The Heart of Newman*, edited by Erich Przywara, S. J. San Francisco, CA: Ignatius Press, 1997.
Niebuhr, H. Richard, "The Ego-Alter Dialectic and the Conscience," *Journal of Philosophy*, vol. 42, no. 13 (June 21, 1945).
Niebuhr, H. Richard, *The Responsible Self*. New York: Harper and Row, 1963.
Nietzsche, Friedrich, *Beyond Good and Evil*. New York: Cambridge University Press, 2002.
Nietzsche, Friedrich, *On the Genealogy of Morals*. New York: Cambridge University Press, 1994.
O'Donovan, Oliver, *Resurrection and Moral Order: An Outline for Evangelical Ethics*. Second edition. Grand Rapids, MI: Eerdmans, 1994.

O'Donovan, Oliver, *Self, World, and Time: Ethics as Theology*. Grand Rapids, MI: Eerdmans, 2013.
O'Donovan, Oliver, *The Ways of Judgment*. Grand Rapids, MI: Eerdmans, 2005.
Pattison, George, *Kierkegaard and the Crisis of Faith*. London: SPCK, 1997.
Pattison, George, *Kierkegaard, Religion, and the Nineteenth Century Crisis of Culture*. New York: Cambridge University Press, 2002.
Pattison, George, *Kierkegaard and the Theology of the Nineteenth Century: The Paradox and the Point of Contact*. New York: Cambridge University Press, 2013.
Pattison, George, *Kierkegaard's Upbuilding Discourses: Philosophy, Theology, Literature*. London: Routledge, 2002.
Pattison, George and Shakespeare S., eds. *Kierkegaard: The Self in Society*. Basingstoke: Macmillan, 1998.
Paul II, John, *Veritatis Splendor*. Boston, MA: Pauline Books, 1993.
Perkins, William, *A Discourse on Conscience*. Nieuwkoop: B. De Graf, 1966.
Piety, M. G., *Ways of Knowing: Kierkegaard's Pluralist Epistemology*. Waco, TX: Baylor University Press, 2010.
Polk, Timothy Houston, *The Biblical Kierkegaard: Reading by the Rule of Faith*. Macon, GA: Mercer University Press, 1997.
Pope Francis, *Laudato Si: On the Care of Our Common Home*. Vatican City: Libreria Editrice Vaticana, 2015.
Potts, Timothy, *Conscience in Medieval Philosophy*. New York: Cambridge University Press, 1980.
Rae, Murray, *Kierkegaard and Theology*. New York: T&T Clark, 2010.
Rae, Murray, *Kierkegaard's Vision of the Incarnation: By Faith Transformed*. Oxford: Clarendon Press, 1997.
Ricoeur, Paul, "The Summoned Subject," in *Figuring the Sacred: Religion, Narrative, and Imagination*. Minneapolis, MN: Fortress Press, 1995.
Rose, Tim, *Kierkegaard's Christocentric Theology*. Aldershot: Ashgate, 2001.
Rossi, Philip, and Michael Wren eds. *Kant's Philosophy of Religion Reconsidered*. Bloomington: Indiana University Press, 1991.
Schleiermacher, Friedrich, *Introduction to Christian Ethics*, translated by John C. Shelly. Nashville: Abingdon Press, 1989.
Schleiermacher, Friedrich, *The Christian Faith*. New York: T&T Clark, 1999.
Schneewind, J. B., *The Invention of Autonomy*. New York: Cambridge University Press, 1997.
Schneewind, J. B., "Natural Law, Skepticism, and Methods in Ethics," *Journal of the History of Ideas*, vol. 52, no. 2 (April–June 1991).
Smith, Adam, *The Theory of Moral Sentiments*. New York: Cambridge University Press, 2002.
Smith, Christian, "On 'Moralistic Therapeutic Deism' as U.S. Teenagers' Actual, Tacit, De Facto Religious Faith," in *The 2005 Princeton Lectures on Youth, Church, and Culture with Imagination and Love: Leadership in Youth Ministry*. Princeton Theological Seminary, 2005. Available at http://youthlectures.ptsem.edu/?action=tei&id=youth-2005-05, accessed on June 2018.
Smith, Christan and Melina Lundquist Denton, *Soul Searching: The Religious and Spiritual Lives of American Teenagers*. New York: Oxford University Press, 2005.
Smith, James K. A., *Who's Afraid of Postmodernism: Taking Derrida, Lyotard, and Foucault to Church* Grand Rapids, MI: Baker Academic, 2006.

Sponheim, Paul, *Kierkegaard on Christ and Christian Coherence*. London: SCM Press, 1968.
Stendhal, Krister, *Paul among Jews and Gentiles and Other Essays*. Philadelphia, PA: Fortress, 1976.
Sullivan, F. Russell, *Faith and Reason in Kierkegaard*. Lanham, MD: University Press of America, 2010.
Taylor, Charles, *Sources of the Self: The Making of Modern Identity*. Cambridge, MA: Harvard University Press, 1989.
Taylor, Charles, *The Ethics of Authenticity*. Cambridge, MA: Harvard University Press, 1991.
Thielicke, Helmut, *Theological Ethics, Volume 1: Foundations*. Philadelphia, PA: Fortress Press, 1966.
Thulstrup, Niels, *Kierkegaard and the Church in Denmark* (Bibliotheca Kierkegaardiana). Copenhagen: C.A. Reitzels Forlag, 1984.
Thulstrup, Niels, *Kierkegaard: The Descent into God*. Montreal: McGill-Queen's University Press, 1985.
Thulstrup, Niels, *Kierkegaard's Relation to Hegel*, translated by George L. Stengen. Princeton, NJ: Princeton University Press, 1980.
Thulstrup, Niels, *Kierkegaard's View of Christianity* (Bibliotheca Kierkegaardiana). Copenhagen: C.A. Reitzels Forlag, 1978.
Tillich, Paul, "The Transmoral Conscience," in *Morality and Beyond*. Louisville, KY: Westminster John Knox, 1995.
Timmerman, Jens, "Kant on Conscience, 'Indirect' Duty, and Moral Error," *International Philosophical Quarterly*, vol. 46, no. 3 (2006).
Van Creveld, Marin, *Conscience: A Biography*. London: Reaktion Books, 2015.
Walker, Jeremy, *To Will One Thing: Reflection on Kierkegaard's Purity of Heart*. Montreal: McGill-Queen's University Press, 1972.
Walsh, Sylvia, *Living Christianly: Kierkegaard's Dialectic of Christian Existence*. University Park: Pennsylvania State University Press, 2005.
Walsh, Sylvia, *Living Poetically: Kierkegaard's Existential Aesthetics*. University Park: Pennsylvania University Press, 1997.
Walsh, Sylvia, *Kierkegaard: Thinking Christianly in an Existential Mode*. New York: Oxford University Press, 2009.
Watkin, Julia, *Historical Dictionary of Kierkegaard's Philosophy*. Lanham, MD: Scarecrow Press, 2001.
Webster, John B., *Barth*. Second edition. London: Continuum, 2004.
Webster, John B., *Barth's Moral Theology: Human Action in Barth's Thought*. Grand Rapids, MI: Eerdmans, 1998.
Webster, John B., "God and Conscience," in *Word and Church: Essays in Christian Dogmatics*. New York: T&T Clark, 2001.
Westphal, Merold, *Kierkegaard's Critique of Reason and Society*. University Park: Pennsylvanian University Press, 1997.
Wolterstorff, Nicholas, "Conundrums in Kant's Religion," in *Kant's Philosophy of Religion Reconsidered*, edited by Philip Rossi and Michael Wren. Bloomington: Indiana University Press, 1991.
Wood, Allen, *Kantian Ethics*. New York: Cambridge University Press, 2008.
Wright, N. T., *Paul: In Fresh Perspective*. Minneapolis, MN: Fortress Press, 2005.
Wright, N. T., *What Saint Paul Really Said*. Grand Rapids, MI: Eerdmans, 1997.

Zachman, Randall, *The Assurance of Faith: Conscience in the Theology of Martin Luther and John Calvin*. Minneapolis, MN: Fortress, 1993.

Zachman, Randall, "Conscience in the Theology of Martin Luther and Søren Kierkegaard." Available at http://downloads.elca.org/html/jle/www.elca.org/what-we-believe/social-issues/conscience-in-the-theology-of-marti3ef395bf.htm, accessed August 2013.

Zachman, Randall, *Reconsidering John Calvin*. New York: Cambridge University Press, 2013.

Ziegler, Philip, "A Christian Context for Conscience? Reading Kierkegaard's Works of Love beyond Hegel's Critique of Conscience," *European Journal of Theology*, vol. 15, no. 2 (2006), 93–102.

Ziegler, Philip, "'Doing Conscience Over:' The Reformulation of the Doctrine of Conscience in the Theological Ethics of Karl Barth and Paul Lehmann," *Toronto Journal of Theology*, vol. 14, no. 2 (Fall 1998), 213–38.

INDEX

Note: Numbers followed by n refer to note numbers.

abstraction
  contingencies of social context 125
  externality 93
accountability 2, 7, 15, 18, 22, 27, 28, 33, 38, 150
  to community 90
  to God 7–9, 54, 73, 90, 130
  locus of 22, 62
  moral 7, 15, 41, 129, 132, 152, 154
  and self-knowledge 60, 90
  singular 150, 165
  source 61, 134, 157
accounting of eternity 77
activity of conscientiousness 137–44
Adams, Robert 70, 70 n.152, 71
After Virtue (MacIntyre) 16 n.13–14, 121 n.18
AmeriCorps 29
Ameriks, Karl 4 n.9, 44 n.16, 46
Ames, William 13, 13 n.4, 135 n.98
Analogy of Grace, The: Karl Barth's Moral Theology (McKenny) 113 n.204
Anti-Climacus *see* Kierkegaard, Søren
anti-individualistic interpretation, of Pauline epistles 119–23
Apostle Paul and the Introspective Conscience of the West, The (Stendhal) 119
apostolic authority 142
appropriation (autonomy as) 17, 89, 140
Aquinas, Thomas 12, 12 n.1, 18–19
  theory of conscience 20
art and education (socially formative) 157
Augustine 73, 119, 127 n.46, 128, 129 n.58, 131, 135 n.95
authentic community 80 n.20
authenticity 99
authentic morality 15
authority 4, 22–3, 62, 160

autonomous individuals 15
autonomy 4, 6, 7, 15, 16, 74
  Kant's formula of 45
awakening conscience 103 n.154
awareness 95

bad conscience 79 n.16, 82, 82 n.38
Barth, Karl 24, 75, 75 n.1, 122, 122 n.21, 127, 127 n.51, 127 n.53, 128, 128 n.54, 155 n.215
  theory of conscience 127
Bauckham, Richard 118 n.2
Benedict XVI 3 n.6, 14, 14 n.8, 152, 152 n.202–6, 160 n.236
Bernard of Clairvaux 1, 14, 152
the Bible 118, 130, 158, 159, 164
Bonhoeffer, Dietrich 24
Book of Common Prayer 2 n.2
Brunner, Emil 24

Calvin, John 1, 1 n.1, 7, 13, 13 n.2, 134, 134 n.90–1, 135, 135 n.97
center of valuation 29
Christian Context for Conscience, A (Ziegler) 76, 78 n.14
Christian Discourses (*CD*) (Kierkegaard) 76, 77 n.10, 81 n.23, 29, 82 n.35, 82 n.38, 93 n.92–3, 93 n.95, 94 n.97
Christian existence 76 n.2
Christianity 105–9, 112–13, 120
Chrysostom, John 1 n.1, 14, 14 n.6, 134, 134 n.92–4, 135 n.96, 138, 146 n.172
command 22, 47, 54, 99, 160
communal mediation of God's judgment 132
communitarianism 2, 123
  and moral self-awareness 123–5
community 2–3, 8–9, 14, 15, 25
  prohibitions 35

Concluding Unscientific Postscript (Kierkegaard) 76
Confessions (Augustine) 73 n.160, 126–7 n.45–6, 129 n.58, 135 n.95
conscience
  absence of 95
  Ames's definition of 13
  Aquinas's theory of conscience 20
  and autonomy 44–50
  awareness of 97
  Calvin's definition 13
  and community 72–4
  consciousness of guilt 100–3
  in contemporary Christian ethics 15
  decline of 17–25
  defined 1 n.1, 12, 13, 14, 19
  degree of noncontingency 125
  disappearance of 33–7
  dismissal of 7
  divine judgment, approximation of 50–4
  division within ourselves 43
  domestication of 18–19
  drawing closer to God 99–100
  eternal 77
  experience of 45, 50, 59, 78, 113, 134, 136, 137–44
  fear of hypocrisy 58
  forum (conscience as) 134–5
  freedom of 133
  independent entity 3
  indicative-imperative disclosure 94–9
  individualistic connotation 3
  isolating relationship of 88–94
  from its absence 80–3
  judgment 53, 54, 101–3
  judicial disclosure 94
  Kant's theory of 5, 7, 41–74, 118
  as *kardia* of 1 Jn 3:21 131
  Kierkegaard definition of 76–80
  Kierkegaard's theory of 5, 6 n.10, 13
  knowledge of the heart 54–9
  Kuyper's definition 13–14
  locus of accountability 22, 62
  moral repentance 65–9
  nature and function 44
  passive experience 137–44
  Perkins's definition of 13, 14
  and perseverance 69–72
  (non)place in Christian ethics 3–5
  as point of unity 153
  "power" within 19
  protestant theory of 13
  reflexive self-awareness 134
  repentance, conversion, and universality 149–54
  revising out of existence 25–31
  self before Christ 103–7
  self-deception, antidote to 59–65
  against self-deception 144–9
  self-posited morality 4
  singularity and authenticity 87, 94, 154–63
  as singular moral self awareness 1, 1 n.1, 3, 117–19, 136
  social theory of 145
  theories of 1, 1 n.1, 12–13
  Thomistic conceptions of 19
  Timothy's description of 138
  as tribunal 41–4
  as tribunal and self-testimony 133–7
  as voice of 19, 95
  as voice of eternity 93
Conscience and Other Virtues (Langston) 3
Conscience in the New Testament (Pierce) 134 n.87–8
conscientious individual, 2
conscientiousness 138, 149, 157, 162
  activity of 137–44
conscientious self-consistency 122
conscientious self-examination 122, 151
corporate self-awareness 33–7
Critique of Practical Reason (Kant) 46 n.23, 52 n.54, 136 n.109
crowd (*mængden*) 76, 80 n.20, 81
  as immediacy 93
  as public (Publikum) 80 n.20
  as semi-somnolent state 82, 89

Daily Examen of Ignatian spirituality 1 n.1
deed of freedom 54
Denton, Melina Lundquist 122 n.23
desire for self-preservation 55
Despland, Michael 6 n.10
dichotomy 125–33

Discourses at the Communion on Friday
   (*DCF*) (Kierkegaard) 76, 77 n.9,
   89 n.77
divine
   assistance 68–9
   command 4
   judgment, approximation of 50–4
   name 99
domestication of conscience 18–19

Ebeling, Gerhard 24, 25
ego-alter dialectic 27, 90
   constancies in 27, 34
   ultimate community of interaction 29
endorsement (autonomy as) 53, 71–2
Enlightenment 147 n.177
eternity 87, 93
Ethics (Barth) 127 n.51, 127 n.53
EUD 81 n.22, 81 n.24, 81 n.26, 91 n.80,
   91 n.83, 92 n.84–7, 95 n.104, 150
   n.190–2
Evans, Steven 76, 98 n.123, 106 n.159
experience of conscience 45, 50, 59, 78,
   113, 134, 136, 137–44
externality 93

Ferreira, Jamie 7, 83, 84 n.45, 85 n.47
For Self-Examination (FSE) (*Kierkegaard*)
   76, 88 n.70, 111 n.185, 111 n.187,
   111 n.190, 158 n.228–9
freedom in Christ 132
Freud, Sigmund 19, 20

Gaudium et Spes 152
genuine community 84, 107 n.164
genuine sociality 87
glorified selves 86
God 49, 52–4
   authority 161
   bondservant 116
   cares for each person 131
   in conscience 111
   delusional relationship 118
   divine command 22, 47, 54, 99, 160
   forgiveness 130
   holy guardian 137
   human morality and 137
   individual, presence of God to 1 n.1
   internal moral director 3

judge lawlessness 133
judgment of God 131–2
judgment of us 53, 72, 74, 117
mediation of 2
moral self-awareness before
   117–19, 127
person's relation to 78
relation to human beings 76, 77, 97, 118
self-disclosing encounter 77
self-manifestation in creation 93
self-revelation in Jesus Christ 105,
   106, 115
"separate and distinct" relation 98
singular accountability before 7–9, 54,
   73, 90, 130
singular relationship to 86
as Supreme Lawgiver 79
transparency before 151
well-pleasing to 71
word 107–9
see oneself before Christ 110–14
God and Morality (Hare) 47 n.28
God's Call (Hare) 153 n.210–11
Golden Age (Kirmse) 84 n.41, 43,
   100 n.136
*Gospel of Glory: Major Themes in
   Johannine Theology* (Bauckham)
   118 n.2
Groundwork of the Metaphysics of Morals
   (Kant) 42, 45–8, 55, 145 n.169
guilt 11, 12, 21, 27
guilty self-awareness 135

haecceitas 153
Hare, John 4 n.9, 47 n.28, 48 n.34, 68, 71,
   73, 153, 153 n.210–11
Hauerwas, Stanley 2, 3, 3 n.4, 7, 14, 15–17,
   25, 31, 31 n.86, 33–7, 41, 45, 84, 121,
   122 n.20, 123, 124, 124–5 n.29–38,
   127, 127 n.47, 136
   modern morality, objection to 44
Hays, Richard 119, 119 n.9, 120
Hebrew Bible 1, 130, 131
   see also the Bible
Herdt, Jennifer 56, 56 n.75, 57,
   143 n.161–2
Hill, Thomas 6 n.10
holiness 70
Holy Spirit 20

Hopkins, Gerard Manly 153
human beings, predispositions, Kant on
　animality 55
　humanity 55
　personality 55
　respect 55
human race 107 n.163
hypekoe (Paul) 20
　attentiveness of faith and conscience 20

individualism 31, 73, 118
individualistic moral relativism 136
Institutes of the Christian Religion (Cavin) 1, 134 n.90–1
internalization
　of social ethos 31
　of social norms 49 n.40
inward deepening 92
Isaiah 6 1 n.1

Jesus Christ (and conscience) 2, 8, 30, 37, 103, 105, 106, 114
　God is love 108
　God-man 107
　God's self-revelation in 107
　love of God 109
　self before Christ 103–7
　see also God
Journals and Papers (*JP*) (Kierkegaard) 77 n.4, 79 n.15, 80 n.18–19, 80 n.21, 84 n.41, 84 n.44, 84 n.46, 97 n.120, 138 n.122, 158 n. 230–1
Judge for Yourself! (*JFY*) (Kierkegaard) 76, 77 n.5, 79 n17, 82 n.33, 83 n.40, 138 n.121, 150 n.193, 157

Kant, Immanuel 3, 7, 13–16, 19, 37, 39, 136, 155
　Christian ethics 4–5, 56
　conscience and disposition 58
　dear self 63–65, 105
　decline of conscience 17–18
　experience of conscience 78
　grace as cooperation from above 68
　individualism 123
　modern individualism. 121
　modern morality 17
　moral philosophy 15 17
　moral self-awareness 5

　moral theology 67
　notion of autonomy 44, 45
　personal morality 4
　philosophy of religion 4
　self-incurred minority 147
　theory of conscience 3–6, 7, 8, 15, 20, 37, 41–74, 75, 78, 90, 117, 118, 119, 131, 137, 144
　theory of punishment 6 n.10
Kantian Ethics (Wood) 49 n.37
Kierkegaard (Ferreira) 83 n.39
Kierkegaard, Søren 5–6, 7, 8, 13, 14, 37, 71, 139, 140 n.139, 141 n.147, 155, 157
　becoming guilty 139
　colliding with the world 99–100
　consent 97 n.112
　conscience 76–80
　conscience from its absence 80–3
　conscience in judgment 100–3
　deeper self 92, 97 n.112
　on double-mindedness 82, 85, 86
　first self 91–2, 150–6
　God, closer to 99–100
　help of Christ 107–9
　indicative-imperative disclosure 95–9
　isolating the relationship of conscience 88–94
　relationship of conscience 89
　second authorship 75–7, 76 n.2
　self before Christ 103–7
　self-knowledge 75
　single individual 76, 77, 83–7
　singularity and authenticity 87, 94, 154–63
　theory of conscience 5, 6 n.10, 13, 75–6, 79, 84, 89, 94, 104, 117–19, 144
　see oneself before Christ 110–14
Kierkegaard and Golden Age Denmark (Kirmse) 83 n.39
Kierkegaard and Theology (Rae) 76, 84 n.41, 107 n.163
Kierkegaard and the Theology of the Nineteenth Century: The Paradox and the Point of Contact (Pattison) 76
King David 111, 128–9
kingdom of nature 52
Kirk, Kenneth 24

Kirmse, Bruce 83 n.39, 84 n.41, 100 n.136
knowledge of ourselves 13
Kuyper, Abraham 13, 14, 14 n.5, 120 n.14

Langston, Douglas 3, 4 n.7
　and theory of conscience 4
Laudato Si': On the Care of Our Common Home (Pope Francis) 147–8, 147–8 n.180–7, 150, 151 n.194–9, 162 n.245–6
Lectures on Ethics (Kant) 43 n.10–11, 53 n.61, 58 n.88, 64 n.115, 65 n.118, 69 n.144, 74 n.166–7, 136 n.102, 137 n.114, 150 n.188, 155 n.216–17
Lehmann, Paul 7, 14, 15, 17–25, 45, 131, 131 n.71–2
Letter Addressed to the Duke of Norfolk, A: On Occasion of Mr. Gladstone's Recent Expostulation (Newman) 160 n.235
Literary Review, A (*LR*) (Kierkegaard) 81 n.25, 81 n.27, 81 n.30–2, 82 n.36, 84 n.45, 87 n.64, 91 n.81, 162 n.247
Living Christianly: Kierkegaard's Dialectic of Christian Existence (Walsh) 76, 94 n.99, 100 n.140, 103 n.151, 114 n.207
Love's Grateful Striving (Ferreria) 84 n.45, 85 n.47
Luther, Martin 3, 70, 119

MacIntyre, Alasdair 7, 14, 15–17, 32, 45, 84, 121, 121 n.16, 122, 123, 123 n.26–8, 136
　modern morality, objection to 44
　moral identity 121
　narrative self 31–3
Mackey, Louis 76, 103 n.151
madness of Christianity 109
Mattison III, William C. 3 n.5
McKenny, Gerald 113 n.204
mediation of God 2
Metaphysics of Morals (Kant) 6 n.10, 42 n.4, 44 n.12–15, 47 n.30, 48 n.35, 49 n.38, 50 n.42–3, 51 n.44, 53 n.62, 54, 54 n.65, 54 n.67, 55 n.74, 56 n.79, 57, 59 n.94, 63 n.113, 65 n.119, 72 n.158, 135 n.100–1, 136 n.103–8, 137 n.115, 138 n.120, 150 n.189, 155 n.172

Michalson, Gordon 67
modern Christianity 120
　see also Christianity
modern individualism 127
modernity, rise of
　MacIntyre and Hauerwas on 15–17
modern morality 15, 20
　Lehmann and O'Donovan on 17–25
moralistic therapeutic deists 122
moral(ity)
　accountability 7, 15, 41, 129, 132, 152, 154
　agency 155, 165
　autonomy 7
　cognizance of 46
　community 157
　consciousness 127
　discernment 90
　feelings 43, 43 n9
　first principles 21
　formation 72
　identity 7, 15, 33, 41, 90, 121, 128
　law 5, 7, 8, 12, 16, 75
　moral agency 31, 35
　pure principles of 19
　quality 54
　quality of action 75
　relativism 12
　religion and God 51
　repentance 11, 65–9, 102, 149, 152, 155
　role to assess 42
　self-awareness 1–8, 11–13, 15, 21, 78, 94, 124, 128, 147, 153, 154
　self-created 4
　self-hood 127
　self-judgment 53
Moral Mrongovius II (Kant) 48 n.33
Mouw, Richard J. 121 n.19

Newman, John Henry 1, 1 n.1, 14, 160 n.235
New Testament 1, 14, 22, 110, 120
　as mirror 107–9
Niebuhr, H. Richard 7, 15, 24, 25, 26, 28, 30, 33, 41, 45, 49, 51, 78, 91, 91 n.79, 124, 125 n.39, 138

O'Donovan, Oliver 3 n.3, 7, 14, 15, 17–25, 38 n.119, 45, 131, 131 n.74–5, 160–1 n.237–42, 162, 162 n.252
On Conscience (Benedict XVI) 160 n.236
On Wealth and Poverty (Chrysostom) 1 n.1

Pattison, George 76
Paul among Jews and Gentiles and Other Essays (Stendhal) 119, 119 n.5–8
Paul: An Outline of His Theology (Ridderbos) 132 n.81
Paul II, John 3 n.6, 58, 72, 119, 120, 132
  invocation of conscience 142
  theology 120
Pauline corpus 1 n.1, 132, 153
Paul the Apostle 143–4
Peaceable Kingdom (Hauerwas) 121 n.15, 124–5 n.29–38
Perkins, William 13, 13 n.3, 14
perseverance 69, 70
personal identity 32, 126, 142, 165
personal morality 4
Pierce, C. A. 134, 134 n.87–8, 138 n.124, 151, 152 n.200
Piety, Marilyn 76
Points of View: Readings of Kierkegaard (Mackey) 76, 103 n.151
Pope Francis 147–8 n.180–7, 151, 162 n.245–6
Practice in Christianity (PC) (Kierkegaard) 76, 107 n.164, 112 n.196, 114 n.207
principle of our accountability to God 54
Psalm 139 1 n.1, 128, 129, 130, 153 n.212
Purity of Heart 95
purposiveness of freedom 51

Rae, Murray 76, 84 n.41, 107 n.163
Rawls, John 17
Reconsidering John Calvin (Zachman) 6, 76, 99 n.133
Reformation 14, 23
relationship of conscience 89
Religion within the Bounds of Reasons Alone (Kant) 47 n.31, 49 n.38–9, 50 n.41, 51, 51 n.45–51, 52–3 n.55–60, 52 n.52–3, 54–5 n.68–72, 54 n.63–4, 54 n.66, 57, 57 n.80, 57 n.83, 58, 58 n.85–91, 59–60 n.95–9, 59 n.93,

62 n.110, 63 n.114, 65–7 n.120–32, 67 n.137, 68 n.141, 69–71 n.145–55, 73 n.161, 163, 118 n.3–4
repentance 69, 102, 105, 149, 152, 155
rescuing attendant 140
responsibility 7, 15, 19, 19. 25, 25, 28, 29, 31
Responsible Self (Niebuhr) 91 n.79, 125 n.39
Resurrection and Moral Order (O'Donovan) 160–1 n.237–42
Ridderbos, Herman 132, 132 n.81, 134, 134 n.80
Royce, Josiah 28

salvation 67
Schneewind, J. B. 6 n.10, 17
scholastic moral psychology 22
Scotus, Dons 153
self 30, 46
self-accusation 137
self-assertion 12, 144
self-assessment 142, 143
self-awareness (conscience as) 2, 8, 33–7, 132, 155
self-consciousness 81
self-consistency 41
self-deception 59–65, 74, 90, 105
  conscience against 144–9
self-dialogue, conscience as 135
self-disclosing encounter 22
self-disclosure before God 14
self-examination (conscience as) 5, 55, 59, 65, 69, 152
self-incurred minority, Kant's fear of 90, 147
selfishness 145
self-judgment (conscience as) 50 n.42, 53, 137
self-knowledge (conscience as) 5, 7, 8, 15, 39, 41, 60, 75, 88, 129 n.58, 163
self-legislating beings 45, 46, 47, 51
self-love 55
self-posited morality 4
self-revelation of God in Jesus 112
self-sacrificing love 108
self-serving immorality 145
self-testimony 35, 133
sense of shame, conscience as 85

sensus divinitatis 14, 92
Short History of Ethics, A: A History of Moral Philosophy from the Homeric Age to the Twentieth Century (MacIntyre) 121 n.16–17
Sickness unto Death, The (SUD) (Kierkegaard) 76, 77 n.11, 89 n.74, 76, 93 n.96, 96 n.108, 101 n.146, 103 n.152, 153 n.209
singularity, sociality, and authority 87, 94, 154–63
Smith, Christian 122 n.22, 123 n.24–5
Smith, James K. A. 120, 120 n.12–14, 126
sociality 26, 30, 34, 41, 72, 84, 87, 89, 90, 107
social life 34
  in crowd 87
social theory of conscience 145
spiritual aspiration 71
Stendhal, Krister 119, 119 n.5–8
stillness 88
Subjectivity and Religious Belief (Evans) 98 n.123, 106 n.159

theories of conscience 1, 1 n.1, 3–4, 12–13
  Aquinas, Thomas 20
  individualism 118
  Kant, Immanuel 3–6, 7, 8, 15, 20, 37, 41–74, 75, 78, 90, 117, 118, 119, 131, 137, 144
  Kierkegaard, Søren 5, 6 n.10, 13, 75–6, 79, 84, 89, 94, 104, 117–19, 144
  Langston's argument 4
  misinterpretation of 41
Thielicke, Helmut 24
Three Discourses (Kierkegaard) 140 n.139, 140 n.141, 141 n.147
Tillich, Paul 24
Timmermann, Jens 42 n.5
tradition-bearing communities 72
tranquility 88
transparent openness before God 14

Three Upbuilding Discourses (TUD) (Kiekegaard) 88 n.66, 91 n.82, 92 n.88–90, 140 n.143
Two Ages (Kierkegaard) 76

Upbuilding Discourses in Various Spirits (UDVS) (Kierkegaard) 76, 77 n.7–8, 79 n.16, 82 n.34, 82 n.37, 83 n.39, 84 n.42, 85 n.48–52, 86–7 n.53–9, 87 n.60–3, 88 n.67, 88 n.71–3, 92 n.91, 93 n.94, 94 n.98, 95 n.101–3, 96 n.105–7, 96 n.111, 97 n.113, 97 n.116, 97 n.117–18, 97 n.121, 98 n.124–7, 118 n.1, 135 n.99, 139–40 n.127–38, 140 n.140, 140 n.145–6, 143 n.163–5, 147 n.178–9, 153 n.207–8, 158, 158 n.227–8, 162 n.248–50

Walsh, Sylvia 7 n.119, 76, 94 n.99, 100 n.140, 103 n.151, 114 n.207
Watkin, Julia 80 n.20
Ways of Judgment (O'Donovan) 162 n.252
Wealth and Poverty (Chrysostom) 134 n.92–4, 135 n.96, 146 n.172
Webster, John 127, 127 n.48–50
What Is Enlightenment (Kant) 50 n.40, 60 n.101–3, 147 n.177, 161 n.243
What Saint Paul Really Said (Wright) 419 n.9–10
Wood, Allen 49 n.37
Works of Love (WL) (Kierkegaard) 76, 77 n.6, 77 n.12–13, 88 n.65, 88 n.68, 89 n.75, 95 n.100, 97 n.122, 98 n.127, 157
worship as a summons 97
worshipper, single individual as 87
Wright, N. T. 119–20, 119 n.9–10

Zachman, Randall 6, 6 n.10, 76, 99 n.133
zeal 118
Ziegler, Philip 6, 6 n.10, 20, 20 n.34, 76 n.3, 78 n.14, 110 n.183, 111 n.188

www.ingramcontent.com/pod-product-compliance
Lightning Source LLC
Chambersburg PA
CBHW070640300426
44111CB00013B/2187